D1616929

Recovered Writers/
Recovered Texts

...k men and p...

...pproaches, the essays in this book imp...tly raise issues, some of wh... ...Why has the imperative to realign works by and about black women with... ...What are the underlying aesthetic, intellectual, theoretical, and pedagogical... ...fact, what we have called "Black Women's Literature" is to be altered significantly... ...irst century, we must move away from the compartmentalized manner of studying blacks i... ...rd a comprehensive examination of our comparative American identities. Although her poetry... ...ntity as a black person or a woman, Phillis Wheatley (c. 1753–84) produced a body of material fr... ...ives to inaugurate the African American literary tradition. Her sublime couplets reminiscent of neo... ...um obscure her sympathetic assertion that no group has a monopoly on the imagination. She studio... ...hought is free; it should not be exclusively conditioned by race or gender. Women as well as men po... ...ity to see life as exalted and, at the same time, to plumb its unfathomable possibilities. Within the... ...vocation to "On Recollection," Wheatley challenges those who would follow this "vent'rous Afric i... ..." to restate the relation among the literary text, ideology, race, and gender. The imagination is the... ...ire to transform the world. Her architectural metaphor suggests her intent to draw a new patter... ...sumed to be a male enterprise. Hence, Wheatley, a Senegalese woman-child transported to B... ...only redefines what it means to be human but also redefines the parameters of literature. Wh... ...escendants to discover the common critical heritage that links the diverse literatures of Afri... ...n, and Latin America. Black women writers in the Western Hemisphere are aware of the iro... ...nd their place in it. Their unenviable task is to overcome a world which consigns them to a str... ...ines them as undesirable others. It is a world which has plunged some of their sable sisters into... ...ent and others into bleak despair. Wheatley, as a sign and symbol of possibility, inflames the i... ...the Western Hemisphere with writing as a deed of daring or adventure. With Promethean de... ...The spirit of adventure lends a beguiling mystery to the Invocation from "On Recollection," t... ...'s desire to reconstruct a world gendered as European and male. She challenges her literary... ...of humanity that marginalizes and excludes them as blacks and as women. Her language becom... ...but to black women in the Americas to write their own texts. Though their bodies may be bound,... ...free. Writing from the womb of history, black women construct a black feminist discourse to nega... ...linist bias in male texts, both white and black. They fuse life into a suppressed feminist discourse a... ...form themselves from objects in male texts to subjects in female texts. They, thereby, intend for their... ...pe the world, thus authenticating Wheatley's "great design." They repeat and invert familiar literary... ...as the disruption of the familiar plots of domestic fiction and fugitive slave narratives by Harriet E. W... ...859) or the feminization of quest-romance by Zora Neale Hurston in Their Eyes Were Watching Go... ...It is a polyphony of voices rewriting the script of the Americas as these women present us with an... ...in a culture that exalts masculine ideals and universalizes male experience. Whereas Whea... ...ention to her race and gender, Anna Julia Cooper forcefully confronts the issue of fe... ...ley's "great design" in her 1892 A Voice from the South. Just as white me... ...black men, neither can black men "fully and adequately . . . reproduce... ...ooper asserts that the black woman from her marginalized position at... ...darkened stag... ...d. "Only the B...

Recovered Writers/ Recovered Texts

Race,

Class, and

Gender in Black

Women's Literature

Edited by

Dolan Hubbard

TENNESSEE STUDIES IN LITERATURE

Volume 38

The University of Tennessee Press / Knoxville

TENNESSEE STUDIES IN LITERATURE
Editorial Board: D. Allen Carroll, Don Richard Cox, Allison Ensor, Richard Finneran,
Nancy Moore Goslee, Marilyn Kallet, Norman Sanders.

"Tennessee Studies in Literature," a distinguished series sponsored by the Department of English
at The University of Tennessee, Knoxville, began publication in 1956. Beginning in 1984, with
Volume 27, TSL evolved from a series of annual volumes of miscellaneous essays to a series of
occasional volumes, each one dealing with a specific theme, period, or genre, for which the editor of
that volume has invited contributions from leading scholars in the field.

Inquiries concerning this series should be addressed to the Editorial Board, Tennessee Studies in Literature, Department of English, The University of Tennessee, Knoxville, Tennessee 37996-
0430. Those desiring to purchase additional copies of this issue or copies of back issues should
address The University of Tennessee Press, 293 Communications Building, Knoxville, Tennessee
37996-0325.

Excerpt from Barbara Chase-Riboud's *Sally Hemings,* Avon; Viking 1979, used with permission of
Barbara Chase-Riboud.

Material from *The Crisis,* the Official Magazine of the National Association for the Advancement of
Colored People, is reprinted by permission of Genry W. Trotter, Publisher and President.

Excerpt from Mary Prince, *The History of Mary Prince, A West Indian Slave, Related by Herself,* by
Moira Ferguson, University of Michigan Press, 1993, used with permission of the publisher and
Moira Ferguson.

Verse from *The Poems of Phillis Wheatley,* ed. Julian D. Mason Jr., University of North Carolina
Press, 1966, 1989, used with permission of the publisher.

The paper in this book meets the minimum requirements of the American National Standard for
Permanence of Paper for Printed Library Materials.
∞ The binding materials have been chosen for strength and durability.

♻ Printed on recycled paper.

Library of Congress Cataloging-in-Publication Data

Recovered writers/recovered texts: race, class, and gender in Black
women's literature / edited by Dolan Hubbard.—1st ed.
     p. cm.— (Tennessee studies in literature; v. 38)
Includes bibliographical references and index.
ISBN 0-87049-959-9 (cloth : alk. paper)
1. Feminist literary criticism. 2. Feminism and literature. 3. Literature—Black authors—History
and criticism. 4. Literature—Women authors—History and criticism. I. Hubbard, Dolan, 1949– .
II. Series.
PN98.W64R44 1997
809'.89287'0896073—dc20   96-10119
                                                    CIP

To my first-grade teacher at North Cooleemee Elementary School (1956) and the teachers at Granite Quarry Colored Elementary School (1957–63) in North Carolina, who instilled in me a love of learning:

Principal: Mary Davis

1956, First Grade: Daisy Bell Coble-Burk
(March 26, 1898–April 25, 1973)

Principal: Clarence J. Shuford
(May 15, 1923–January 24, 1965)

First Grade: Eva K. Johnson

1957, Second Grade: Helen L. Wood

1958, Third Grade: Pauline Morton-Martin

1959, Fourth Grade: Rosebud Aggrey
(July 7, 1910–February 3, 1990)

1960, Fifth Grade: Geneva I. Oglesby
(May 25, 1905–March 24, 1981)

1961, Sixth Grade: Bessie Craig
(September 10, 1903–July 13, 1989)

1962, Seventh Grade: William Eugene Graeber

1963, Eighth Grade: John Reddick

Contents

Acknowledgments   ix

Introduction: Can I Get a Witness?   xi
  Dolan Hubbard

Witnesses and Practitioners: Attitudes toward Miscegenation in
Barbara Chase-Riboud's *Sally Hemings*   1
  Emma Waters Dawson

**The Two Marys (Prince and Shelley) on the Textual Meeting
Ground of Race, Gender, and Genre**   15
  Helena Woodard

Harriet Wilson's *Our Nig:* The Demystification of Sentiment   31
  Debra Walker King

Gender, Genre, and Vulgar Secularism: The Case of Frances
Ellen Watkins Harper and the AME Press   46
  Frances Smith Foster

Anna J. Cooper: The International Dimensions   60
  David W. H. Pellow

The "Invisible Woman" Abroad: Jessie Fauset's New Horizon   75
  Erica L. Griffin

A Blend of Voices: Composite Narrative Strategies in Biographical
Reconstruction   90
  Sandra Y. Govan

Before the Stigma of Race: Authority and Witchcraft in Ann
Petry's *Tituba of Salem Village*   105
  Trudier Harris

Reading Ann Petry's *The Narrows* into Black Literary Tradition   116
    Joyce Pettis

The Unmasking of Virginia Brindis de Salas: Minority Discourse of Afro-Uruguay   129
    Caroll Mills Young

Selected Bibliography   153
Contributors   163
Index   167

Acknowledgments

I have many people to thank for their assistance and encouragement in helping me write and edit this book. Allen D. Carroll, Chair, and Dorothy M. Scura, former chair, Department of English, University of Tennessee, Knoxville, supported my project from its inception. Particular gratitude goes to Norman J. Sanders and George M. Hutchinson, who encouraged and helped me shape the project. I thank Meredith Morris-Babb, acquisitions editor of the press, who has constantly encouraged me to get a good manuscript into production soon. I also thank the trustees of the Better English Fund established by John C. Hodges and administered by the Department of English at the University of Tennessee, Knoxville, for financial support. During my two years at the University of Georgia, I have had the generous aid of Hugh Ruppersburg, head, Department of English and R. Baxter Miller, director, Institute for African American Studies.

To all of my colleagues in CLA, I owe thanks for their stimulating and supportive friendship. I owe special thanks to Thelma B. Thompson, then CLA president (1990–92), James J. Davis, CLA vice-president, and Filisha Camara-Norman, foreign language representative, who supported me and provided encouragement as I worked on this project.

For their critical comments and insights, I owe particular thanks to Debra Boyd Buggs, Thomas N. Hammond, Karla F. C. Holloway, Elwanda D. Ingram, Marvin A. Lewis, Barbara McCaskill, and Ruby V. Rodney.

While the book was in progress, I was sustained by the encouragement of many friends: Hazel A. Ervin, Mildred White Barksdale, Esme Bhan, Adnee M. Bradford, Chester J. Fontenot Jr., Carolyn Hodges, John O. Hodges, La Vinia Delois Jennings, Sharynn Owens Etheridge, Vera Mitchell, Hollis Earl Pruitt, Paula L. Roper, Rosemary Stevenson,

Gwendolyn A. Thomas, and Joyce Carol Thomas. Thanks are certainly due my research assistants, Erica L. Griffin (University of Georgia) and Michael D. Hill (Harvard University), who had a summer research fellowship at the Institute for African American Studies.

Finally, I thank Ruth, my wife, and Aisha and Desmond, our children, for their patience and understanding.

Introduction:
Can I Get a Witness?

MNEME begin. Inspire, ye sacred nine,
Your vent'rous *Afric* in her great design.

   Phillis Wheatley (1773)

I feel, therefore I can be free.

   Audre Lorde (1977)

Founded in 1937, the College Language Association is the nation's preeminent organization of African American scholars of languages and literature.[1] In April 1992, a group of scholars and critics participated in the Fifty-second Annual Convention of the College Language Association hosted by the University of Tennessee, Knoxville, entitled "Gender and Genre: From Illusion to Reality." More than two hundred scholars and critics presented and considered a variety of papers on pedagogy and literary scholarship. They brought a fresh reading to some of the more significant unread as well as underread works by black women writers, many of whom have been marginalized by critics of African American, Caribbean, and Latin American literature. My daily involvement with the conference and its intellectual thrust served as an inspiration for this volume.

    The essays contained in *Recovered Writers/Recovered Texts* reflect ways in which this black feminist criticism informs and alters our understanding of cultural history and our understanding of aesthetic value. They represent the feminization of black American literary scholarship and the extent to which this dynamic scholarship "has transformed the intellectual base of our profession" (Lauter xii). The critics take the black woman writer out of the hegemonic shadow of the racial mountain as traditionally defined by white and black men and present her in all of her rich complexity.

    Beyond the varying approaches, the essays in this book implicitly raise issues, some of which I wish to examine briefly in this introduction: Why has the imperative to realign works by and about black women within New World black literature arisen? What are the underlying aesthetic, intellectual, theoretical, and pedagogical questions that must be addressed if, in fact, what we have called "Black Women's Literature" is to be altered significantly? As we move into the twenty-first century, we must move away from the compartmentalized manner of studying blacks in the New World and toward a comprehensive examination of our comparative American identities.[2]

Although her poetry reflects little of her identity as a black person or a woman, Phillis Wheatley (c. 1753–84) produced a body of material from a variety of narratives to inaugurate the African American literary tradition. Her sublime couplets reminiscent of neoclassical decorum obscure her sympathetic assertion that no group has a monopoly on the imagination. She studiously asserts that thought is free; it should not be exclusively conditioned by race or gender. Women as well as men possess the capacity to see life as exalted and, at the same time, to plumb its unfathomable possibilities.

Within the critical play of her Invocation to "On Recollection," Wheatley challenges those who would follow this "vent'rous *Afric* in her great design" to restate the relation among the literary text, ideology, race, and gender. The imagination is the key for those who aspire to transform the world. Her architectural metaphor suggests her intent to draw a new pattern on what had been presumed to be a male enterprise. Hence, Wheatley, a Senegalese woman-child transported to Boston against her will, not only redefines what it means to be human but also redefines the parameters of literature.[3]

Wheatley invites her literary descendants to discover the common critical heritage that links the diverse literatures of African America, the Caribbean, and Latin America. Black women writers in the Western Hemisphere are aware of the ironic context of history and their place in it. Their unenviable task is to overcome a world which consigns them to a structural silence and defines them as undesirable others. It is a world which has plunged some of their sable sisters into mindless detachment and others into bleak despair. Wheatley, as a sign and symbol of possibility, inflames the imagination of blacks in the Western Hemisphere with writing as a deed of daring or adventure. With Promethean defiance, she steals the fire. The spirit of adventure lends a beguiling mystery to the Invocation from "On Recollection," thereby suggesting Wheatley's desire to reconstruct a world gendered as European and male. She challenges her literary daughters to resist a model of humanity that marginalizes and excludes them as blacks and as women. Her language becomes heuristic as it calls out to black women in the Americas to write their own texts. Though their bodies may be bound, their spirits remain free.[4]

Writing from the womb of history, black women construct a black feminist discourse to negate the masculinist bias in male texts, both white and black. They fuse life into a suppressed feminist discourse as they transform themselves from objects in male texts to subjects in female texts. They, thereby, intend for their narratives to reshape the world, thus authenticating Wheatley's "great design." They repeat and invert familiar literary constructs, such as the disruption of the familiar plots of domestic fiction and fugitive slave narratives by Harriet E. Wilson in *Our Nig* (1859) or the feminization of quest-romance by Zora Neale Hurston in *Their Eyes Were Watching God* (1937). The net result is a polyphony of voices rewriting the script of the Americas as these women present us with an empowering self-image in a culture that exalts masculine ideals and universalizes male experience.

Whereas Wheatley obliquely draws our attention to her race and gender, Anna Julia Cooper forcefully confronts the issue of feminist cultural politics embedded in Wheatley's "great design" in her 1892 *A Voice from the South*. Just as white men cannot speak through the consciousness of black men, neither can black *men* "fully and adequately . . . reproduce the exact Voice of the Black Woman" (iii). Cooper asserts that the black woman from her marginalized position at the bottom of society in the Americas illuminates the darkened stage of history; her voice must be heard: "Only the BLACK WOMAN can say 'when and where I enter, in the quiet, undisputed dignity of my womanhood, without violence and without suing or special patronage, then and there the whole . . . *race enters with me*'" (31).

Without the black woman's voice included in the overarching discourse, Cooper aptly points out, the world is visually impaired: "The world has had to limp along with the wobbling gait and one-side hesitancy of a man with one eye. Suddenly the bandage is removed from the other eye and the whole body is filled with light. It sees a circle where before it saw a segment. The darkened eye restored, every member rejoices with it" (122–23).

As a bridge that black women in the 1920s could cross, Cooper's feminist statement made it possible for black women to situate themselves in the historic project of reclamation and reconstruction. Black women writers of the Harlem Renaissance, the Caribbean, and Latin America began to explore the full range of black women's voices. For example, Jessie Fauset, Zora Neale Hurston, Gwendolyn Bennett, and Virginia Brindis de Salas give us four distinct portraits of the black woman's engagement with self and society. Their works reflect the continual exploration of the infinite complexity of the experience of black people in the Americas. These writers do not flinch before the awareness of themselves as black women in the Western Hemisphere. In this respect, Larsen's quicksands of representation is a recognizable metaphor for black women confronted with racism and sexism.

The legacy of black women writers from the 1920s to the 1950s, which reached a full flowering in the dawn of the United States civil rights movement, is their growing perception of themselves bound up with codes of domination and subordination. At bottom their lives reflected the inner crisis of black life in the Americas. Out of this matrix, we can begin to discern, as Hazel Carby observes, "the theoretical and historical questions raised by the construction of a tradition of black women writing."[5]

The civil rights, black power, and feminist movements spawned a new generation of black women critics such as Brenda Berrian, Hazel Carby, Barbara Christian, Carol Boyce Davies, Elaine Fido, Maryemma Graham, Trudier Harris, Karla F. C. Holloway, bell hooks, Joyce Joyce, Gloria Joseph, Deborah McDowell, Hortense J. Spillers, Barbara Smith, Valerie Smith, Cheryl A. Wall, Sherley Ann Williams, Miriam DeCosta-Willis, and Ann Venture Young. As Mary Helen Washington notes, these critics challenge us "to learn to read the African American literary tradition in new ways" (xxv). They raise issues of race and sex and make us more conscious of gender politics and the politics of gender. They present us with a more comprehensive model of literary maturity that causes us to rethink how we teach African American literature or mainstream American literature.

While the literary production of black women in the Americas was often impressive in the first half of the twentieth century, it was corseted and worn to support and shape the literary waistline of a male and feminist discourse. The unseen shaped the seen without having its presence acknowledged. Black women's writings as figurative undergarments become the sign for the legitimization of marginalization, not fit for discussion in public discourse. The work of black women slipped through the cracks of literary scholarship and into oblivion. With a few notable exceptions, it existed on the margins in a luminous darkness.

Robert E. Hemenway and Alice Walker ushered in a new era in the historic project of reclamation of black texts, especially those by and about black women, with the landmark publications of *Zora Neale Hurston: A Literary Biography* (1977) and *In Search of Our Mothers' Gardens* (1983). Other notable reclamation projects have been carried out by Frances Smith Foster and Melba Joyce Boyd (Frances E. W. Harper), Henry Louis Gates (Harriet Wilson), Gloria Hull (Alice Dunbar-Nelson), Charles R. Larson and Thadious M. Davis (Nella Larsen), Miriam DeCosta Willis (Ida Wells Barnett), and Jean Fagan Yellin (Harriet Jacobs). Perhaps the most impressive project of recovery and reclamation is the publication of *The Schomburg Library of Nineteenth-Century Black Women Writers,* edited by Henry Louis Gates Jr. in 1988. With the availability of all these texts, scholars can begin the assessment of the ideologies of womanhood represented in literature by and about black women.[6]

First and foremost, women are prominent participants and agents in the making a vibrant black literary tradition. In the very process of telling our collective (his)tory, their positionality endows them with a secondary vision that is missing from male texts. Building upon the heuristic call of Wheatley, these women reveal how gender affects genre. They also force the reader to confront "a theory of selfhood that is always under examination" (Benstock 1). In the process, they demystify many of the narrative codes governing literary discourse and ideology and their work resists easy definition.

As a result of the inclusion of these texts, scholars and critics are more attuned to an *aesthetics of intimacy,* with a focus on the interior life of the community. Richard Wright's *Native Son* (1940) and Ann Petry's *The Street* (1946), for example, place a different emphasis on the politics of interpretation and the way in which gender affects the texture of a fictive universe. Wright tends to identify the dilemma of black America with that of the oppressed male only. The black woman reminds him of his diminished status in patriarchal society. She is sacrificed on the altar of recrimination. In this regard, Petry offers a subtle revision of a patriarchal literary tradition by undermining its claim to a privileged objectivity. Emblematic of her literary foremothers, she transforms her generic subject position into a positive, collective one.

Finally, the inclusion of texts written by women from the Afro-Caribbean and Latin America not only makes possible a radical reassessment of New World black literature but also energizes our reading of the literature within the tradition. As sites for the construction of comparative black identities, the Caribbean and Latin America enable us to examine the structural affinities we have in common. Historically, we have examined the work of black men writers from this part of the diaspora to see what they have to tell us about the intellectual, cultural, and political implications of their lives as blacks in the New World. Rosemary Geisdorfer Feal reminds us that a "feminist consciousness" has emerged in the second half of the twentieth century in the Caribbean and Latin America "in societies that a few decades ago were closed to it for the most part" (10). By bringing together women writers from the Caribbean and Latin America such as Mary Prince (Bermuda and Antigua) and Virginia Brindis de Salas (Uruguay), scholars transform the canon, producing a dynamic interaction between black women of the United States, the Afro-Caribbean, and Latin America. The inclusion of Prince and Brindis de Salas is consistent with a growing movement that discusses New World black writers in a pan-American approach.[7]

Although in a matter of style, the women discussed in this volume clearly differ from each other, and although one needs to take some account of geography when studying their practice as writers, their thought bears witness to the stories told to them by their mothers and grandmothers. It is in this sense that we can speak of the synoptic overtones of their writings. They emphasize self and society, the artist's place within the community, the reconstruction of black sexuality, and the representation of a self that is black and female. Through their art, they minister to a discredited community. They call and respond to each other's testimonies. They attach much importance to the long memory of (her)story, a story they tell with great passion.

Through stratagems of appropriation and resistance, these black women writers assume and anticipate "a brighter coming day," when their heroism would be celebrated in a variety of media by their literary descendants, thereby altering our canons of knowledge and standards of beauty.

As viable hermeneutical devices for interpreting the works of black women writers, these works present no significant dichotomy in their articulation of what it means to be black and female in the New World. Other than the obvious distinctions between time and geography, these works share a striking similarity in historical *continuities.*

The first three essays are governed by what Fredric Jameson refers to as "the dialectics of difference and the paradoxical reversals of Identity and Difference."[8] Applying a political interpretation to literary study, he unearths the contradictions behind the unspoken assumptions about the nature of language, of interpretation, and of culture. Each of these essays moves from a criticism of displacement to a criticism of replacement. In the ways their very suggestive readings alter the terms of the discourse, they prompt us to realign our critical vision.

In "Witnesses and Practitioners: Attitudes Toward Miscegenation in Barbara Chase-Riboud's *Sally Hemings,*" Emma Waters Dawson's project is twofold: first, she rescues from critical obscurity Chase-Riboud's meticulously researched book and, second, she examines Chase-Riboud's construction of her text. The research yields a willful, resourceful, and gentle protagonist. The relationship between a Founding Father of the Republic—Thomas Jefferson—and his reputed slave mistress has been relegated to the underground national discourse, and this traps Hemings outside of history and effectively renders her silent.

Jefferson's relation with Hemings cannot be reduced to a simple interaction between master and slave. It is an event that is affected and controlled by a dialectic of economic materialism mediated by race and gender. Chase-Riboud recovers this legend of miscegenation from the resisting white American public and places it at the center of American discourse. She asserts her right to write a national (counter)romance.

It serves as a metaphor for the antihuman message at the heart of lofty national documents couched in a rhetoric of freedom. A careful reading of *Jefferson's Notes on the State of Virginia* (1787) reveals that he was intimately involved in an intense philosophical and scientific debate which would dominate much of nineteenth-century thought: What is a human being? How is a human being different from animals (or machines) that can perform labor? This heated debate, which raged on both sides of the Atlantic, involved luminaries such as Karl Marx, Charles Darwin, Frederick Douglass, John Stuart Mill, and Mary Shelley.

In *Frankenstein* (1816), Mary Shelley imagined an illusionary world inhabited by a ghoulish creation born of the human imagination. Dr. Frankenstein exercises unlimited powers of creation, dominance, and reproduction over the Monster that he creates. Shelley's Gothic illusion conjured up in the idle imaginings of privileged, nineteenth-century English romantic writers had a real-life counterpart in the New World. On a West Indian plantation under the ownership of an English slaveholder, a real life Frankenstein, Mary Prince, in her slender slave narrative (1831), depicts genocidal powers gone awry, reproductive aberrations, and attempts to make barren the human spirit.

In "The Two Marys (Prince and Shelley) on the Textual Meeting Ground of Race, Gender, and Genre," Helena Woodard reveals the paradoxical conditions of Mary Prince's existence as living, breathing proof of England's true-to-life Gothic horror story, and she addresses the silencing and marginalization of such stories by the literary establishment. Woodard's discussion of Mary Prince brings into sharp focus what Toni Morrison termed "the unspeakable things unspoken."[9] The life of Mary Prince illustrates that Mary Shelley's indulgence in the politics of deformation was no mere idle intellectual formulation; rather, it was an extension of the homogenizing—indeed even totalitarian—tendencies of a politics of deformation, and the erasure of her gender is reminiscent of Douglass's observation that "slavery abolished manhood and womanhood."

In "Harriet Wilson's *Our Nig:* The Demystification of Sentiment," Debra Walker King engages Henry Louis Gates's description of *Our Nig; or, Sketches from the Life of a Free Black* (1859) as the fusing of "an autobiographical, sentimental novel" and the slave narrative in "a deeply ironic" work. King contends that by inverting expected thematic tensions and subverting social ideologies, Wilson reveals the illusory nature of the constructs nineteenth-century America considered proper, conciliatory, and just. Rejecting the conventional aesthetics in favor of her own creation, Wilson presents a "uncategorized, intergeneric form" to her white, middle-class readers. In its most ambitious moments, this essay reveals several postmodern impulses within the novel which expose the contradictions and ambiguities of nineteenth-century hegemonic rhetoric.

The following four essays analyze those texts which have been neglected as a result of the sexuality and ideology of the author as well as the artist's place in the community. The writers articulate the discourse and context in which the works were produced. The women under discussion share a common concern for connecting the personal with the political. They were concerned with questions of power, equity, representation, and authority in a racist and sexist world. Gender, as a critical factor in the equation, adds another dimension to the struggle for human dignity.

Frances Smith Foster turns her attention in this collection to a reexamination of the position of a noted lecturer, author, and reformer in "Gender, Genre, and Vulgar Secularism: The Case of Frances Ellen Watkins Harper and the AME Press." Although the recognized canon of early African American literature does not ignore Harper as a writer, Foster, a major Harper scholar, argues that the critical community has tended to misrepresent Harper's achievements and to misread her texts. Her works are often used as a barometer to measure the paucity of African American literature prior to her arrival or to anticipate themes that would flourish in her wake. Foster attributes the patronizing attitudes toward Harper's work to sexism and to the bias of academic critics toward her writing style and subject matter. Foster historicizes both the attitudes and the art of the mid-nineteenth century, especially the ways in which Harper drew on traditions that were unabashedly sentimental, religious, and didactic. Foster situates Harper within the aesthetics and values of the churchgoing black middle class and shows us how one of the foremost writers of her era brought innovation to a socially conservative tradition.

In "Anna J. Cooper: The International Dimensions," David W. H. Pellow positions the essayist Cooper among her more celebrated colleagues, such as W. E. B. Du Bois, Alain Locke, and Marcus Garvey. An astute observer of the geopolitical situation of her day, Cooper made incisive observations on the political dynamics in Haiti, Canada, Africa, and Europe. This pivotal figure in the feminization of pan-African discourse drew upon her knowledge of imperialist aesthetics with its codes of domination to critique the colonial mindset. Pellow observes that her Sorbonne Ph.D. thesis, "L'Attitude de la France à l'égard de l'esclavage pendant la Révolution" (1925), is as much a history of the Saint-Domingue (Haiti) revolution as it is of French racial attitudes at the time. Cooper's work is original and creative, as it demonstrates insights and sensitivity which most others on the subject lack. In his discussion of Cooper, Pellow thus brings to bear an interpretative pressure on pan-African discourse that many in the intellectual community have chosen to ignore.

By the same token, many in the intellectual community have tended to ignore the travel literature of Jessie Redmon Fauset. Much praised for her role as the midwife of the Harlem Renaissance and as a novelist who delineated upper-middle-class black life, Jessie Fauset, Ivy League educated, also traveled extensively. In "The 'Invisible Woman' Abroad: Jessie Fauset's New Horizon," Erica L. Griffin contextualizes Fauset as a Francophile and maintains that "a comprehensive analysis of Fauset's fiction is incomplete without examining her six travel essays" that appeared in *The Crisis*. Griffin not only reveals an image of Fauset that counters the portrayal of her as being "prim and proper" but also demonstrates how Fauset incorporated her European and North African experiences into her fictive world.

In "A Blend of Voices: Composite Narrative Strategies in Biographical Reconstruction," Sandra Y. Govan details her fifteen-year odyssey of recovery and reclamation of Gwendolyn Bennett. Govan moves beyond W. E. B. Du Bois's paradigm of the divided self, the "two warring ideals in one dark body" from in his 1903 *Souls of Black Folk*, to expand this image of black psychology in her study of Bennett. In addition to traditional resources, Govan uses a composite narrative strategy drawing from diaries, scrapbooks, and letters, "in an active rather than passive manner," and oral testimony from peers, colleagues, and friends. Govan also adheres to the admonition of Arnold Rampersad that the writer of black autobiography must "[seek] insights from a psychoanalytic perspective." Rampersad charges the black autobiographer to address forthrightly the "full spectrum of the human personality, politics, sexuality, and artistic sensibility" (197) without fear of "overprotectiveness toward the subject or toward the race" (196). Bringing this sympathetic critique to her study of Gwendolyn Bennett, Govan helps us to better understand our own lives and our society.

The next two essays reflect the resurgent interest in Ann Lane Petry, whose work has been displaced traditionally by the masculinist discourse and spatial configuration of Richard Wright, Ralph Ellison, and James Baldwin. Her tightly crafted novels are read as distant literary cousins to her more acclaimed male models. Petry is recognized by African American scholars as a central figure in the tradition of women's writing, but mainly through reference to her depiction of environmental determinism in *The Street* (1946). In a paradigm shift, Trudier Harris and Joyce Pettis show how the Connecticut-born Petry in two of her neglected novels critiques masculine ideology and aesthetic judgment.

In "Before the Stigma of Race: Authority and Witchcraft in Ann Petry's *Tituba of Salem Village*," Harris examines history and ideology as a shaping influence on character. Seldom does our meditation on history involve religion and conjuration to consider how black women may have fared in the colonies in the early days of the Republic when women, often simply because they were women, were believed to be something other than human, even in league with the devil. In *Tituba* (1964), Ann Petry presents a slightly different view of how a black woman came to be maligned. Petry rewrites the history of a slave woman from Barbados who was accused of witchcraft. Harris's project is to reclaim Petry's historical novel from the juvenile bookshelf.

In "Reading Ann Petry's *The Narrows* into Black Literary Tradition," Joyce Pettis sees *The Narrows* (1953) as an overlooked minor classic that is important to our understanding of black women's writing and positions it as a text worthy of recovery. *The Narrows* is as unyielding in its presentation of place and character as is *The Street;* it offers a tight study of several inhabitants of The Narrows, a riverside community where "Negroes had replaced those other earlier immigrants, the Irish, the Italians and the Poles." Thematically, *The Narrows* surpasses *The Street* in complexity since several extensively developed subplots are connected to the story of protagonist Lincoln Williams.

In "The Unmasking of Virginia Brindis de Salas: Minority Discourse of Afro-Uruguay," Caroll Mills Young examines the mystery surrounding the authenticity of the poetry of the Afro-Uruguayan de Salas and illuminates the ideology her poetics. According to Alberto Britos Serrat, who edited the first anthology of Afro-Uruguayan poetry, *Antologia de Poetas Negros Uruguayos* (1990), those works published by de Salas in *Pregón de Marimorena (The Call of Mary Morena)* in 1946 are not her original compositions but the works of Julio Guadalupe, her contemporary. Young reexamines Virginia Brindis de Salas as one of the most celebrated writers of African-Uruguayan descent and addresses the issues of authorship and authenticity of *Pregón de Marimorena.*

The essays here collected invite us to take another look at writers whose works have been neglected and marginalized in black and feminist traditions. They may be read as a series of meditations on denial and resistance to marginalization. These essays cause us to refocus our critical vision and the way we construct a canon. The community of scholars who contribute to this volume provide suggestive readings that free us from the tyranny of masculinist texts and acknowledge the central role black women in the Americas have played in the production of meaning.

NOTES

The epigraphs are taken from Phillis Wheatley, "On Recollection," *The Poems of Phillis Wheatley,* ed. Julian D. Mason (1966; Chapel Hill: U of North Carolina P, 1989), 76 and Audre Lorde, "Poetry Is Not a Luxury," *Sister Outsider: Essays and Speeches* (Trumansburg, NY: Crossing P, 1984), 38.

1. CLA has played a pivotal role in African American intellectual formation. For additional information on this association, see Therman B. O'Daniel, introduction, *A Twenty-Five-Year Cumulative Author-Title Index to the CLA Journal (1957–1982)* (Baltimore: J. H. Furst, 1985), xi–xxx; Carolyn Fowler, *The College Language Association: A Social History* (Ann Arbor, Mich.: University Microfilms, 1988); and Dolan Hubbard, "Why CLA Still Prospers," *Black Issues in Higher Education* (25 Aug. 1994): 57.

2. Hortense J. Spillers, "Introduction: Who Cuts the Border? Some Readings on 'America,'" *Comparative American Identities: Race, Sex, and Nationality in the Modern Text,* ed. Spillers (New York: Routledge, 1991), 1–25. In her introduction to this provocative collection of essays, Spillers maps out a dynamic terrain of "New World" cultural identities, questions, and problems. Also see Gustavo Pérez Firmat, ed., *Do the Americas Have a Common Literature?* (Durham, NC: Duke UP, 1990) and Edward Mullen, "Afro-Hispanic and Afro-American Literary Historiography: Comments on Generational Shifts," *College Language Association Journal* 38.4 (June 1995): 371–89. None of the essays in the Firmat volume specifically address the issue of race and ethnicity.

3. After an exhaustive search, Mason concludes that he cannot substantiate Senegal as the home of Wheatley (3 n. 2). In his chronology, John Shields suggests that she was born "perhaps along the Gambia River" (337). Wheatley was the first African American (the second woman, after Anne Bradstreet) to publish a book of poetry in the United States (1773). In *Notes on the State of Virginia,* Jefferson did not consider the compositions of Wheatley to be poetry (1787; Chapel Hill: U of North Carolina P, 1955), 140. Others who have offered a more complimentary view of Wheatley include such writers as Gertrude Mossell, F. E. W. Harper, and W. S. Scarborough. See also Barbara Christian, "Afro-American Women Poets: A His-

torical Introduction (1982)," *Black Feminist Criticism: Perspectives on Black Women Writers* (New York: Pergamon, 1985), 119–25 and Alice Walker, who, quite correctly, noted that Wheatley preserved for her descendants "the notion of song" in the only manner she could (qtd. in Christian 120). In "In Search of Our Mothers' Gardens," Walker identifies only three literary foremothers: Phillis Wheatley, Nella Larsen, and Zora Neale Hurston. See also Houston A. Baker, *The Journey Back: Issues in Black Literature and Criticism* (Chicago: U of Chicago P, 1980), 6–15, passim; Sondra O'Neale, "A Slave's Subtle War: Phillis Wheatley's Use of Biblical Myth and Symbol," *EAL* 21.2 (Fall 1986): 144–65; and Ann Allen Shockley, *Afro-American Women Writers: 1746–1933* (New York: Meridian, 1989), 17–25.

4. Eleanor W. Traylor, Response, *Afro-American Literary Study in the 1990s*, ed. Houston A. Baker Jr. and Patricia Redmond (Chicago: U of Chicago P, 1989), 129.

5. Hazel Carby, *Reconstructing Womanhood: The Emergence of the Afro-American Woman Novelist* (New York: Oxford UP, 1987).

6. Others who joined in this project of reclamation include: Mari Evans, ed., *Black Women Writers (1950–1980): A Critical Evaluation* (Garden City, NY: Anchor/ Doubleday, 1984); Frances Smith Foster, *Witnessing Slavery: The Development of the Ante-Bellum Slave Narratives* (Westport; CT: Greenwood P, 1979); Stanlie M. James and Abenia P. A. Busia, *Theorizing Black Feminisms: The Visionary Pragmatism of Black Women* (New York: Routledge, 1994); Ann duCille, *The Coupling Convention: Sex, Text, and Tradition in Black Women's Fiction* (New York: Oxford UP, 1993); Michael Awkward, *Inspiriting Influences: Tradition, Revision, and Afro-American Women's Novels* (New York: Columbia UP, 1989); Gloria T. Hull, *Color, Sex and Poetry: Three Women Writers of the Harlem Renaissance* (Bloomington: Indiana UP, 1987); Hortense J. Spillers and Marjorie Pryse, eds., *Conjuring: Black Women, Fiction, and Literary Tradition* (Bloomington: Indiana UP, 1985); Houston A. Baker Jr., *Workings of the Spirit: The Poetics of Afro-American Women's Writing* (Chicago: U of Chicago P, 1991); Claudia Tate, *Domestic Allegories of Political Desire: The Black Heroines' Text at the Turn of the Century* (New York: Oxford UP, 1992); and Margaret Busby, ed., *Daughters of Africa: An International Anthology of Words and Writings by Women of African Descent: From the Ancient Egyptian to the Present* (New York: Pantheon, 1992). Other restoration projects are being carried out by Beacon Press in its Black Women Writers Series under the editorship of Deborah E. McDowell and by Rutgers University Press.

7. Recent works that examine the construction of a New World identity include those by Marvin A. Lewis, *Afro-Argentine Discourse: Another Dimension of the Black Diaspora* (Columbia: U of Missouri: P, 1996); Carol Boyce Davis and 'Molara Ogundipe-Leslie, eds., *Moving Beyond Boundaries*, vol. 1, *International Dimensions of Black Women's Writing*, and vol. 2, *Black Women's Diasporas* (New York: New York UP, 1995); Margaret Busby (see note 6 above); Miriam DeCosta Willis, "Afra-Hispanic Writers and Feminist Discourse," *NWSA Journal* 5.2 (1993): 204–18; Karla F. C. Holloway, *Moorings and Metaphors: Figures of Culture and Gender in Black Women's Literature* (New Brunswick, NJ: Rutgers UP, 1992); Hortense J. Spillers (see note 2 above); Gustavo Pérez Firmat (see note 2 above); A. La Vonne Brown Ruoff and Jerry W. Ward Jr., eds., *Redefining American Literary History* (New York: MLA, 1990): 1–5; Ian Isidore Smart, *Nicolás Guillén: Popular Poet of the Caribbean* (Columbia: U of Missouri P, 1990); Carole Boyce Davies and Elaine Fido, eds., *Out of the Kumbla: Caribbean Women and Literature* (New York: Africa World P, 1990); and Ann Venture Young, *The Image of Black Women in 20th Cen-*

tury *South American Poetry: A Bilingual Anthology* (Washington, DC: Three Continents P, 1987). For trenchant reappraisal of the movement toward a pan-American aesthetic, see Edward Mullen, (See Note 2 above) and Rosemary Geisdorfer Feal, "The Afro-Latin American Woman Writer: Drumming with a Difference," *Afro-Hispanic Review* 14.2 (Fall 1995): 10–12.

8. Fredric Jameson, foreword, *Caliban and Other Essays,* by Roberto Fernandez Retamar, trans. Edward Baker (Minneapolis: U of Minnesota P, 1989), viii.

9. Toni Morrison, "Unspeakable Things Unspoken: The Afro-American Presence in American Literature," *Michigan Quarterly Review* 28 (Winter 1989): 1–34.

WORKS CITED

Baker, Houston A., Jr. *The Journey Back: Issues in Black Literature and Criticism.* Chicago: U of Chicago P, 1980.

Busby, Margaret, ed. *Daughters of Africa: An International Anthology of Words and Writings by Women of African Descent: From the Ancient Egyptian to the Present.* New York: Pantheon, 1992.

Carby, Hazel V. *Reconstructing Womanhood: The Emergence of the Afro-American Woman Novelist.* New York: Oxford UP, 1987.

Christian, Barbara. "Afro-American Women Poets: A Historical Introduction (1982)." *Black Feminist Criticism: Perspectives on Black Women Writers.* New York: Pergamon, 1985. 119–25.

Davies, Carole Boyce, and Elaine Fido, eds. *Out of the Kumbla: Caribbean and Literature.* New York: Africa World P, 1990.

Davies, Carole Boyce, and 'Molara Ogundipe-Leslie, eds. *International Dimensions of Black Women's Writing.* New York: New York UP, 1995. Vol. 1 of *Moving Beyond Boundaries.*

———. *Black Women's Diasporas.* New York: New York UP, 1995. Vol. 2 of *Moving Beyond Boundaries.*

Firmat, Gustavo Pérez, ed. *Do the Americas Have a Common Literature?* Durham, NC: Duke UP, 1990.

Fowler, Carolyn. *The College Language Association: A Social History.* Ann Arbor, Mich.: University Microfilms, 1988.

Holloway, Karla F. C. *Moorings and Metaphors: Figures of Culture and Gender in Black Women's Literature.* New Brunswick, NJ: Rutgers UP, 1992.

Hubbard, Dolan. "Why CLA Still Prospers." *Black Issues in Higher Education* (25 Aug. 1994): 57.

Jameson, Fredric. Foreword. *Caliban and Other Essays.* By Roberto Fernandez Retamar. Trans. Edward Baker. Minneapolis: U of Minnesota P, 1989.

Jefferson, Thomas. *Notes on the State of Virginia.* 1787. Chapel Hill: U of North Carolina P, 1955.

Lorde, Audre. "Poetry Is Not a Luxury." *Sister Outsider: Essays and Speeches.* Trumansburg, NY: Crossing P, 1984. 36–39.

Morrison, Toni. "Unspeakable Things Unspoken: The Afro-American Presence in American Literature." *Michigan Quarterly Review* 28 (Winter 1989): 1–34.

Mullen, Edward. "Afro-Hispanic and Afro-American Literary Historiography: Comments on Generational Shifts." *College Language Association Journal* 38.4 (June 1995): 371–89.

O'Daniel, Therman B. Introduction. *A Twenty-Five-Year Cumulative Author-Title Index to the CLA Journal (1957–1982).* Baltimore: J. H. Furst, 1985. xi-xxx.

O'Neale, Sondra. "A Slave's Subtle War: Phillis Wheatley's Use of Biblical Myth and Symbol." *EAL* 21.2 (Fall 1986): 144–65.

Shockley, Ann Allen, ed. *Afro-American Women Writers: 1746–1933.* New York: Meredian, 1989.

Smart, Ian Isidore. *Nicolás Guillén: Popular Poet of the Caribbean.* Columbia: U of Missouri P, 1990.

Spillers, Hortense J., ed. *Comparative American Identities: Race, Sex, and Nationality in the Modern Text.* New York: Routledge, 1991.

Tate, Claudia. *Domestic Allegories of Political Desire: The Black Heroines' Text at the Turn of the Century.* New York: Oxford UP, 1992.

Traylor, Eleanor W. Response. *Afro-American Literary Study in the 1990s.* Ed. Houston A. Baker Jr. and Patricia Redmond. Chicago: U of Chicago P, 1989. 128–34.

Walker, Alice. *In Search of Our Mothers' Gardens.* New York: Harcourt, Brace, Jovanovich, 1983.

Wheatley, Phillis. *The Collected Works of Phillis Wheatley.* Ed. John Shields. New York: Oxford UP, 1988.

———. *The Poems of Phillis Wheatley.* Ed. Julian D. Mason. 1966. Rev. and enl., Chapel Hill: U of North Carolina P, 1989.

Willis, Miriam DeCosta, ed. *Blacks in Hispanic Literature: Critical Essays.* Port Washington, NY: Kennikat, 1977.

Willis, Miriam DeCosta, "Afra-Hispanic Writers and Feminist Discourse." *NWSA Journal* 5.2 (1993): 204–18.

Young, Ann Venture. *The Image of Black Women in 20th Century South American Poetry: A Bilingual Anthology.* Washington, DC: Three Continents P, 1987.

Witnesses and Practitioners:
Attitudes toward Miscegenation in Barbara Chase-Riboud's *Sally Hemings*

EMMA WATERS DAWSON

In 1979, amid widely varied critical reception—much of it controversial—Barbara Chase-Riboud published an epic novel, *Sally Hemings*. Prompted, in part, by Fawn Brodie's 1974 biography *Thomas Jefferson: An Intimate History*, Chase-Riboud revisions history as she reinserts into it the slave woman's voice.[1] She adapts to fiction the life and experiences of Sally Hemings, the reputed mistress of American statesman Thomas Jefferson. Basing her novel upon the much disputed thirty-eight-years' affair between Jefferson and Hemings following the death of his wife—the half-sister of Sally—and resulting in the birth of seven children, Chase-Riboud raises many questions about their illicit and illegal love affair.[2] As the slave mistress of Jefferson, Hemings was placed in a highly contradictory position—connected, yet excluded from the dominant discourse of American politics. She had no recognizable public presence. The novel *Sally Hemings* captures Hemings's public presence, places her at the center of American political discourse, and questions the issue of marriage and property.

Hemings's public voice is silenced not only because she is an unmarried woman but also because she has the blood of Africa flowing in her veins; consequently, she does not conform to the dominant ideologies of womanhood which excluded her from the definition of woman.[3] Chase-Riboud recovers and reconstructs the vibrant presence of the enslaved Hemings, whose voice is silenced by the political and sexual ideologies of the nineteenth century. She produces an alternative American romance—one that counters the official national romances of George and Martha Washington and James and Dolly Madison.

Though consigned to live in darkness (shadows), Hemings fires the emotions of Jefferson. Their love disrupts the social text, for it reveals a split between public and private self-representations. Specifically, it is the notion of a private romance between master and slave expressed through Jefferson's ritual visits to her cabin at the end of the road that forms the link between his ruminations on race and our continuing debate on race and rights. Of Sally Hemings, Chase-Riboud states, "That she loved [Jefferson]—in the way we interpret love today—is still a question. . . . it still hangs in the air, even after you've read the book. And you will have to make up your own mind" (Wilson 13). Significantly, the novel challenges conventional notions of what was possible for black slave women. In her quiet way, Chase-Riboud's Hemings transgresses the boundaries of slave etiquette. Finally, the novel challenges us to read African American women's literary tradition in new ways.

To assist in this process, I suggest an examination of the diverse attitudes toward miscegenation, as believed, questioned, professed, voiced, lived, and affirmed by the characters in the eighteenth-century Albemarle County, Virginia, setting where American cultural etiquette has relegated the Jefferson-Hemings love story to the back pages of American history. Passed down from generation to generation, this dramatic love story, nevertheless, survives in black folklore.[4] Within the parameters of an 1830s setting, Chase-Riboud, through flashback technique, explores the consciousness of various characters and affirms codes of conduct for the practitioners and witnesses of miscegenation.

Despite condemnatory rebuttals by apologists who have defended Jefferson's character and not Hemings's, Chase-Riboud published her work as fiction, not history; consequently, the present discussion will consider *Sally Hemings* as a novel based on historical fact. I will survey the text in its adherence to features of the novel such as chronological progression, continued presence of leading characters, the dramatic re-creation of a world through action, dialogue, and images which recall this larger than life love story between Jefferson and Hemings. Through a series of shifts in the consciousness of various characters and fragmentary dialogue, Chase-Riboud reveals the unsanctioned romantic codes that caused love to blossom in the heart of master and slave. Thus, the novel is an attempt to revision, reclaim, and empower an African American slave woman denied her place in historical texts. In effect, Chase-Riboud re-creates the 1830s Albemarle County, Virginia, setting with its easy gentility that masks the cruel nature of "the peculiar institution."

By depicting the various interactions between slave and master, black and white, and male and female through shifts in consciousness and dialogue between characters, Chase-Riboud transforms *Sally Hemings* into a vehicle of rage directed not only against the ironies present in Thomas Jefferson's personal "history" but also against the principles of the Founding Fathers, resulting in her empowerment of a black female slave protagonist never freed by her master and lover. The proximity of this comely slave concubine to the "apostle of freedom" posed a clear and present danger to our national myth of Anglo-American superiority.

The central theme in *Sally Hemings,* however, is miscegenation and the effect of the power of love between slave master and concubine, manifested not only through the relationship between the fictional Thomas Jefferson and Sally Hemings but also through other relationships: public official–slave, parent-child (master and slave), slave woman–slave mistress, slave mother–daughter, slave master–slave mistress, and male-female slave. Through a careful review of the historical record, Chase-Riboud juxtaposes the characters to reveal their corresponding and opposing attitudes toward miscegenation. She empowers Hemings through dialogue, snippets of conversation, testimonials, and indirection. Through backhanded compliments and unconscious slips of the tongue, characters depict a woman of great integrity. The net effect is that Chase-Riboud provides Hemings with a measure of authority unknown to her in real life.[5]

My purpose here in focusing upon the black female protagonist and her assertions and reactions to the behavior of others is to establish Chase-Riboud's empowerment of the black female slave. Hemings, as metaphor for slave women, displaces the criticism heaped upon her by historians and other critics of oral history.[6] Specifically, I intend to examine Chase-Riboud's development of the theme of miscegenation and its meaning to key figures in the novel who either witnessed or practiced miscegenation within the dramatically re-created experience of slavery in this historical romance. By representing the tension between Jefferson's desire to be a gentle lover in private and his public objection to social intercourse between whites and blacks (his concord with prevailing political and sexual ideology), Chase-Riboud illuminates the chasm between the proper mulatta and respectability.[7]

Chase-Riboud recognizes the problem of unity in her historical reconstruction. As a partial solution, she introduces the seven sections and a majority of the novel's forty-five chapters with quotations from an ecumenical array of political personalities and social critics (e.g., Abigail Adams, Thomas Carlyle, Margaret Douglas, Edmund Burke, Friedrich Engels, Mary Boykin Chestnut, Harriet Beecher Stowe, Frederick Douglass, and W. E. B. Du Bois) on the contradictions inherent in both slavery and love. The cumulative effect of these quotations serve to remind the reader of the racist and sexist attitudes that inform America's august national documents, such as the Declaration of Independence and Constitution. In spite of state-sanctioned oppression, the democratic impulse of love transcends the socially constructed barriers of class and caste.

The epigraph that introduces chapter 1 sets the tenor and tone of the historical romance and ironically foreshadows events to unfold. Jefferson's own words from the privately published *Notes on the State of Virginia* (1790) function as metaphor for the new Republic's struggle with the dark night of its national soul and present the reader with the difficulty many American citizens have in transcending race and color: "There must doubtless be an unhappy influence on the manners of our people produced by the existence of slavery among us" (162).[8]

In this astute analysis, Jefferson acknowledges that the institutionalization of slavery began the nation's descent into sin. Miscegenation is the scarlet letter of national shame. Miscegenation derives from two Latin words, *miscere* (to mix) and *genus* (race), to denote the abstract idea of the mixture of two or more races.[9] The mulatta is the physical manifestation of white, male America's libertine manners—and of its strident refusal to acknowledge patrimony. In the retelling of the Jefferson-Hemings romance, Chase-Riboud places a human face on this contradiction in the American national character.

The novel begins in flashback in Albemarle County, Virginia, twenty-six years after the death of Thomas Jefferson. Chase-Riboud develops first the relationship existing between the public official and slave through the consciousness of the white census taker, Nathan Langdon, and his thoughts on the "myths" of slavery as he approaches the cabin of Sally Hemings and her two sons, Eston and Madison, the only remaining two of the five living children who have not yet "strolled away," that is, passed for white. Langdon recalls his northern education and his experience of convincing northerners about the realities of slavery and dispelling popular tales to establish that Virginian slave owners did not own thousands of slaves that they starved and beat, that the slave owners' and slaves' breeding habits were not aberrant, and that neither possessed an inordinate number of abnormalities, such as "tails, two heads."[10]

Chase-Riboud explores the consciousness of a white public official as his southern white male perspective questions others' (northerners') misconceptions about slave ownership, treatment of slaves, and irregular physical and sexual dispositions of slave owners and slaves. Langdon, who embodies the sensibility of the landed gentry, disclaims such myths while simultaneously relying upon a belief in the inherent, "God-given" superiority of whites over blacks. He accepts uncritically the offspring of slave master and slave as proof of sin against the moral order. Langdon represents the eighteenth- and nineteenth-century southern, white, male slave owner and his peculiar attitude toward miscegenation.

Pondering his inability to explain the system to northerners so that they might understand, Langdon asserts to himself that the intimate nature of miscegenation hybridizes a superior and inferior race; "to intermingle them was an error against God, Nature and Society. No matter how many mulattoes, quadroons, octoroons, metis issued from lust or passion" (8). The expectation that either party engaged in miscegenation should have behaved in an ethically straightforward decorum is somewhat presumptuous and incredible when such liaisons were deemed illegal and taboo despite the pervasiveness of its practice. Hence, at the core of Langdon's belief system is a society vastly different in its protocol for masters and slaves as well as for men and women.

Even after the New England–educated Langdon visits the home of Sally Hemings, a former slave who looks white, he finds it extremely difficult to address her as a respectable woman. Her gentility negates everything he has been taught to believe about the supposedly inferior race. When the census taker meets the much discussed but seldom seen mystery woman of Albemarle

County, her very presence causes the rumors of her affair with Thomas Jefferson to recede into the background. No longer the invisible woman, Hemings calls into question the irrational basis for the racial stereotypes that trap her outside of history. Full of ambivalence, Langdon resolves the conflict in a manner consistent with his socialization in a white, patriarchal society. He refuses to acknowledge that Thomas Jefferson could be guilty of miscegenation—a tabooed practice if acknowledged publicly.

Accordingly, Langdon analyzes the implications behind the rumored affair between Jefferson and Hemings when he considers Sally Hemings's rumored identity and the liaison with Jefferson, concluding that the statesman may, indeed, have violated the law against miscegenation (17). Langdon not only records the ages, family status, and occupation of Sally Hemings and her two sons, but he also writes in their race as white. As census taker, he denies the American slave woman Sally Hemings her rightful place in history. Chase-Riboud's depiction of Langdon's identifying Hemings as white illustrates his manipulation of public documents and symbolizes how history may be altered by the recorder, whether he be historian or census taker.

Interestingly enough, historian Fawn Brodie alludes to the one missing record in the letter-index volume recording Jefferson's incoming and outgoing letters for the critical year of 1788. Jefferson went on vacation to Holland and Germany while he was ambassador in Paris; Sally Hemings accompanied him there as maid to his two daughters. Brodie wrote: "This raises the question whether or not someone at some time went through Jefferson's papers systematically eliminating every possible reference to Sally Hemings. Letters from Jefferson to Sally's brothers, and from her brothers to him, are extant. But no letters or notes exchanged between Sally Hemings and Thomas Jefferson have yet ever found their way into the public record" (301). The novel *Sally Hemings,* therefore, becomes a necessary response not only to historical texts but also to white, male reality manifested in the control of history. Hence, in changing Sally Hemings's racial identity, Langdon also erases Jefferson's "sin" and legal violation, miscegenation—actions depicted and implied through Chase-Riboud's creative response to Langdon's character (21–22).

Chase-Riboud also explores miscegenation through a parent-child relationship in shifting consciousness to center upon the offspring of a mixed relationship. The chapter's maxim characterizing the state of this relationship also excerpts from Jefferson's *Notes on the State of Virginia, 1790.* It reads: "The parent storms, the child looks on, catches the lineaments of wrath, puts on the same airs in the circle of smaller slaves, gives a loose to his worst of passions, and thus nursed, educated, and daily exercised in tyranny, cannot but be stamped by it with odious peculiarities" (22).

Literally, this epigraph relates to the behavior of the slave owner's white child. As he becomes heir to his parent's property, he assumes the father's conduct. Because the prevailing code of conduct dictated that the white father not acknowledge his slave offspring, his children followed suit, resulting in generations of perpetual silence, as well as a lack of self-identity for the mixed offspring. In the context of the Hemings' family status as former slaves in Virginia, where it was illegal for free blacks to reside, Sally's son Madison tries to understand his mother's refusal to leave Monticello. Through his character, Chase-Riboud imagines the impact of miscegenation upon the offspring of such a liaison. Madison, for example, realizes gradually that his mother is mute on the subject of his paternity; her silence on his origins is consistent with the way slave children were reared. In his or her confrontation with the silence of history, the slave child's main source of information regarding paternal identity remained older slaves, mammies, and whites' conversations. Received in such a covert manner, the information provided bitterness, pain, and humiliation "without alleviating the burden" (26).

Manifesting "odious peculiarities," as Jefferson described the effect of slavery upon children, Madison recalls his self-inflicted pain which prompted him to butt his head against the fence, producing blood, because "he couldn't understand why his father didn't love him" (26). Built out of impotence, Madison's rage is the result of miscegenation's effect upon the offspring, yet it is also indicative of the erasure of self-identity that characterizes the plight of slave children.

Chase-Riboud's depiction of the legacy of the slave son in her historical romance is similar to the recent characterization of Golden Gray in Toni Morrison's latest novel, *Jazz* (1992). After learning the identity of his father, Gray, a child of mixed parentage—the white mistress and black male slave—initially seeks his father, Hunters Hunter (Henry Les Troy or Lestory), in order to kill him. However, in comparing his emptiness (the loss of a father) to an amputated arm, the character reveals the feelings and emotions of the mulatto offspring who has been raised ignorant of his father's identity. Though *Sally Hemings* and *Jazz* contrast the racial identities of the fathers, both children still experience a void in their lives life—a lack of self-identity.

A rhetoric of silence undermines the ideology of motherhood in the slave community. Truth is corrupted; motherhood is a lie, for it is incompatible with the ideology of slavery. Placed in an untenable position, the slave mother tries to comply with her dual and contradictory roles as worker and concubine. In "Somebody Forgot to Tell Somebody Something," Barbara Christian comments on the challenge before the African American woman writer. The African American woman writer must recover the voice of the black woman and displace a deafening silence surrounding her active role of heroic resistance. The cost of this silence still undermines the social fabric of the African American community. It stunts the vitality of the community, as is evident in the concern that post–World War II generation of African Americans have for their children's lack of knowledge of their history (326).

Similarly Chase-Riboud sees a parallel situation in post-revolutionary America. Sally Hemings maintains a deafening silence as she strives to protect the identity of her children's father. In a cruel irony, she protects the identity of Jefferson, a Founding Father of the new Republic, while simultaneously blocking their just claim to their patrimony as sons of the founder. The post-revolutionary setting of the novel serves to heighten the irony. This Founding Father did not intend for freedom to apply equally to the enslaved Africans, even if they had his blood flowing through their veins. Jefferson's public denial of Hemings underscores the pervasive influence of the tabooed behavior not only upon them, but also upon future generations. Future generations are heirs to the denial of patrimony. Figuratively and literally, the curse of the father would be visited upon future generations. It is in this sense that Chase-Riboud's recreation of the Jefferson-Hemings relationship is a mediation on history. Surely, the exploration of miscegenation via the adult examination of childhood knowledge underscores the pervasive influence of the tabooed behavior not only upon the couple involved in the illicit relationship but also upon future generations.

In the Albemarle County setting of 1830, Sally Hemings flashes back to an earlier time, 22 August 1807, when her mother, Elizabeth Hemings, dies at age seventy-two. Present at her bedside are Sally and Martha Jefferson Randolph, Jefferson's daughter and Sally's niece, since Martha is the offspring of Jefferson and his wife, Martha Wayles Jefferson, Sally's half-sister. John Wayles, another white slave owner, fathered both Martha Wayles Jefferson and six of Elizabeth Hemings's twelve children. It is through this bedside scenario of the women's interactions with each other that Chase-Riboud develops relations between slave mistress and slave woman concubine, the slave woman's compliance to her dual roles of worker and concubine, and the oral inheritance from slave-mother concubine to slave-daughter concubine.

On her deathbed, Elizabeth recounts her life—serving the passions of John Wayles and running his household for eleven years—her connection with his white children (especially Martha), and her love for both the black and white children. Elizabeth's confession implies an ethic of laboring benignly as a mammy figure, yet adapting to her forced state without malice. Certainly, the scene responds to historical fact, for, according to C. Minrose Gwin, "it is not the smallest irony of the slavocracy that its codes of conduct demanded moral superiority from white women and sexual availability from black, yet simultaneously expected mistress and slave woman to live and work in intimate physical proximity" (39). Continuing inquiry into another relative effect of miscegenation, Chase-Riboud describes "a strange and southern circle of complicity: the concubine, daughter, the mistress and the slave; the aunt and the niece.

The three women reflected the intricate and convoluted ties that bound them one to the other: blood, love, servitude, hate, womanhood, time" (28).

The bonds of family revolve around the white slave master, who—as father, master, husband, and lover—creates feelings of love, servitude, hate, and acceptance.[11] Though the slave master's role is framed by the connection existing between slave mistress and slave woman, Chase-Riboud focuses on the bond between slave mother and daughter. She creatively inquires into another relative effect of miscegenation, the code of silence regarding the slave master's miscegenation in a patriarchal society. However, in Elizabeth's deathbed account of John Wayles's dying and not freeing her or any of her children, Elizabeth reminds Sally of the advice she has given all of her beautiful daughters: "Don't love no masta if he don't promise in writing to free your children. Don't do it. Get killed first, get beaten first. The best is not to love them in the first place. Love your own color if you can, and if you're chosen, get that freedom for your children. . . . He never promised and I never asked. I just expected. A terrible thing for a slave to do. Expect" (31).

Elizabeth's admonishment gives valuable insight to the study of the link between written language and power, for without written documentation to free them, both Elizabeth and Sally, two generations witnessing and practicing miscegenation, remain merely a slave master's concubine, his legal property. In her deathbed litany, Elizabeth Hemings announces to Sally and Martha why Jefferson years earlier had lost a case defending a mulatto claiming freedom because his great-grandmother was a white woman who had a child by a black slave father. She tells them that the state of Virginia did not want to hear anything about a white woman committing miscegenation, for they felt that all of her babies would be born black. Furthermore, she tells them, such a white woman found guilty of amalgamation risked being sold into slavery for five years and having her child sold for thirty years. She wonders why the law did not apply as well to a black woman having a "white" baby.

In "The Darkened Eye Restored," a cogent review of black women in the making of American literary history, Mary Helen Washington shows that two generations later a caravan of black women scholars fulfill her expectations. Busy about their mother's house, black women scholars explore the manifold dimensions of the life lived by their foremothers and smash pernicious stereotypes. Drawing upon feminist cultural history and literary theory, they drive a truth train across the missing pages of American history, picking up the stories told by their wayfaring sisters. Washington notes, "Their literature [black women writers'] is about Black women; it takes the trouble to record the thoughts, words, feelings, and deeds of Black women, experiences that make the realities of being black in America look very different from what men have written" (35). In the above passage, Chase-Riboud not only captures the material conditions under which so many black women were forced to live but she also reveals the willing suspension of belief on the part of many white women. Hence, Chase-Riboud considers the sexual determination of both black and white women in exploring Elizabeth's testimony to the power the slave master wielded. She confesses her errors in mothering Sally and her daughters in the only way she knew how. She ultimately realizes that her vision of the perfect slave had coincided with Jefferson's vision of the perfect woman. The mother dies full of contempt and love, convinced her daughter not only loved Thomas Jefferson, but also that Sally "was still childish, rancorless, detached, except for that which concerned what she loved" (39).

As Barbara Christian reminds us, "Re-memory is a critical determinant in how we value the past, what we remember, what we select to emphasize; what we forget" (1990, 333). When Sally recalls a scene that occurred more than twenty years earlier, she forces herself to acknowledge both her mother's and her own past. She realizes that both she and her mother had erred in their blind trust of their masters/lovers. At a time when Sally feels her aloneness, she remembers the urgency of her mother's dying confession, as well as Elizabeth's reprimand years earlier in the spring of 1795, after her return to Monticello following Sally's sojourn in Paris. In Elizabeth's advising and reproving Sally, the mother points out the trapped state of both women. She upbraids Sally for foolishly returning from her state of freedom in Paris to slavery in Virginia, endangering her life, gambling with her fate as a slave woman, and testing the power of love in her liaison with Jefferson. Elizabeth justifiably voices her disapproval of the affair as a mother who has not only witnessed miscegenation but also practiced it as well. She rants: "You forgot the first lesson of slavery, your blackness. And you forgot the second, loving somebody you ain't got no business loving. . . . The man you got has no business loving, either. He's put himself in danger as well—don't forget that when you start feeling sorry for yourself. In danger from his own white folks, loving somebody, he, with all his money and power, ain't got no right to love" (209).

The abolitionists' slogan that complete power corrupts is nowhere more apparent than in Elizabeth's assessment of Hemings's and Jefferson's violations of the slave woman's and slave master's ethics of miscegenation. Sally recognizes years later the full impact of her daring to love Jefferson at the coinciding of two pivotal events in the novel: Langdon's altering of Sally Hemings's racial identity and the insurrection and execution of Nat Turner. Finally, Sally understands the meaning of power.

Chase-Riboud's epigraph foreshadows Sally Hemings's reaction to the news of Nat Turner's insurrection and alludes to another effect of slavery upon its practitioners: "With the morals of the people their industry also is destroyed. For in a warm climate, no man will labour for himself, who can make another labour for him" (41). Though Jefferson's reference is obviously to the proprietors of slavery, Chase-Riboud innovatively structures the novel so that the epigraph ironically predicts Sally's acknowledgment of her powerlessness in her affair with Jefferson. "In her loneliness and weariness," Sally recalls, "she had failed to remember the first lesson of Black womanhood: never touch a white man" (47). She echoes her mother's sentiments, yet her knowledge of Langdon's altering her history forced Sally to act independently and assert herself in a way that she had never done in her life. She explodes and informs Langdon of her tiredness of white men playing God with her flesh, spirit, children, and life. Unlike the woman she had been at her mother's death, the fifty-four-year-old Sally denounces Langdon in telling him: "Instead of being black and a slave, I'm now free and *white.* . . . You've left me nothing of my own. Not even my color! . . . I can't forgive another man" (58–59).

Sally's denunciation is a precursor of the silent scream in Sherley Anne Williams's *Dessa Rose* (1987). Dessa screams her rage to herself at the scene of miscegenation involving her male slave friend Nathan and the slave mistress Rufel by exhorting, "Can't I have nothing? Can't I have nothing?" (175). Both scenes challenge conventional notions of what is possible for black women characters, dissenting from exclusively subordinate roles; moreover, dissenting not only empowers the characters but also retrieves the collective history of the black slave woman.

Sally Hemings's personal quest for self-assertion extends to the depiction of communal support. It is another man, however, in the figure of Nat Turner, who spiritually saves Sally in her efforts to face the consequences of miscegenation affecting her throughout her life. The chapter's epigraph anticipating this emancipation reads: "The spirit of the master is abating that of the slave rising from the dust, his condition mollifying, the way I hope preparing . . . for a total emancipation" (63). In 1831, Sally forces her son to take her to Jerusalem, Virginia, to witness Nat Turner's execution, preceded by the insurrection itself, which forces her to face "the truth of her life: she had loved the enemy" (64).

Ralph Reckley observes that Chase-Riboud never lets the reader forget "Sally Hemings is Black, female, slave. . . . And while the character is deluded into believing that she is something more than property, the realization slowly comes to her that she is, and her love for Jefferson becomes an ambiguous, bitter thing" (35). In realizing the error in her action, Sally comes to see Turner as a real symbol of power. She finally understands, "This man had killed her enemies. For her! He had taken them on and fought them to his last breath. . . . He had stood while she had done nothing for herself all these years except submit" (65). Though Sally's attendance at Nat Turner's execution signals her support of a black man on a collective quest in the slave community, it also signifies her individual pursuit of self-assertion by affirming the unity of the aggregate racial struggle against slavery. By witnessing Nat Turner's execution, Sally is empowered, even though she had thought she knew all about real power, having spent forty years of life daily with Thomas Jefferson and having witnessed Jefferson's friends and enemies seek power or pay homage to it. Nat Turner's insurrection, however, magnifies the significance of power for her as Chase-Riboud explores Sally's psyche and reveals that Sally

> had never understood until now, however, why men lusted after it with such ferocity; why they fought, killed, slandered, flattered, begged, worshipped, begot sons in its name. All the Burrs, the Hamiltons, and the Washingtons that she had seen come and go had never been able to convey the meaning of it as well as this black man about to have terrible things done to him. He was now being dragged, spit upon, and kicked. He seemed half-crazy; wounded, a hunted animal, caught. Yes, this man's dignity had become real power to her. (65)

Sally Hemings asks forgiveness to God for ever having loved Thomas Jefferson, for as Chase-Riboud notes in a hard tone, "He didn't free her because he didn't want to—men don't free what they love" (Kissel 4). Relative to Chase-Riboud's assessment, Reckley reminds us that "possibly the most valuable character in the novel is Sally herself, for she begins her relationship enamoured of her master, and she ends that relationship hating him" (35). Thus, Chase-Riboud's examination of the powerfully rumored relationship between Jefferson and Hemings reclaims and empowers yet another invisible black slave woman who was a victim of miscegenation. The exploration of the theme of miscegenation and the effect of the power of love between slave master and concubine illustrate the pervasive influence such an illegal liaison had not only upon the fictional lovers but also upon others, such as the white male census taker, the slave children, the white mistress, the black slave mother, and even the black male slave.

In daring to imagine the romantic coupling of black and white historical figures, one famous and another obscure, Barbara Chase-Riboud provides us with a dynamic meditation on history. She rips the veil that covers the official white male–dominated texts of United States history. She questions the void in these historical texts; she reclaims in *Sally Hemings* an intimate vision of the black slave woman's experience. Through her project of historical reclamation, Chase-Riboud forces the reader to revision history. She moves Sally Hemings from the darkened wings of history and places her beneath the bright lights at center stage.

Through her manipulation of character consciousness and dialogue, Chase-Riboud presents Sally Hemings as a well-rounded character, replete with her ambivalence for the man who forces her into the contradictory role of concubine and mother. From her object position, Sally Hemings draws on the politics of black women's sexuality to exert control over her life. In concert with men and women in her community, she challenges the conventional notions of prescribed social space for black women, departs from exclusively subordinate roles, and dares the reader to dismiss her humanity. As a result, Sally Hemings becomes infinitely more powerful and resonant than the void in the American slavery experience could ever be.

NOTES

1. In this regard, Chase-Riboud's novel is similar to many other works written by contemporary African American women novelists: Margaret Walker's *Jubilee* (1966), Gayl Jones's *Corregidora* (1975), Octavia Butler's *Kindred* (1985), Sherley Anne Williams's *Dessa Rose* (1986), Toni Morrison's *Beloved* (1987) and *Jazz* (1992), J. California Cooper's *Family* (1990), and Paule Marshall's *Daughters* (1991). All of these novels are fictional responses to a historical void—the dismissing of the American slave woman's experience.

2. Revisioning history, however, is characteristic of the African American literary tradition as is evident in William Wells Brown's *Clotel; Or, The President's Daughter: A Narrative of Slave Life in the United States* (London, 1853).

3. Hazel V. Carby, *Reconstructing Womanhood: The Emergence of the Afro-American Woman Novelist* (New York: Oxford UP, 1987), 6. See also Frances Ellen Watkins Harper, *Iola Leroy* (1892; Boston: Beacon, 1987).

4. Consider the recent controversial article by Laura B. Randolph, "Thomas Jefferson's Black and White Descendants Debate His Lineage and Legacy," in *Ebony* 48.7 (July 1993): 25–29. The article examines the question whether Jefferson fathered children by or even had a sexual relationship with Hemings. It points out that the controversy has been debated for almost two centuries, even causing a major scandal in 1802, during Jefferson's presidency, when a Richmond newspaper published an article about the affair. A celebration of Jefferson's 250th birthday in April 1993 and a seminar at the University of Virginia on "Jefferson, Race, and Slavery" recently rehashed the controversial discussion between the opposing factions.

5. Through their silence or overt denial of its existence, early biographers of the Jefferson-Hemings affair, such as Henry S. Randall and James Parton, ignored its larger implications. John Chester Miller postulates that Hemings fabricated the relationship to excuse her commission of out-of-wedlock motherhood and miscegenation. He conjectures that Hemings's naming a man of Jefferson's high station as the father of her children tempered both acts. In "Clotel, Thomas Jefferson, and Sally Hemings," *CLA Journal* 17.2 (Dec. 1973): 147–75, W. Edward Farrison counters such arguments by noting that while Jefferson was living he never seemed to have affirmed or denied a liaison with Hemings.

6. Barbara Christian, *Black Women Novelists: The Development of a Tradition, 1892–1976* (Westport, CT: Greenwood, 1980), 35–71. See also Carby 20–39.

7. Valerie Smith, *Self-Discovery and Authority in Afro-American Narrative* (Cambridge: Harvard UP, 1987), 2.

8. Thomas Jefferson, *Notes on the State of Virginia* (1787; Chapel Hill: U of North Carolina P, 1955). This slender volume originated in 1781 as a body of information on Virginia for a small audience of French statesmen and intellectuals. Jefferson opposed publishing the enlarged manuscript, in part because of his strictures on slavery. Intended for strictly private circulation, *Notes* was published in an anonymous edition in *France in Age of Revolution: 1770–1823* (Ithaca, NY: Cornell UP, 1975): 176–77.

9. Daniel Aaron, "The 'Inky Curse': Miscegenation in the White American Literary Imagination," *Social Science Information* 22.2 (1983): 171. See also Werner Sollars, "'Never Was Born': The Mulatto, An American Tragedy?" *Massachusetts Review* 27 (1986): 293–316.
10. Barbara Chase-Riboud, *Sally Hemings* (New York: Avon, 1979), 3. Subsequent references to Sally Hemings are from this source and referenced in the text.
11. Christian, *Black Women Novelists;* C. Minrose Gwin, *Black and White Women of the Old South: The Peculiar Sisterhood in American Literature* (Knoxville: U of Tennessee P, 1985); Anne Firor Scott, *The Southern Lady from Pedestal to Politics, 1830–1930* (Chicago: U of Chicago P, 1970); and Carolyn Alpine Watson, *Prologue: The Novels of Black American Women, 1891–1965* (Westport, CT: Greenwood, 1985) are a few critics who discuss the corresponding images of the southern white lady and the loose black and the mammy as they appear in fact and in fiction in American history and literature.

WORKS CITED

Aaron, Daniel. "The 'Inky Curse': Miscegenation in the White American Literary Imagination." *Social Science Information* 22.2 (1983): 169–90.
Brodie, Fawn M. *Thomas Jefferson: An Intimate History.* New York: Bantam, 1974.
Carby, Hazel V. *Reconstructing Womanhood: The Emergence of the Afro-American Woman Novelist.* New York: Oxford UP, 1987.
Chase-Riboud, Barbara. *Sally Hemings.* New York: Avon, 1979.
Christian, Barbara. *Black Women Novelists: The Development of a Tradition, 1892–1976.* Westport, CT: Greenwood, 1980.
———. "Somebody Forgot to Tell Somebody Something." *Wild Women in the Whirlwind.* Ed. Joanne M. Braxton et al. New Brunswick, NJ: Rutgers UP, 1990. 326–41.
Dabney, Virginius. *The Jefferson Scandals: A Rebuttal.* New York: Dodd, 1981.
Davis, David Brion. *The Problem of Slavery in the Age of Revolution: 1770–1823.* Ithaca, NY: Cornell UP, 1975.
Farrison, W. Edward. "Clotel, Thomas Jefferson, and Sally Hemings." *CLA Journal* 17.2 (Dec. 1973): 147–74.
Gwin, Minrose C. "Green-Eyed Monsters of the Slavocracy: Jealous Mistresses in Two Slave Narratives." *Conjuring: Black Women, Fiction, and Literary Tradition.* Ed. Marjorie Pryse and Hortense J. Spillers. Bloomington: U of Indiana P, 1985. 39–52.
Harper, Frances Ellen Watkins. *Iola Leroy.* 1892. Boston: Beacon, 1987.
Jefferson, Thomas. *Notes on the State of Virginia.* 1787. Chapel Hill: U of North Carolina P, 1955.
Jordan, Winthrop D. *White over Black: American Attitudes toward the Negro, 1550–1812.* Chapel Hill: U of North Carolina P, 1968. 430–36.
Kissel, Howard, "Sally Hemings: Little Fictional Embroidery." *Chicago Tribune* 3 July 1979, sec. 2: 4.
McHenry, Susan. "'Sally Hemings': A Key to Our National Identity." *Ms* (Oct. 1980): 35–40.
Morrison, Toni. *Jazz.* New York: Knopf, 1992.
Randolph, Laura B. "Thomas Jefferson's Black and White Descendants Debate His Lineage and Legacy." *Ebony* 48.7 (July 1993): 25–29.
Reckley, Ralph. "The Love-Hate Syndrome of Master-Slave Relationships in Sally

Hemings." *20th Century Black American Women in Print.* Ed. Lola E. Jones. Baltimore: Morgan State UP, 1991. 33–43.

Smith, Valerie. *Self-Discovery and Authority in Afro-American Narrative.* Cambridge: Harvard UP, 1987.

Sollars, Werner. "'Never Was Born': The Mulatto, an American Tragedy?" *Massachusetts Review* 27 (1986): 293–316.

Welter, Barbara. "The Cult of True Womanhood, 1820–1860." *Dimity Convictions: The American Woman in the Nineteenth Century.* Athens: Ohio UP, 1976. 21–41.

White, Deborah Gray. *Ar'n't I a Woman: Female Slaves in the Plantation South.* New York: Norton, 1985.

Williams, Sherley Anne. *Dessa Rose.* New York: Berkley, 1986.

Wilson, Judith. "Barbara Chase-Riboud: Sculpting Our History." *Essence* 10.8 (Dec. 1979): 12–13.

The Two Marys (Prince and Shelley) on the Textual Meeting Ground of Race, Gender, and Genre

HELENA WOODARD

At first glance, the separate circumstances under which Mary Prince and Mary Shelley appeared as storyteller and writer, respectively, seem to preclude any viable canonical links between them. In *Frankenstein* (1818, 1831), Shelley merged Gothic and science fiction elements to sustain a semblance of idealized romanticism and an added dimension of metaphysical grotesqueness. Prince's *History of Mary Prince, A West Indian Slave* (1831), categorically a slave narrative, is the actual story of her life as a slave in the British West Indies and later in England. Shelley grew up financially secure and intellectually stimulated as the daughter of prominent literary parents, William Godwin and Mary Wollstonecraft. (Wollstonecraft died from complications of giving birth to Mary Shelley.) Prince was enslaved from birth, circa 1788, and her parents, though enslaved nearby, were virtually powerless to intercede for their daughter, who suffered numerous cruelties associated with slavery.

For Mary Prince, any suggestion of an artistic or literary association with Mary Shelley inevitably conjures past canonical circumstances that validated a black text solely by its stylistic similarity with texts typically by white, male, Western authors. Meanwhile, Mary Shelley's literary reputation was circumscribed by critical assessments that cast her as the shadowy extension of William Godwin (father) and Percy B. Shelley (husband). Perhaps a notable example is William Veeder, who, in *Mary Shelley and Frankenstein: The Fate of Androgyny* (1986), argues that *Frankenstein* "grows in part from Mary's frustration at failing" to be the son that Godwin wanted, the "antitype" that Percy craved, and the intellect that Byron admired (13). Hence, both Prince and Shelley have been marginalized (albeit differently) by some in the literary establishment, and they have been subjected to certain exclusionary canonical practices.

But revisionist readings that now confront rather than silence or bracket discomforting perspectives on race, gender, and slavery have precipitated a textual "recovery" and a reexamination of outmoded assumptions about Prince's and Shelley's literary value. For example, recent articles by Moira Ferguson

("Introduction to the *History of Mary Prince*") and Sandra Pouchet Paquet ("The Heartbeat of a West Indian Slave: *The History of Mary Prince*") have restored authorial agency to Prince as the primary voice and activist force in the narrative rather than assign that role to her British patrons, Susanna Strickland and Thomas Pringle. (Strickland was Prince's ghostwriter, and Pringle was largely responsible for the narrative's publication.)

Similarly, Mary Poovey, "My Hideous Progeny: Mary Shelley and the Feminization of Romanticism," and Barbara Johnson, "My Monster/My Self," are among those who have removed Mary Shelley from the critical nexus of both William Godwin and Percy Shelley. Within this revisionist context, my reading of Prince and Shelley, *together,* hardly forces a mainstreaming of either by assimilative strategies; rather, it reinforces their *differences,* the ways in which they have been marginalized on the ground of race, gender, and genre.

Indeed, it is in the pivotal zone of gender and ethnography that Prince's artistic identification with Shelley intersects and diverges in ways that I find most enriching and appealing for the purposes of this essay. The worlds of the economically privileged English woman and the enslaved West Indian woman converge where a "mythical" literary aesthetic leaves off. A mythical literary aesthetic is one that, among other things, gauges authorial intentionality as a prime barometer in locating meaning in a text, and it strictly separates meaning from ideological considerations. But it is impractical to assess Prince's and Shelley's impact broadly within such an aesthetic. I therefore apply a reading of "the two Marys" that denies any intertextual, intercultural, or interdisciplinary separations and/or exclusions in deriving meaning.

This essay explores how Prince's and Shelley's personal and artistic identities as women who broke into a traditionally male literary environment are "differently" informed by race and gender. Further, it identifies Shelley's artistic invention, a fictitious "monster" created in a single instance of ego-mongering by an isolated individual and subsequently rejected by a totalizing social power structure, as an ironic reading of Prince's *actual existence* as an enslaved black woman. My claims engage new-historicist precepts—not the unlikely notion that Shelley ever knew Prince or her work. I argue in the tradition of Stephen Greenblatt (*Learning to Curse: Essays in Early Modern Culture;* 1990), Terence Hawkes (*Shakespeare's Talking Animals;* 1973), and others who apply colonialist readings to Caliban in *The Tempest.* Hawkes, for instance, reads Shakespeare as a dramatist who metaphorizes the role of the colonist in *The Tempest* because of the island's construction as a New World environment which Prospero enters to establish command over. Hawkes's observations about the dramatist's *art* are quite appropriate to my exploration of Shelley's work, however.

Alluding to Shakespeare, Hawkes writes that the dramatist's "art penetrates new areas of experience, [and] his language expands the boundaries of our culture" (212). Similarly, I argue that Shelley's art metaphorizes some aspects of a slaveholding society and thus performs a cultural function similar to that which Hawkes describes in *The Tempest*. Victor Frankenstein codifies the language of New World, colonialist conquest in his desire to create, dominate, and subjugate a new species that would idolize and obey him. The ideological implications of such language make strictly aesthetic readings of Shelley's work inadequate.

Both Shelley and Prince grappled with the credible presentation of their stories, though for Shelley, it meant an artistic conformity commensurate with the nineteenth-century English romantic literary tradition. For Prince, whose narrative was ghostwritten, "self" presentation more than literary meritocracy was essential in order to influence an English readership coming to terms with an antislavery momentum in Britain. To explore how race and gender differently informed Prince's and Shelley's struggle for recognition, I first cite Mary Poovey, who very plausibly attributes conflicting readings of *Frankenstein* to Shelley's "attempt to conform simultaneously to two conflicting prescriptive models of behavior" (332), one for authors and one designated for women. Those conflicting readings show that *Frankenstein* conforms to and departs from a romantic credo that, among other things, embraces a belief in the unbridled, uncensored imaginative faculty to spark creativity.

Shelley effectively neutralizes Victor Frankenstein's "crime" of invention by eliminating both maker and monstrous "other," thus ending "their" abominable line of descent. Shelley thus reasserts a universal order more fictionally reminiscent of neoclassical dogma than romantic creed. The novel's outcome, as Poovey reads it, allows Shelley to adhere to a prescribed romanticism and to a studied conformity particularly appropriated for mothers, wives, and daughters. Shelley's authorial ambivalences, then, Poovey continues, "simultaneously fulfill[s] and punish[es] her desire for self expression" (332). Yet, these ambivalences purportedly *enrich* a formerly misunderstood text by inaugurating a neofeminist discourse not uncommonly found in period texts by other women authors.[1] In other words, by first exposing, then neutralizing the imaginative largess, the creative energies that Victor Frankenstein required to construct an alien being, Shelley pays homage to the romantic credo, preserves authorial integrity, and retains a position in the cult of true womanhood.[2]

It is precisely within this cult—a code of behavior that stresses chastity and femininity for women—that I take leave of Poovey in order to demonstrate the first of several ironies in Shelley's "neo-feminist discourse" that renders her artistic separation from Prince. While Shelley sought artistic merit, recognition, and validation in a virtual all-male writers' environment in part by negating unlimited indulgence in imaginative excess in *Frankenstein,* Mary Prince had to first prove herself morally worthy as a woman and as an individual *before* she could credibly tell her story to an English readership. Furthermore, in order for Prince's *History* to be effective as an antislavery document, she had to engender sympathy for her *inability* to participate in the cult of womanhood. As a slave woman, Prince's compromised abilities to maintain sexual and reproductive control disqualified her for moral consideration.

Born around 1788 at Brackish-Pond, Devonshire Parish, in Bermuda, then colonized by Britain, Prince was first enslaved, along with her mother, by the Darrell family. Captain Darrell had purchased Prince as a slave for his young granddaughter, Betsy Williams. Prince called the years she spent with Williams her happiest, though she added that she was too young to understand her condition as a slave at that time. While in the Williams household, Prince was under the care of her own mother, and her father was enslaved nearby as a sawyer to Mr. Trimmingham, a shipbuilder at Crow-Lane. This demographic proximity with her parents surely provided some psychological if not authoritative reinforcement for Prince. At around the age of twelve, she was sold, along with two sisters, to a slave owner from Spanish Point whom she identified only as Captain I.

After five years, she was sold to "Mr. D" at Turk's Island, where she labored in the salt ponds. Prince's final purchaser was John Wood, who took her to Antigua. In December 1826, while enslaved to the Wood family, Prince married a free black carpenter, Daniel James. And when the Woods went to England to place their son in school, they took Prince with them. While in England, Prince sought asylum with Moravian church missionaries who brought Prince before Thomas Pringle, a Methodist secretary for the British antislavery society in November 1828.[3]

While living in the Pringle household, Prince met Susanna Strickland, who transcribed her narrative before Pringle published it in 1831. Prince told the story of her enslavement primarily to expose slavery as inhumane. In formulating a credible (self) presentation and in creating an acceptable "feminine" persona, Prince had to transcend liminalities imposed on the narrative's "ghosted" form, an inception steeped in orality and documented by another's hand. (It is poignant to note here that Prince's editor, Thomas Pringle, placed an explanatory note in the narrative claiming that these words were expressed "verbatim" by Prince to an amanuensis, Susanna Strickland.)

Prince transcends these "liminalities," in part, by manipulating traditional, Western, European language forms. Hence, her articulation of self-identity is an empowering act, crafted in oral *and* written form. She was well aware of the need to counter negative perceptions about blacks, particularly women. As a result, Prince employs language that is poetic, demonstrative, and sentimental. She purposely constructs an oppositional narrative strategy that connects the narrator with an English readership under a moral hegemony and an English nationalism.[4] Prince appeals to Britain's moralistic and legalistic sense of its nationalist identity, particularly as a purported "slave-free" land.

With no constitutional basis for its laws, British judicial officials decided cases narrowly and inconsistently and largely denied the country's slavocracy. Two cases in point: In *Historical Collections of Private Passages of State, Weighty Matters in Law, Remarkable Proceedings,* John Rushworth records a 1569 judicial decision that declared English air "too pure . . . for slaves to breathe in" (2: 468). William Cowper echoes Rushworth's sentiments in "The Task": "Slaves cannot breathe in England; if their lungs Receive our air that moment they are free" (2.40–41). Writers and judicial officials could easily vent such emotionalism without disturbing profitable West Indian and American slave colonies for the British.

In relating the barbarities of slavery, Prince excludes from Britons' nationalist coalition those West Indian slave owners and overseers whom she calls "Buckras," and she depicts them as callous, immoral supporters of slavery. Prince binds this group as collective misfits whose verbal and physical abusiveness to slaves is deemed offensive to England as a nation. For example, on more than one occasion, Prince writes that after displeasing her slave owners, they abused her with words that were so vile that they could not be spoken in *England.* She thus appeals particularly to English readers with whom she clearly seeks a moral and verbal alliance, recognizing fully the supportive strength of the antislavery climate in Britain at this time.

Prince's "immorality equation" also includes hardhearted bystanders and proslavery sympathizers who surrounded the slave auction block where she and her sisters were sold in a show of indifference for the grief of Prince's mother and other family members: "They were not all bad, I dare say, but slavery hardens white people's hearts towards the blacks; and many of them were not slow to make their remarks upon us aloud, without regard to our grief—though their light words fell like cayenne on the fresh wounds of our hearts" (52).

Prince pointedly uses emotionally charged similes that she relates to the human heart. Only God knows "the thoughts of a slave's heart," she writes (51). And she observes that the stones and the timber in the home of one slave owner and his wife were not nearly "so hard as the hearts of the owners" (54).

Sandra Paquet aptly notes that Prince's emotive language of the heart is "an alternative to the material measure of the marketplace as a measure of the moral and ethical sensibility that governs the well-being of individuals in society" (142). Prince connects an abject materiality with those who own and sell human beings for profit; moreover, she abjures any associations between "feelings" and profit. Meanwhile, the "profitless" individuals—Prince and fellow slaves—demonstrate a subjective and responsive grief over being separated from one another.

Prince's liberal use of sentimental language is a well-established formulaic convention of eighteenth- and nineteenth-century slave narratives.[5] Clearly, such language helped to foster antislavery sentiment. The so-called sentimental literary tradition in eighteenth-century England has long been recognized as a transition between neoclassicism and romanticism, though more current studies point out artificialities in such constructions. The artificiality in these trends is traceable to rigid dating patterns. Both Prince and Shelley tapped into sentimentalism and romanticism, respectively, as vibrant and timely literary trends that governed the success of their work. Additionally, issues pertaining to race and gender further informed their efforts.

For example, I find it interesting that Mary Poovey's identification of Shelley's "neo-feminist" discourse, produced by her divided loyalties to art form and gender expectations, strikingly resembles discursive formations in black literature, particularly in the slave narrative and black autobiography. Similar neodiscursive beginnings characterize "resistance" literature and are commonly associated with oppressed and/or colonized groups. As long argued by diverse observers such as W. E. B. Du Bois, Paulette Nardal, Frantz Fanon, Albert Memmi, Audre Lorde, and Henry Louis Gates, black literature commonly depicts individuals who are conflicted by living as blacks in a culturally alienating Western society.[6]

Prince's dilemma is shared in varying degrees by other slave narrators, especially those whose works were ghostwritten. James Ukawsaw Gronniosaw, *A Narrative of the Most Remarkable Particulars in the Life of James Albert Ukawsaw Gronniosaw* (1770), was among other African British narrators who struggled for similar recognition. Ottobah Cugoano, *Thoughts and Sentiments on the Evil of Slavery* (1787), and Olaudah Equiano, *The Interesting Narrative of the Life of Olaudah Equiano or Gustavus Vassa, the African* (1789), wrote their own works and achieved greater recognition and visibility, but still suffered racially biased scrutiny in newspaper and other accounts. Equiano's impressive command of story and presentation of self is filtered through his use of defamiliarization, signification, and other literary motifs.[7] Cugoano counters the Hamitic Hypothesis as a biblically based defense of slavery used by many supporters of slavery.

Unlike her black male counterparts, however, Prince had to prove sexual purity as an added requirement in promoting a valid self. In her introduction to Prince's Narrative, Moira Ferguson speculates that the paucity of pre-nineteenth-century black women's narratives may result from abolitionists' reluctance to address in print the morally thorny issues of sexual abuse and reproductive control that slave owners inflicted on black slave women.[8]

In order to widen the moral chasm between herself and the West Indian slave owners who exercised sexual and reproductive control over slaves, Prince detailed the sadistic, albeit sexually *implicit,* nature of beatings that she received from slave owners. But ever mindful of a self-identity and a verbal or written presentation that were compliant with abolitionist dictates, Prince carefully encodes the language of sexual abuse amid other forms of physical abuse, such as beatings. Interestingly enough, even though Prince's composite feminine persona is devoid of *overt* sexual language, its *subtext* is still discernible. For example, she contrasted two methods of punishment by two enslavers, Captain I and Mr. D. Prince described a particular beating inflicted upon her first by the slave mistress and later the same day by Captain I for having accidentally broken an earthen jar. Captain I's frenzied style was to inflict a rapid succession of strokes until exhaustion completely overtook him, followed by periods of rest, then more beatings.

Prince described Mr. D's brutality more ritualistically, using subtle language that has sadistic overtones. The implication is that Captain I and Mr. D likely derived some perverted pleasure from administering these beatings: "There was this difference between them; my former master used to beat me while raging and foaming with passion; M. D—was usually quite calm. He would stand by and give orders for a slave to be cruelly whipped, and assist in the punishment, without moving a muscle of his face; walking about and taking snuff with the greatest composure" (62).

In the narrative, Prince is the embattled recipient of these increasingly vicious beatings for the most innocuous infractions, for example, the cow getting into the sweet potato slips. Contrary to perception, then, Prince dispels the notion that, as a black woman, she is responsible for the moral degradation of the white male slave owner.

For example, Prince leaves enshrouded in obscurity details of another ritual that Mr. D engaged in; he forced her to bathe his naked body. But she does not discuss further improprieties that might have attended such a ritual. Yet Prince's disgust is so great that she eventually asks to be transferred to the service of her eventual owner, John Wood. In a very revealing passage, Prince details the beatings that she received on her naked body by Mr. D, and writes that these beatings were for her far more tolerable than the bathing ritual:

> He had an ugly fashion of stripping himself quite naked, and ordering
> me then to wash him in a tub of water. This was worse to me than all
> the licks. Sometimes when he called me to wash him I would not come,
> my eyes were so full of shame. He would then come to beat me. One
> time I had plates and knives in my hand, and I dropped both plates
> and knives, and some of the plates were broken. He struck me so se-
> verely for this, that at last I defended myself, for I thought it was high
> time to do so. I then told him I would not live longer with him, for he
> was a very indecent man—very spiteful, and too indecent; with no
> shame for his servants, no shame for his own flesh. So I went away to a
> neighbouring house and sat down and cried till the next morning, when
> I went home again, not knowing what else to do. (67–68)

Prince's words leave open speculation that other untold abuses may have occurred. But more revealingly, they show Prince's struggle to maintain personal dignity in opposition to the indecency of Mr. D and others. As previously stated, Prince's struggle for moral propriety is an essential aspect of a credible self-presentation.

Significantly, a number of British women abolitionists, especially those with religious affiliations, relied on their own recognizable moral grounding to argue that slave women were innocent victims of an unjust practice.[9] Though Prince's sexual persona in the narrative is consistent with abolitionists' objectives, the work's construction resists clear patronage. Prince, no passive voice, defies efforts to restrict her to an objectified, victim's status. By way of self-presentation, then, she achieves something artistically.

In *Reconstructing Womanhood: The Emergence of the Afro-American Woman Novelist,* Hazel Carby points out the ideological polarities between perceptions about black and white womanhood: "Black women, in gaining their public presence as writers, would directly confront the political and economic dimensions of their subjugation. They had to define a discourse of black womanhood which would not only address their exclusion from the ideology of true womanhood but, as a consequence of this exclusion, would also rescue their bodies from a persistent association with illicit sexuality" (32).

And as Moira Ferguson writes in the introduction to Prince's narrative, the antislavery society that sponsored the publication of Prince's narrative had to present slave women as "victims" whose moral stature was beyond reproach in order to win public support for them and to turn sentiment against slavery. This stringent moral code was observed even when women were forced to comply with sexual demands against their will. "Christian purity, for those abolitionists, overrode regard for truth," Ferguson writes (introduction, 4). Like Shelley, then, Prince was entrapped by the cult of true womanhood. But unlike Shelley, Prince faced societal expectations of chastity for women by a populace that saw black women as lewd and lascivious.

As I have illustrated through Prince's employment of sentimental and other language forms, she was unable to divorce (self) identity from artistry; to the contrary, her identity is rooted in the narrative's artistry. Prince's presentation thus fulfills the challenges stipulated by the cult of womanhood, and it reinforces her "suitability" for moral recognition by readers. For the slave woman as narrative voice this effort (recognition as credible and morally pure) was doubly challenging.

In fact, Thomas Pringle's appendix to Prince's narrative provides some clues to her complex sexual history, clues that she could not relate because of marketing concerns. These clues reveal that "measured" empowerment for Prince could likely be achieved through sexual means. John Wood, Prince's former enslaver, sued Thomas Pringle for publishing Prince's damaging accusations of brutality against him. Furthermore, Wood charged Prince with immorality. In defending Prince, Pringle reveals a relationship that she had with a white man that occurred prior to her marriage to a free black man. Pringle also charged Wood and slave owners, in general, with hypocrisy and sexual misconduct with slave women. In the narrative, Prince is preoccupied with cleansing her life of past indiscretions that she does not identify, and she later seeks moral healing by embracing the Moravian religious sect. "I never knew rightly that I had much sin till I went" to the Moravian church, she writes. "When I found out that I was a great sinner, I was very sorely grieved, and very much frightened" (73).

Though initially angered by Prince's marriage to a free black, Wood claims to have provided the couple domicile to encourage her faithfulness to her husband. Discrepancies and omissions in the narrative and in Pringle's appendix show that Prince's struggle to achieve recognition and respectability as a narrator and even as a victim of slave abuses were connected, inextricably, to her sexual persona. Prince's struggle to maintain sexual and reproductive control is similar to that of African American slave narrator Harriet Jacobs, whose work, *Incidents in the Life of a Slave Girl* (1861), was published some thirty years later. Prince shares with Jacobs the complexities of formulating an acceptable self-presentation that included feminine purity. Both Prince and Jacobs relied on white feminist patrons to edit their narratives. Susanna Strickland and Lydia Maria Childs downplayed their roles as editors. But the mere presence of an authenticating (white) voice in a slave's narrative was a critical marketing strategy.

Ironically, Shelley also employs the "disclaimer" that editors provided to mask their roles in writing and/or producing black narratives, though for vastly different reasons. Consider Shelley's explanation for narrative differences between the 1818 and 1831 editions of *Frankenstein:* "I will add but one word to the alterations I have made. They are principally those of style. I have changed no portion of the story nor introduced any new ideas or circumstances. I have mended the language where it was so bald as to interfere with the interest of the narrative" (xii).[10]

Shelley writes to delineate the "novel" differences between the 1818 and 1831 editions of *Frankenstein.* She attempts to diffuse criticism that she received for composing an "immoral" story that featured an individual's tampering with divine and natural laws. How could a "lady" entertain such hideous notions—even abstractly? The irony is in Shelley's need to diffuse criticism for producing a fictional model that easily stood alongside the *non*fictional model that Prince's story provided.

After all, Shelley need not have looked very far to find rampant inhumanity and the suspension of moral and divine laws in the "real" world. In one of those sweet ironies of history, Prince's *History* was published in the same year that

Shelley's 1831 edition of *Frankenstein* appeared. I certainly do not find it incredulous that sexism indeed influenced the (re)shaping of Shelley's art. In a somewhat related example, Moira Ferguson argues convincingly that British women abolitionists battled slavery (especially its impact on black women and family dissolution) even while showing remarkable restraint in fighting, *simultaneously,* for equal protection under the law for England's female population. Indications are that English women found it easier to make strides by engaging in strategic oppositional maneuvers rather than in resistance outright.[11] The feminists' fight for slave women was a plea for their right to function as wives and mothers in the domestic arena—a pleas that was safe, of course, from white male dissension.

In the 1818 edition of *Frankenstein,* Shelley seems to show sensitivity to the claims of the critics that the novel was an unthinkable invention for *pretty minds* better suited for officiating over domestic affairs. Movey Poovey notes that the 1831 edition diffuses certain radical overtones found in the 1818 edition. Shelley's decentered narrative position provides the key to her authorial dilemma. Shelley asserts that she did not make herself the heroine of her own stories because "life appeared too commonplace an affair" (viii). Shelley's declaration of narrative intent does seem to reflect her limited exposure, perhaps, to a world socially, politically, and economically antithetical to the one in which she lived. Though she had suffered some personal tragedies, including several miscarriages by the time she wrote *Frankenstein,* Mary Shelley likely had little knowledge of what Mary Prince's world was like.[12]

Realizing that such inventiveness had to be spun out of chaos, Shelley had to search outside herself—even beyond her world, literally and metaphorically—to gather suitable moments of reflection for composition. To evoke a tale of sheer metaphysical horror, steeped in a willing suspension of disbelief, required aberrations of monstrous proportions. The most striking candidates derived from scientific possibilities, unthinkable as they may have seemed, of the human capacity for altering nature, for restoring life to the lifeless. The specter of invention loomed large. Shelley wrote the following: "Frightful must it be, for supremely frightful would be the effect of any human endeavor to mock the stupendous mechanism of the Creator of the world. His success would terrify the artist; he would rush away from his odious handiwork, horror-stricken" (xi). Shelley's "ghost story," then, showed nineteenth-century England and the world what a *fictitious* abuse of the powers of natural science could render.

In contrast with Shelley, Mary Prince featured herself at the center of her narrative, and Prince's life was anything but commonplace, though her self-conscious artistry is also rooted in the mechanics of productivity. Prince wanted the story of her enslavement on a West Indian plantation told so that the "good people in England might hear from a slave what a slave had felt and suffered."[13] Yet, Prince's story filtered through a complex productive webbing that included the "authenticating" words of Thomas Pringle and Susanna Strickland. But Pringle and Strickland had to be effective and convincing in their "representation" of Mary Prince while, simultaneously, they had to downplay their own roles in Prince's creation as character. Thus, Pringle provides a statement in the narrative that seeks to lend authority and credibility to Prince's own voice: "It [the narrative] is essentially her own, without any material alteration farther than was requisite to exclude redundancies and gross grammatical errors, so as to render it clearly intelligible" (preface, 45).

Ironically, the grammatical roughness of the narrative flaunted the bareness of Prince's literacy skills and actually served to authenticate her slave past. The production of the narrative would lend its voice to a growing number of voices set to expose slave cruelties in the hope that England would outlaw the practice. Thus, Mary Prince's individuality was secondary to "cause" for which her story provided needed evidence. Coincidentally, Prince's "devaluation" enhanced her usefulness for the antislavery society, while it posed a liability in her struggle for identity beyond that of an ennobled, primitive, untutored being.

Both the presence of patrons and their need, simultaneously, to affirm and to deny the extent of their own function in Prince's presentation are familiar paradoxes in slave narrative methodology. Pringle's introduction, however well intentioned, and the growing antislavery climate attending the publication of the narrative diminish Prince as "subject" and threaten to privilege the conditions that portray her as slave rather than as enslaved. In addition, the shared roles between Prince and amanuensis, between verbal artist and the guiding hand of written expression place Prince in a liminal position as controlling artist and makes her struggle for self-identity and empowerment all the more challenging. Prince's narrative was never destined to find its way among the Bunyanesque spiritual autobiographies.

Its presentation to the reading public was a political act, a plea for Britain's complete outlawing of slavery. In addition, the very presence of a battery of authenticating voices *and* their ambivalent "affirming/denying" posture threatened to delimit the voice of the enslaved woman that patrons sought to empower. Simply stated, Prince's word was not her "bond" but was, at least in part, her bondage. The irony, of course, is in the nonfictional status of Prince's *History*—a story seemingly with questionable veracity for some eighteenth-century readers.

I have explained how the entrance of Prince and Shelley into a traditionally male literary environment is "differently" informed by race and gender. This section examines the two works, intertextually, in order to discover their collaborative signifying function. For example, I will show how Shelley's text metaphorizes a slave-holding society, codified in Victor Frankenstein's "New World conquest" language, and played out in a society intolerant of the Monster's "otherness." I will make explicit the connection between the Monster's alienation from, and Prince's rejection by, a society unwilling to accord either of them human status. Interestingly, this reading analogizes Prince much more definitively with the Monster, Shelley's artistic invention, rather than with Shelley herself.

A racist ideology perceived Prince as inhuman. Ironically, then, she wore the *real* face of the unimaginable "other" that Shelley cast as an *invented* model in *Frankenstein*. The world could easily "imagine" Shelley's invention perhaps because she expels the monstrous ogre and retrieves readers safely from a nightmarish abyss. Indeed, Victor's refusal to create a promised bride for the Monster is based on his fear that a race of undesirable beings would inhabit the earth. It is the ultimate fear, a colonial power's worst nightmare: Caliban's threat to Miranda to people the world with "little Calibans." (Ironically, Queen Elizabeth expressed similar fears when she ordered the deportation of blacks from Britain in 1596.)[14] Prince's narrative forces a recognition of slavery and other atrocities in the human world, and therefore functions as a signifying text for *Frankenstein*. Meanwhile, Shelley's engineering and subsequent displacement of an "alien" being enables her *fictional* work to function dramatically as an ethnographic reading of Prince's *nonfictional* work.

Frankenstein sets forth a precolonial dictum predicated upon the Monster's expulsion from the human world. Predictably, the instant Victor met his monstrous Creation—a malformed replica of himself—he wished for and sought its annihilation. The Monster was a misfit, a virtual slave who depended wholly upon his Maker for his well being. The Great Experiment was doomed to failure, however, because of Frankenstein's attestation to the limitations of the pseudo-scientific Creator and because the "sin" of the "Master" was destined to be fulfilled in the "slave's" refusal to participate in his own annihilation. For the Monster would not only haunt his maker, but he would assume empowerment in proportion to his Master's diminishing capacity for absolute power and control.

The Monster's personal horror is isolation, the realization that he can never hope for accommodation within a society in which exclusionary practices read "difference" as innate inferiority. The Monster says to Victor Frankenstein, "All men hate the wretched; how, then, must I be hated, who am miserable beyond all living things! Yet you, my creator, detest and spurn me, thy creature to whom thou art bound by ties only dissolvable by the annihilation of one of us. How dare you sport thus with life" (95). Needless to say, the Monster's words in this passage bring to mind Prince's complaints about her treatment at the hands of numerous enslavers. Prince wrote that slave buyers treated her as a nonhuman and that buyers openly commented on her physicality in animal terms as though she could not understand their meaning (4).

Victor seemed unable to recognize, let alone atone for, his inhumanity when the mere sight of his gangly creation proved repulsive to him. The Monster was further rejected by the cottagers and other individuals who were unable to accept his inhuman form in spite of his self-instruction in the manners and customs of the human world. The Monster's teachings revealed mixed messages on the value and proportion that knowledge and wealth held in that world. These messages influenced the bourgeois Victor Frankenstein to seek knowledge and power obsessively and destructively. The Monster's observations of the cottagers led to his pronouncement on the human species that is eerily remonstrative of Mary Prince's predicament as a slave in an industrialized society: "I learned the possessions most esteemed by your fellow creatures were high and unsullied descent united with riches. A man might be respected with only one of these advantages, but without either he was considered, except in very rare instances, as a vagabond and a slave, doomed to waste his powers for the profits of the chosen few!" (114).

Reminiscent of Britain's own empowerment through slavocracy, Victor Frankenstein creates a Monster to fulfill his obsessive quest for self-empowerment and recognition. He blithely announces that "a new species would bless [him] as its creator and source" and that "many happy and excellent natures would owe their being to [him]—" (52). I liken Frankenstein's comment to a widely perpetuated proslavery notion which held that Africans enslaved in European colonies were merely "rescued" from a worse fate in their homelands, and that Europeans offered slaves "enlightenment" through Christianity and civilization, as is evident in Phillis Wheatley's poem "On Being Brought from Africa to America."[15]

While the Monster's speech aids *Frankenstein*'s treatment as a social reform novel, such readings invoke the French Revolution and do not connect such reform to slavery. Yet, Mary Prince, Olaudah Equiano, and other former slaves saw their human worth commodified by the dictates of a market economy. When Frankenstein's Monster is unable to gain acceptability from the human world (a world that included his own maker), he systematically destroys the perpetrators of an insidious ethnocentrism lodged at society's core.

When Shelley closes *Frankenstein*, though, on one man's hapless journey into a metaphysical disaster, the rest of the world suffices in moderately restorative vignettes. Meanwhile, the Monster's alienation from it, and expulsion by it, are unreconciled. Hence, she represents Victor Frankenstein's "crime" of invention as the isolated deed of a wayward prodigal son, and therefore only *narrowly* exploits the systemic source of Frankenstein's crime—an inherently corrupt hegemonic power structure—of which he is only symptomatic. Shelley's textual sanitation, here, stems more from personal and artistic divisiveness than from the ghosts of God(win), the father, or Percy B. Shelley, the husband. Her structural compromise is actually reinforced by her entrenchment in, and entrapment by, the cult of true womanhood. And as I previously stated, Shelley lacked the lived and/or known experiences that might have exposed her to an existent, universal model of pathological dominance and control befitting a Dr. Frankenstein and his fictitious society. Yet, the pseudo-scientific apparatus for such a society already existed in Shelley's world in grotesque form in the system of chattel slavery in faces that were typically black and "other." It was the face and the world of Mary Prince, who, reconstructed and regendered, lived the Gothic science fiction horror that Mary Shelley fictionalized.

As signifying texts, *The History of Mary Prince* and *Frankenstein* invite reflexive critiques on colonialism and slavery, colonizer and colonized, power and resistance, and other dichotomies. A reading of Prince's narrative does not suspend disbelief *willingly;* it disrupts the imaginative process and disallows a cathartic freeing of the soul. The narrative is a gloss on Britain's slavocracy, and it forces a collective national (un)conscious to confront its sins (as Victor Frankenstein confronts his own). Prince readily indicts a systemic malignancy that, in the words of her editor, Thomas Pringle, dehumanized both oppressor and oppressed. This systemic exposure in the *History of Mary Prince* is muted in Shelley's *Frankenstein* to all but, perhaps, the Monster himself. An intertextual reading of Prince and Shelley's works mediates the dialectic between an *unauthorized* European slavocracy and an *authorized* literary didacticism. I have tried to show how the broad impact that each work has on the other is most discernible when readers explore them intertextually. Such a reading meshes not only inside versus outside and fiction versus nonfiction, but it transgresses the boundaries of contemporary cultural experiences.

NOTES

1. Writers who are instrumental in exploring a neofeminist discourse include: Mary Poovey, *The Proper Lady and the Woman Writer* (Chicago: U of Chicago P, 1984); Nancy Armstrong, *Desire and Domestic Fiction* (New York: Oxford UP, 1987); and Moira Ferguson, *Subject to Others: British Women Writers and Colonial Slavery, 1670–1834* (New York: Routledge, 1992).
2. For an examination of the cult of true womanhood, see Elizabeth Fox Genovese, *Within the Plantation Household: Black and White Women of the Old South* (Chapel Hill: U of North Carolina P, 1988). Hazel V. Carby explores "the dialectical relationship with the alternative sexual code associated with the black woman" in *Reconstructing Womanhood: The Emergence of the Afro-American Woman Novelist* (New York: Oxford UP, 1987), 30. See also bell hooks, *Feminist Theory: From Margin to Center* (Boston: South End, 1984).
3. A published poet, Thomas Pringle provides a continuation of the life of Mary Prince in a supplement to the first edition. The narrative went through three editions. For more information on Pringle, see John Robert Doyle Jr., *Thomas Pringle* (New York: Twayne, 1972) and Moria Ferguson's excellent introduction to Mary Prince, *The History of Mary Prince, A West Indian Slave, Related by Herself* (1831; Ann Arbor: U of Michigan P, 1993), 38–40 n. 44 and 30–31 n. 15. All citations are from this edition and are hereafter noted by page numbers within the text. A convenient edi-

tion of Prince's narrative (without the Ferguson introduction) is, of course, *The Classic Slave Narratives*, ed. Henry Louis Gates Jr. (New York: Mentor, 1987).

4. See Homi K. Bhabha's "Introduction: Narrating the Nation," *Nation and Narration*, ed. Homi Bhabha (London: Routledge, 1990), 1–7; for specific references to Britain's historical nationalism, see Linda Colley, "Britishness and Otherness: An Argument," *Journal of British Studies* 31 (Oct. 1992): 309–29.

5. See John Sekora and Darwin T. Turner, eds., *The Art of Slave Narrative: Original Essays in Criticism and Theory* (Macomb: Western Illinois UP, 1982).

6. W. E. B. Du Bois, *Writings* (New York: Library of America, 1986); Paulette Nardal, *La Revue du Monde Noir* (Paris, 1930); Frantz Fanon, *Black Skin, White Masks*, trans. Charles Lam Markmann (New York: Grove, 1967); Albert Memmi, *The Colonizer and the Colonized*, trans. Howard Greenfeld (Boston: Beacon, 1965); Audre Lorde, *Sister Outsider* (Trumansburg, NY: Crossing P, 1984); and Henry Louis Gates Jr., ed., *"Race," Writing and Difference* (Chicago: U of Chicago P, 1985). See also Eslanda Goode Robeson, "Black Paris," *New Challenge: A Literary Quarterly* (Jan. & June 1936); Robert P. Smith Jr., "Rereading Banjo: Claude McKay and the French Connection," *CLA Journal* (Sept. 1986): 46–58; and Janet G. Vaillant, *Black, French, and African: A Life of Leopold Sedar Senghor* (Cambridge: Harvard UP, 1990).

7. Henry Louis Gates Jr., *The Signifying Monkey: Towards a Theory of Afro-American Literary Criticism* (New York: Oxford UP, 1988).

8. Moira Ferguson, Introduction to Mary Prince, *The History of Mary Prince, A West Indian Slave, Related by Herself* (1831; Ann Arbor: U of Michigan P, 1993), 4. Ferguson speculates that Prince encodes her abusive, sexual experience through accounts of general physical abuse from her enslavers.

9. These British women writers include Ann Yearsley, Hannah More, Helen Maria Williams, Mary Scott, and Mary Wollstonecraft, Mary Shelley's mother. See Ferguson's *Subject to Others*.

10. Mary Shelley, *Frankenstein* (1831; New York: New American Library, 1965), xii. All subsequent references made to this work are cited in the manuscript. Shelley's 1818 text is edited, with variant readings, and an introduction and notes, by James Rieger. See Mary Wollstonecraft Shelley, *Frankenstein, or, The Modern Prometheus*, ed. James Rieger (1818; Indianapolis: Bobbs-Merrill, 1974).

11. This is a familiar narrative strategy. Ross Chambers's *Reading the Opposition(al) in Narrative* is useful here.

12. See Ellen Moers, "Female Gothic," *Literary Women* (Garden City, NY: Doubleday, 1976), 92; Also see Alan Bewell, who links Mary Shelley's creative influences for *Frankenstein* to her "experience of pregnancy and loss" as biological, social, and discursive events in "An Issue of Monstrous Desire: *Frankenstein* and Obstetrics," *Yale Journal of Criticism* 2 (Winter 1988): 105–28.

13. Prince 1–43.

14. Queen Elizabeth herself ordered the deportation of blacks from England on 11 July 1596 in an open letter to the lord mayor of London and the mayors of other cities. The queen wrote that "there are of late divers blackmoores brought into this realme, of which kinde of people there are allready here to manie" (*Acts of the Privy Council of England* n.s. 26: 20–21). For an excellent study on black people in Britain, see Peter Fryer, *Staying Power: The History of Black People in Britain* (London: Pluto, 1984).

15. Phillis Wheatley, *The Poems of Phillis Wheatley*, ed. Julian D. Mason (Chapel Hill: U of North Carolina P, 1989), 53.

WORKS CITED

Bewell, Alan. "An Issue of Monstrous Desire: Frankenstein and Obstetrics." *Yale Journal of Criticism* 2 (Winter 1988): 105–28.

Cowper, William. *The Poems of William Cowper.* Ed. J. C. Baily. London: Methuen, 1905.

Ferguson, Moira. *Subject to Others: British Women Writers and Colonial Slavery, 1670–1834.* New York: Routledge, 1993.

Hawkes, Terence. *Shakespeare's Talking Animals: Language and Drama in Society.* London: Edward Arnold, 1973.

Johnson, Barbara. "My Mother/My Self." *A World of Difference.* Baltimore: Johns Hopkins UP, 1987. 144–54.

Paquet, Sandra Pouchet. "The Heartbeat of a West Indian Slave: *The History of Mary Prince.*" *African American Review* 26 (Spring 1992): 131–46.

Poovey, Mary. "My Hideous Progeny: Mary Shelley and the Feminization of Romanticism." *PMLA* 95 (May 1980): 332–47.

Prince, Mary. *The History of Mary Prince, A West Indian Slave, Related by Herself.* 1831. London: Pandora, 1987.

Rushworth, John. *Historical Collections of Private Passages of State, Weighty Matters in Laws, Remarkable Proceedings.* 8 vols. London: D. Browne, 1721–22.

Shelley, Mary Wollstonecraft. *Frankenstein, or, The Modern Prometheus.* 1818. New York: New American Library, 1965.

Veeder, William. *Mary Shelley and Frankenstein: The Fate of Androgyny.* Chicago: U of Chicago P, 1974.

Wheatley, Phillis. *The Poems of Phillis Wheatley.* Ed. Julian D. Mason. 1966. Rev. and enl., Chapel Hill: U of North Carolina P, 1989.

Harriet Wilson's *Our Nig:*
The Demystification of Sentiment

DEBRA WALKER KING

Harriet Wilson's novel *Our Nig; Or, Sketches From the Life Of a Free Black, In a Two-Story White House, North* (1859) was written during an era when the dictates of a patriarchal, white society determined the models by which social, religious, and cultural acceptability was defined and judged. It was the era of the white woman's sentimental novel and the African American's slave narrative. While narratives by African Americans were expected to praise the North as a "promised land" and condemn the South for its exploitation and inhumane treatment of an entire race of captive people, novels written about and by women were expected to promote the cult of True Womanhood and its incorporation of the cult of domesticity. Harriet Wilson took advantage of her subject position as both a black and a woman when deciding the shape and content of *Our Nig;* in so doing, she crossed the color line. Since there were no novels written by African American women prior to *Our Nig,* both Wilson and her audience were entering new territory. At the gates of this new territory stood the traditions of women's fiction—demanding that Wilson either respect the formula and ideals of the sentimental novel or adopt the black, autobiographical form. Wilson did neither.

Instead she creates a patchwork quilt of nineteenth-century literary expression. Wilson frames her story to "frame-up" her reader, sews stitches where stitches do not belong, lays a familiar pattern only to disrupt its intimate flow, and places all upon a lining of indignation and rage. The finished product defies categorization, mocks hypocrisy, and demystifies the biased rhetoric of popular nineteenth-century modes of acculturation. Nothing escapes Wilson's hand of parody, subversion, and disclosure. Her novel challenges the rules governing discourse, behavior, and caste as proposed by white, Victorian culture and asks why such a culture should be the model by which blacks measure their humanity and define themselves. At every turn, *Our Nig* circumvents the expectations of its nineteenth-century readers by directly attacking the systems of order they used to define their world. *Our Nig* is a "critical narrative," a rewriting of the sentimental novel and the slave narrative. It moves beyond formulaic standards and emerges as an uncategorized, intergeneric form. Wilson rejects conventional aesthetics in favor of her own creation, a creation that challenges the literary and social contingencies of her time boldly and without reservation.

The story she tells takes place in Massachusetts. Jim, a black man, befriends a white woman in trouble (named Mag Smith) and later marries her. From this union two mulatto children are born, both girls. A few years later, Jim dies from consumption and Mag marries his black business partner, Seth Shipley. Unable to secure work, Seth suggests that they give the children away and move to a better place. Mag leaves with Seth, abandoning only one of her daughters, Frado, whom she leaves at the home of the Bellmonts. Frado becomes an indentured servant, suffering many abuses at the hand of the evil Mrs. Bellmont and her daughter, Mary. Privileges such as school and church are taken away from Frado because Mrs. Bellmont feels that blacks are unfit for both. Frado's only friendships are found with Aunt Abby (Mr. Bellmont's sister) and the male members of the family—especially James, who introduces her to Christianity and promises to take her from the Bellmont home to live with him and his wife in Baltimore. This plan is spoiled by his death and Frado is once again abandoned.

After James's death, Frado seeks comfort in religion, but "resolve[s] to give over all thought of the future world" when she discovers that her cruel mistress expects to hold a space in heaven beside James (104). Throughout this period, Frado continues to experience abuse and cruelty at the hand of her mistress until she learns to speak for her rights. Although her new "voice" frees her from undeserved beatings, this freedom comes too late. At age eighteen, Frado discovers that the physical abuse she suffered while in the Bellmont home has left her in poor health. She is continually in need of public charity until she learns a trade, needlework, and begins to experience freedom for the first time. This cherished freedom is suspended when she marries Samuel, a "professed fugitive" from slavery, has his child, and is once again abandoned (126). Still suffering poor health, she puts her son in the foster care of a friend and goes to a county home. Frado later encounters kidnappers (slave traders) and abolitionists whose dishonesty and hypocrisy soil the world she inhabits. In the end, the protagonist learns how to dye hair and writes a book about her life so that she might provide for herself and her son.

Wilson's narrative technique opens and ends with repetition and radical revisions of the "norm," the expected. The revision of genre, for instance, begins with a title designed to claim an affinity with black, autobiographical narratives. The titles of slave narratives are peculiarly explicit about the boundaries they set. They usually consist of a main heading, identifying the subject of the autobiography or biography, followed by a subtitle, summarizing the life revealed within the text, and a signatory, identifying the writer: "By Himself," "By Herself," or the name of the amanuensis. Of course there are variations, but the basic structure remains the same. Compare the title of Chloe Spear's 1832 narrative, *Memoir of Chloe Spear, a Native of Africa, Who Was Enslaved in Childhood. By a "Lady of Boston,"* and Sojourner Truth's 1850 narrative, *Narrative of Sojourner Truth, a Northern Slave, Emancipated from Bodily Servitude by the State of New York in 1828. Narrated to Olive Gilbert, including Sojourner Truth's Book of Life, and a Dialogue,* with the title of Wilson's novel, *Our Nig; or, Sketches from the Life of a Free Black, In a Two-Story White House, North. Showing That Slavery's Shadows Fall Even There, "By Our Nig."* The similarities are clear. Each follows the formulaic structure of the conventional framing device. Because *Our Nig*'s title is constructed in the tradition of the slave narrative, it suggests that the text following the frame is a slave narrative set in the North.[1] It is not.

Our Nig's title is a formulaic framing device that parodies a tradition. Slave narratives traditionally open with a statement concerning the author's birth: "I was born." *Our Nig* opens with a tale reminiscent of the sentimental novel—not the slave narrative. It begins, "Lonely Mag Smith! See her as she walks with downcast eyes and heavy heart" (5). The narrator doesn't mention the protagonist's birth until the second chapter—and then only as an aside: "Time levied an additional charge upon him [Mag's husband, Jim], in the form of two pretty mulattos" (14). Frado, the novel's protagonist, isn't identified as one of these two mulatto children until three pages later. Because *Our Nig*'s title follows the formulaic style of the traditional slave narrative frame, it signals the inability of titles to mandate the text by indicating genre. This failure to mandate genre also informs readers that in this text convention will not dictate nor override Wilson's creative authority.

If the first chapter followed faithfully the form of the slave narrative, the ability of the opening frame to establish the boundaries of form would be intact. This ability is circumvented by a textual deception that forces a contradiction between what the title announces and what the text provides. Wilson's opening frame is a frame up, a deception that accentuates a dislocation between itself and the internal structure it introduces. But this shrewd frame-up does not stop with one revision. After announcing itself as a slave narrative and opening with a tale reminiscent of sentimental fiction, Wilson's novel again challenges the idea of genre. This time it revises the sentimental novel. Wilson's initial characterization of Mag Smith imitates that of the heroines of sentimental novels. Following the introduction of "Lonely Mag Smith," the reader is told, "She had a loving, trusting heart. Early deprived of parental guardianship, she was left to guide her tiny boat over life's surges alone and inexperienced" (5). This whisper of the sentimental novel is quickly undermined by loud, unexpected echoes of the seduction tale: "There fell on her ear the music of love. . . . She knew the voice of her charmer, so ravishing, . . . alluring her upward and onward. . . . She surrendered to him a priceless gem which he proudly garnered as a trophy, with those of other victims" (6).

"Lonely Mag Smith," a white woman, is seduced and abandoned by the father of her unborn child (5). Unlike the fallen women in novels of seduction, Mag Smith does not experience a religious conversion and neither does she die as a result of her impropriety. She is ostracized by society and lives alone in poverty for years after the birth and death of her illegitimate daughter. The merging of the sentimental novel and the seduction tale is developed within the first two pages of the novel and further thwarts any claim that tradition governs the text of this radical, black, female writer.

After framing up her reader, Wilson uses the characterization of her protagonist to design a pattern of subversion that undermines the cult of True Womanhood, a pattern she repeats throughout the novel with a multitude of colorful variations. Frado, the indentured servant, is *every black woman*. Burdened by the stereotypes and prejudices defining blackness in America, most often poverty stricken, and as members of the (so-called) weaker sex, nineteenth-century African American women often found themselves standing outside of Victorian standards of acceptability. Even their position as women was tentative when measured against the requirements of the popular cult of True Womanhood.

In *Dimity Convictions*, Barbara Welter describes the cult of True Womanhood this way: "The attributes of True Womanhood, by which a woman judged herself and was judged by her husband, her neighbors and society, could be divided into four cardinal virtues—piety, purity, submissiveness, and domesticity. . . . Without them, no matter whether there was fame, achievement or wealth, all was ashes. With them [a woman] was promised happiness and power" (21). In other words, women were given limited "power" in the home as long as they were always submissive to male authority, including the masculine power structure of the church. True women did not work outside the home. Their place was inside the domestic sphere; therefore, they could have no direct influence in the world beyond it. Paula Giddings adds that "to be lacking in any of these qualities meant a woman was unnatural, unfeminine, and thus a species of a different—if not lower—female order" (48). Gender constructs such as this defeminized black women mainly because of the economic and social paradoxes they presented. To be a "true" woman required a financially secure husband and a favorable reputation—to say nothing of leisure time. Most African American women were not afforded such privileges. Stereotyped by race as ignorant, licentious Jezebels and driven to work outside the home by financial necessity, most black women simply didn't measure up.

Wilson refused to pay homage to the economically exclusive and socially biased definition of womanhood upheld by the cult of True Womanhood. She comments upon the unsexing of black womanhood in America by inverting her description of the novel's only black, female character. Initially, Frado is described as an androgynous being, "one who could so well adapt herself to all departments—man, boy, housekeeper, domestic, etc." (116). Frado's defeminization is contradicted later in the novel when she marries and achieves the ultimate accomplishment of a true woman: she has a child. This proof of Frado's gender boldly points out the contradictions within the rules governing True Womanhood. Within that context it asks how an androgynous being like Frado, someone who is obviously not a true woman by cult standards, could bear a child? Although the question is merely implied, it does emphasize the poor, black woman's subject position as one both inside and outside of traditional definitions of womanhood, a position which offers no honor or dignity that a nineteenth-century, white audience would acknowledge.

Wilson does not stop with the subversion of Victorian standards for True Womanhood. She goes a step further and undermines the cultural understanding of motherhood as upheld in the sentimental novel. By presenting motherhood as the destruction of a white woman's hope and independence and as the source of her social degradation, Wilson demystifies the exalted image of white motherhood and white purity. Although the mother in sentimental novels is usually separated from her child, it is not a separation of choice, and the time spent with the child, although brief, is filled with love and tender dedication, a demonstration of the mother's piety and merit. The reader is not led to despise this representative of True Womanhood, but is led to sympathize with her. The conventional plot of sentimental novels would never allow a mother to succumb to the fate of Mag Smith, nor would it allow her to enter into an interracial marriage.

First depicted as innocent and without family or friends, Mag's image is quickly contaminated by the news of her illegitimate pregnancy. Her hope is crushed and she is further degraded by her marriage to a black man and the birth of their mulatto children. Mag is certainly outside the realm of acceptability. Her attitude toward self-sacrifice is so exaggerated that it might be described best as selfishness and self-pity, a parody of a mother's self-sacrificing nature. Unlike the heroine of sentimental novels, Mag nurtures her despair, "morose and revengeful, refusing all offers of a better home than she possessed . . . hugging her wrongs, but making no effort to escape" (8). And, as if this were not enough, the novel demonizes Mag as both a mother figure and as a heroine. She falls willingly into miscegenation and her character mutates into a symbol of evil who refers to her legitimate mulatto children as "black devils." The narrator describes Mag as suffering "fits of desperation, bursts of anger and uttering curses too fearful to repeat" (16). She not only rejects Victorian standards of motherhood but also the standards of morality and virtue. The narrator tells us that Mag "had no longings for a purer heart, a better life. Far easier to descend lower. . . . She asked not the rite of civilization or Christianity" (16).

Black motherhood is presented quite differently. Like the mothers of sentimental novels, Frado is *forced* to leave her child in someone else's care. She does not abandon him; she does not lose her hope nor faith in God. Claudia Tate examines Wilson's novel as the symbolic reproduction of a black mother as historical subject. She explains that Wilson "mothers" her text through an allegory which revises "the condition of black people . . . by replacing the alienation inherent to that oppression with symbolic mother-love" (112). Wilson effaces the highly esteemed definitions of white motherhood while presenting black motherhood as the embracing of an entire race. Her symbolic mother-love carefully critiques nineteenth-century sociocultural ideals by offering the familiar and alienating only to challenge the racist ideological structures supporting them.

By mirroring that which it challenges in order to announce a deceit, Wilson's novel is often locked inside a rhetorical mode which appears to promote the very concepts the authorial voice rejects. It is within patterns of repetition, parody, and self-irony that the novel critiques that which it opposes. Wilson's novel uses hypocrisy and deception to nullify the validity, or usefulness, of the parodied material. Such is the case as the novel chastises abolitionists who promote the publication of narratives that denounce southern attitudes toward slaves while practicing racism and exclusion at home. The narrator describes Frado's encounters with abolitionists this way: "[She was] . . . maltreated by professed abolitionists, who didn't want slaves at the South, nor niggers in their own houses, North. Faugh! to lodge one; to eat with one; to admit one through the front door; to sit next to one; awful!" (129). The tone of authorial indignation present within this quote parodies the malice of racism and clearly opposes it. The statement repeats the hypocrisy of abolitionists, but does so in the manner of an outraged self-presentation.

During the Victorian age, such anger—when displayed by the powerless or by a true woman—was considered taboo. In an analysis of how women disguise and express anger, Jane Marcus explains that "anger and righteous indignation are the two emotions that provoke the most hostility from the powerful when expressed by the powerless" (122). The powerful of society demand the suppression of anger in women, slaves, children, and servants. Expressions of anger among these groups often lead to excommunication, ostracism, or obscurity—the type of obscurity that hid *Our Nig* in silence for over 120 years. Even in the face of these social pressures, expressions of anger among the powerless do not disappear. Instead, they are used as teaching tools to expedite a lessons in self-control and quiet obedience to authority.

Displays of angry defiance in the sentimental novel are not blatant; they occur in subtle forms. Dee Garrison comments that "the heroine's steel fist is concealed in a prim silken glove" (81). In Susan Warner's *Wide Wide World* (1850), the nation's first "best seller," the protagonist, Ellen, defies her guardian, Miss Fortune, and rebels against her verbal abuse: "'Stop! Stop!' said Ellen wildly,—'you must not speak to me so! Mamma never did, and you have no right to! If Mamma or papa were here you would not dare talk to me so'" (193). As a result of this open display of anger and rebellion, Ellen is slapped across the face and suffers a guilty conscience. The intended lesson is learned and Ellen thereafter restrains her anger with "tight-lipped obedient acceptance of the inevitable" (Dodson 230). In a similar scene in Wilson's novel (discussed later), the violent hand that threatens to teach Frado a lesson is stilled by her angry outburst.

When the writers of sentimental novels protest social standards, they often do so within the boundaries of indirect discourse. They announce obedience to social and cultural ideologies while undermining that ideology through the very act of writing. Their novels appear to promote traditional power relations, but, in fact, subvert them through their characterization of the powerful as abusive or easily manipulated. Characters in these novels announce an acceptance of religious convention, for instance, but subvert the institutions of religion by meeting God directly—in private moments outside of the male-dominated structure of the church (Baym 1978, 44). Obvious deviations from the formulaic standards of genre and acceptable social behavior are most often rebuked by the novel's end, however.

Nina Baym identifies E. D. E. N. Southworth as a "flagrant transgressor" of formulaic standards (1978, 110). But even Southworth, the most controversial of nineteenth-century women writers, does not completely defy tradition. Southworth inverts the entire feminine stereotype in her depiction of Capitola, the independent, self-sustaining, and tomboyish heroine of *The Hidden Hand* (1859).[2] Joanne Dodson comments that even though Southworth inverts the feminine stereotype, she "protects herself from censure by presenting Capitola not as a serious heroine, but as a great joke" (232). Like many other writers of sentimental novels, Southworth ultimately cloaks her rebellion against gender-specific, social standards beneath a "prim silken glove." She conforms to audience expectations and ends her tale by allowing Capitola to repent and marry.

Wilson discards the prim silken glove and replaces it with the bare knuckles of fury.[3] She spares nothing, not even religion, from her angry interpretations and appraisals. Her novel questions and attacks the hypocrisy of the pious, the authenticity of "professed fugitives from slavery" (126), and the charity of "professed abolitionists" (129). Her female characters flaunt their anger in forms of violence and abuse that reach beyond incidents of rhetorical play and indirect discourse into condemnation and rage. Acts of violence occur most often as a means of controlling Frado's emotions, behavior, and voice (although, at times, she is punished for no apparent reason). We are told that "no matter what occurred to ruffle her [Mrs. Bellmont], or from what source provocation came, real or fancied, a few blows on Nig seemed to relieve her of a portion of ill-will" (41). Frado is locked in a dark room, attacked with a knife, threatened with death and disfigurement, beaten with a rawhide, and kicked across a floor. On three occasions she is silenced both figuratively and literally with towels stuffed into her mouth or wood wedged between her teeth. Whenever she shows evidence of traits that are considered feminine, such as emotion or physical vulnerability (even illness), in the presence of either Mrs. Bellmont or her daughter Mary, Frado is attacked, threatened, or beaten.

The opposition between speech and silence motivates many these acts of violence—mostly because Frado is forbidden to speak or to make any sounds at all. But this is only one of the hierarchical tensions at issue in these frequent appearances of violence and abuse. Opposition between obedience (or submissiveness) and disobedience is another. Most of Frado's punishments are administered because of what Mrs. Bellmont considers Frado's disobedience. The protagonist accepts the unjust abuses and even tries to comply with Mrs. Bellmont's wishes by silencing her own voice and by hiding her true emotions. This behavior ends once the opposition between obedience and disobedience is redefined in terms of power relations and Frado becomes self-aware. Refusing to suffer an unwarranted beating, she challenges her persecutor: "'Stop!' shouted Frado, 'strike me, and I'll never work a mite for you'; and throwing down what she had gathered, stood like one who feels the stirring of free and independent thoughts. . . . *She did not know, before, that she had a power to ward off assaults*" (105, my emphasis).

Unlike Ellen in Warner's novel, Frado is not punished because of her sudden outburst and neither does she suffer a guilty conscience. On the contrary, she finds strength as a result of her actions and the violent hand that threatened her is stilled. By not surrendering herself to Mrs. Bellmont's torture, Frado finds the power to reject imposed definitions of her desires and her behavior. The narrator explains this new-found power and Frado's plans for its use a few pages later as Frado contemplates leaving the Bellmont home: "She remembered her victory at the wood-pile. She decided to remain to do as well as she could; to assert her rights when they were trampled on; to return once more to her [church] meeting in the evening, which had been prohibited. She had learned how to conquer; she would not abuse the power" (108).

If we halt the process of word supplementation at this point in the novel, we find that obedience is defined as submission, immolation, effacement, deprecation, and self-sacrifice; while disobedience is freedom, independence, victory, power, self-awareness, and self-possession. Frado's act of resistance and anger empowers her and unlike those who wielded power before her, she, being more virtuous than them, decides not to abuse it. This new "power" gives Frado freedom of choice and command of her own existence. No longer does she accept her desires and emotions as signs of disobedience. Frado can now define herself, assert her rights, and make her own decisions. She has learned the importance of self-possession, a lesson she did not learn through submission and self-denial. The opposite is often true in sentimental novels where obedience yields freedom and independence from the sin of resistance; and self-awareness and self-possession are the rewards of quiet submission.

Further examination of the novel's many incidents of violence and abuse reveal new insights into the work's intertextual relationship with the sentimental novel and the ideological differences this relationship disseminates. *Our Nig* intertextualizes the thematic discourse of sentimental novels concerning the relationship between religious piety and poverty. Wilson challenges the nineteenth-century belief that merit is the foundation for economic success. By repeating and inverting a scene from Warner's *Wide Wide World* and by continually announcing the prison of poverty in which Frado (and many other meritorious, nineteenth-century, African American women) live, Wilson challenges the conventional relationship between piety and poverty.

Poverty, a condition to be scorned, was considered the just manifestation of an individual's lack of merit. For most writers of sentimental novels (who, like their readers, were of the middle class), the subject of poverty was met with ambivalence. Nina Baym explains that although "they recognized that merit might exist among the poor, they tended to believe that American society was designed to permit such merit naturally to push itself up the social scale, and hence that those who remained poor were the less meritorious" (1978, 46). Because of this ideology, many women promoted the idea that the solution to poverty was the installment of good manners and piety. The pursuit of this notion as a worthy cause, an honorable mission, was promoted by more than a few midcentury women.

Our Nig challenges these beliefs by exposing the hypocrisy practiced by nineteenth-century "Christians" and by undermining the Victorian idea that merit yields economic success. Frado is depicted as more pious and meritorious than either of her persecutors. Yet, it is she who remains poverty-stricken and in need of assistance throughout the novel. Both Mrs. Bellmont and her daughter are characters whose piety goes no further than empty rituals and whose merit is more than questionable. The epigram Wilson chooses to introduce the novel underscores this type of piety and merit: "That hell's temptations, clad in heavenly guise / And armed with might, lie evermore in wait / Along life's path, giving assault to all." Frado rejects the hypocrisy ingrained in this type of religion and meets God on her own terms.

James, a Christ figure, symbolizes the masculine power structure of nineteenth-century Christian dogma; Mrs. Bellmont is the symbol of its hypocrisy. After James's death, Frado realizes that Mrs. Bellmont considers her religion and his to be the same. Allowing hypocrisy to roam freely among the pious is not attractive to Frado. She rejects it and "resolve[s] to give over all thought of the future world" (104). This is the most misunderstood passage of Wilson's novel. Many readers interpret this as Frado's rejection of a spiritual life, of religion. Just the opposite occurs. Frado rejects the hypocrisy ingrained in Mrs. Bellmont's interpretation of Christianity, not religion. She also rejects the Christian concept of life in death—the future world, a belief strongly held and romanticized by blacks as well as whites. Frado's religion is one in which she meets God directly—while here on earth. This change is symbolized by the Bible, "her greatest treasure," which she carries with her when she leaves the Bellmont home (117). Frado achieves piety. But even with the requirement of inner piety and merit achieved, she remains poor.

Wilson's inversion of the conventional relationship between merit (or piety) and poverty is symbolically portrayed during Frado's encounter with Mary at a stream. Jealous of Frado's popularity among the school children, Mary plans to "punish" Frado by pushing her into the stream. Unfortunately, it is Mary who ends up in the water. Again, Wilson borrows and revises a similar incident from Warner's *Wide, Wide, World*. A poor girl, Nancy, who is depicted as cruel and less meritorious than the novel's heroine, Ellen Montgomery, urges the protagonist to cross a brook:

> The only thing that looked like a bridge was an old log that had fallen across the brook, or had at some time or other been put there on purpose; and that lay more than half in the water; what remained of its surface was green with moss and slippery with slime. . . . Slowly and fearfully, and with as much care as possible, she [Ellen] set step by step upon the slippery log. Already half of the danger was passed, when, reaching forward to grasp Nancy's outstretched hand, she missed it,—perhaps that was Nancy's fault,—poor Ellen lost her balance and went in head foremost. (151–52)

As suggested by the text, Nancy arranges or precipitates Ellen's fall into the water, thereby demonstrating a lack of merit and refinement. Compare the same scene in Wilson's novel:

> There was, on their way home, a field intersected by a stream over which a single plank was placed for a crossing. It occurred to Mary that it would be a punishment to Nig to compel her to cross over; so she dragged her to the edge, told her authoritatively to go over. Nig hesitated, resisted. Mary placed herself behind the child, and, in the struggle to force her over, lost her footing and plunged into the stream. (33)

In both Warner's novel and in *Our Nig*, the child who falls into the water goes "to the nearest house, dripping, to procure a change of garments" (Wilson 34). The scenes are very similar, except in Wilson's version the parameters of merit are redefined and its relationship to economic status is reversed. In Warner's novel, it is the almost saintly, middle-class Ellen who is victimized by the poor and evil Nancy. Wilson inverts the hierarchical oppositions of good and evil and wealth and poverty that is traditional in both the sentimental novel and in nineteenth-century social ideology. Frado, the poor but meritorious intended victim, remains dry and safe while Mary, the middle-class and evil abuser, is punished with a dangerous fall. Consequently, the equating of merit with wealth is negated and replaced by the correlation of evil with wealth.

Two chapters later a similar scene is depicted. This time, however, Frado's encounter is with a sheep, "a willful leader, who always persisted in being first served, and many times in his fury he had thrown down Nig" (54). This episode parodies the biblical parable describing a shepherd's lost sheep but subverts that parable by depicting Frado as a shepherd who causes one of her sheep's fall into a river. Her actions ultimately separate the sheep from the rest of the flock until nightfall. Later, scenes describing Mary's departure from the Bellmont home and her subsequent death mirror this parody and, in doing so, they not only subvert religious ideologies but also subvert nineteenth-century racial ideologies. When Mary leaves the Bellmont home, Frado is exuberant. Aunt Abby interprets Frado's wish that Mary never return as a wish for Mary's death. Frado does not deny this and reiterates the wish as a premonition. Still trying to correct the child, Aunt Abby reminds her that Mary is James's sister. To this Frado comments: "So is our cross sheep just as much, that I ducked in the river; I'd like to try my hand at curing her too" (80). When Mary dies, Frado brings up the subject of the river once again: "She got into the river again, Aunt Abby, didn't she; the Jordan is a big one to tumble into any how. S'posen she goes to hell, she'll be as black as I am. Wouldn't mistress be mad to see her a nigger!" (107).

Extending the imagery of immersion in water to include the sheep as well as Mary's death thematically links the two events. The novel's juxtaposition of Mary with the sheep suggests allegorically a distinct social commentary. The separation of the sheep from the flock foreshadows Mary's separation from her mother, her co-conspirator in self-righteous and prejudicial evil. It also symbolizes the separation of racism from American society. Mary, a "sheep" separated from the flock of Frado's tormentors, symbolizes the evil which infiltrates nineteenth-century ideologies promoting the separation of blacks from whites, the color line. Frado's comment that she wishes to "cure" Mary, just as she did the sheep, expresses symbolically the author's wish for a cure which would purge America of racial prejudice.

In addition, the salvation of the Jordan River is transformed into a hell which does not cleanse but burns and chars Mary until she is black.[4] The Jordan River is the place where John the Baptist preached of repentance and baptized converts. The Pharisees, a sect of Jews who upheld their own interpretations of the Mosaic Law regardless of how it nullified God's Word, were required to give proof of their repentance so as to discourage outward religious show without inward commitment to "truth" (Dake N.T., 2). John the Baptist warned them that "every tree which bringeth not forth good fruit is hewn down, and cast into the fire" (Matt. 3:10). It is to this burning and charring of hypocrisy that Frado refers.

Throughout the novel, Frado's life is filled with horrors of bondage and racial prejudice which find no equal outside of the slave narrative. But unlike the heroic slave, *Our Nig*'s narrator does not tell a story of success (Foster 31). The protagonist of Wilson's novel remains in bondage as the story ends, an economic bondage. Regardless of whatever else we may discern, economic circumstances contribute to Mag and Seth's abandonment of Frado at the Bellmont home. Poverty is even more central to Frado's inability to mother her son and ultimately forces her to relinquish his care to a friend. It is also what motivates the protagonist/author to write her narrative. *Our Nig*, like the slave narrative, self-consciously crosses the boundaries separating fact from fiction and art from life in order to point out the defects of nineteenth-century American society. But, unlike the slave narrative, Wilson's novel crosses these boundaries in a manner that masks its social implications and forbids closure. *Our Nig* invites the reader to play a role in writing its ending, an ending which is still being written today by everyone who reads the text and responds to it. *Our Nig* blends the fictional recreation of a life with lived experiences, binding the reader to them both only to undermine this relationship through hidden discourse.

This hidden discourse is disguised beneath the novel's radical merging of life and art and can be understood best through a close reading of the author's pleas for assistance. Through her open requests for aid, Wilson prevents closure of the text, thereby summoning the present and the future of lived experience to enter at will. Her first request appears in the preface of the novel: "I sincerely appeal to my colored brethren universally for patronage, hoping they will not condemn this attempt of their sister to be erudite, but rally around me a faithful band of supporters and defenders" (3). Within the final chapter, she requests the reader's assistance for a second time: "Still an invalid, she asks your symyathy [sic], gentle reader. Refuse not. . . . Enough has been unrolled to demand your sympathy and aid" (130). Unless the reader is a borrower, financial assistance through the purchase of the book has been given prior to the time he or she encounters this second request. Why does Wilson repeat her request in the final chapter? Perhaps she hoped the reader might encourage others to purchase the book; or perhaps there is another reason hidden beneath the rhetoric of her request.

On its most primary level, Wilson's request is purely an appeal for financial support. It is not until the second request is made that a second meaning of her words is revealed. When the novel begins, Wilson's authorial voice is refracted and another voice, the narrative voice, surfaces. While the narrator describes the situations Frado encounters, the refracted authorial voice speaks from behind the main story and expands the meaning of the original request to include a foreshadowing of events within the novel. Throughout the story, a "faithful band of supporters and defenders" is literally what Frado is seeking. In the novel's seventh chapter, "Spiritual Conditioning of Nig," James tells Aunt Abby of Frado's disheartening laments concerning the protagonist's solitary life:

> "No one cares for me only to get my work. . . . Work as long as I can stand, and then fall down and lay there till I can get up. No mother, father, brother or sister to care for me." . . . I [James] took the opportunity to combat the notions she seemed to entertain and want of sympathizing friends. I assured her that . . . in our part of the country there were thousands upon thousands who favored [supported] the elevation of her race, disapproving of oppression in all its forms; that she was not unpitied, friendless, and utterly despised; that she might hope for better things in the future. (75) [5]

Frado discovers a small "band of supporters and defenders" while at the Bellmont home, but in each case the relationship is broken by either the removal of one member of the bond or by the restrictions placed upon the friendship by Mrs. Bellmont. Jack leaves the home; and, as a result, he is forced to abandon his relationship with Frado. Although Frado finds a friend in James, this relationship ends when death takes him away from her. Left with only the friendship of Aunt Abby, Frado continues to suffer in solitude until she leaves the Bellmont home. Ultimately, this and all other friendships Frado develops fall to waste.

Unlike the heroines of sentimental novels, around whom a surrogate family forms, Frado is left alone, still seeking "a faithful band of supporters and defenders" at the conclusion of the novel. Outside of the few, brief bonds of friendship she experiences, Frado's search for "sympathy and aid" continually leads her into the cold arms of public charity and abandon. Frado is abandoned by those she expects to support and defend her at least four times. Death is the cause of two incidents of abandonment, her father's and James's; economic conditions force Mag to abandon her; and Frado's husband's irresponsibility (and ultimate death) results in another incident of abandon. The relationship between Frado's search for kinship ties and the author's request for supporters and defenders is harmonic. With this in mind, it is easier to understand how Wilson's second request for aid coaxes the audience to enter the tale—and how it refines the parameters and conditions of the action she solicits. Although it appears that the writer is simply restating her appeal for financial assistance, Wilson's appeal for "sympathy and aid" also calls for social change through faithful bonds of friendship and communal action.

By making a second direct appeal at the end of the narrative, Wilson not only crosses the boundary between art and life, she revises the meaning of her request. The appearance of an appeal at this point in the novel forces the reader to recognize that society's responses to the conditions of poverty and racial oppression as expressed by James and as mirrored throughout the novel are comforting but highly illusory. They are not answers to society's problems, but cloaks for them. They yield nothing in the way of support or dignity for those who suffer, but merely allow those securely within the realm of comfort to feel self-righteous and vindicated morally.

This novel places a few sharp pins beneath the bed of those lying within the realm of comfort while demystifying many of the rules governing nineteenth-century literary discourse and social ideology. *Our Nig* pushes against the boundaries of the formulaic and conventional to expose that which is masked by these imposed boundaries. It defines "Slavery's Shadows" as race and gender prejudice as well as socioeconomic bondage. In its most challenging moments, the novel condemns American society for its continual proliferation of these evils. It thwarts the ability of nineteenth-century rules governing acceptable modes of acculturation to mandate its use of literary form and it denounces the value of the cult of True Womanhood. In the end, *Our Nig* issues a call for community bonding and action by asking others to rally around and support a radical, black woman writer. Henry Louis Gates's response to *Our Nig* was to search for its author. The results of this search afforded him an opportunity to "write" an ending for the novel. In his book *Figures in Black*, Gates summarizes the end of the novel this way: "The text concludes in Harriet Wilson's voice, a direct appeal to her readers to purchase her book so that she might retrieve her son. Six months later, we know, her son is dead" (141). This is only one ending. Wilson's appeals for support demand that we do many more revisions.

NOTES

1. Hazel Carby argues that because of its title, its condemnation of northern racism, and the main character's oppressive situation, the novel is an allegory of the nineteenth-century slave narrative, "a 'slave' narrative set in the 'free' North" (43).
2. The story was first published in serial form in the *New York Ledger* in 1859 as "Capitola's Triumph." It was not published as a book until 1889.
3. At almost every point in the novel anger controls language, plot, and structure. The book's epigram, quoted from Josiah Gilbert Holland's book-length poem *Bitter-Sweet* (1858), states a truth: this is a text "giving assault to all." Considering the venom of the author's pen and her attentiveness to almost everyone in her apologia, it is possible that *Our Nig* was not written with a particular au-

dience in mind at all—especially not an audience seeking examples of true womanhood and Victorian values.

4. This inversion of the Jordan as hell also facilitates the inversion of white and black as color designations for good and evil as noted by Gates in his introduction.

5. Whether the friends who support the uplift of the black race referred to here are within the black "community" or are white abolitionists is not clear. Like Frado, the reader is left without a clue.

WORKS CITED

Baym, Nina. *Novels, Readers, and Reviewers: Responses to Fiction in Antebellum America*. Ithaca, NY: Cornell UP, 1984.

————. *Woman's Fiction: A Guide to Novels by and about Women in America*. Ithaca, NY: Cornell UP, 1978.

Carby, Hazel. *Reconstructing Womanhood: The Emergence of the Afro-American Woman Novelist*. New York: Oxford UP, 1987.

Dake, Finis Jennings. *Dake's Annotated Reference Bible*. Lawrenceville, GA: Dake Bible Sales, 1963.

Davis, Charles T., and Henry Louis Gates Jr., eds. Introduction. *The Slave's Narrative*. Oxford: Oxford UP, 1985. xi–xxiv.

Dodson, Joanne. "The Hidden Hand: Subversion of Cultural Ideology in Three Mid-Nineteenth-Century American Women's Novels." *American Quarterly* 38.2 (Summer 1986): 233–42.

Foster, Frances Smith. "Adding Color and Contour to Early American Self-Portraitures: Autobiographical Writings of Afro-American Women." *Conjuring: Black Women, Fiction, and Literary Tradition*. Ed. Marjorie Pryse and Hortense J. Spillers. Bloomington: U of Indiana P, 1985. 25–38.

Garrison, Dee. "Immoral Fiction in the Late Victorian Library." *American Quarterly* 28.1 (Spring 1976): 71–89.

Gates, Henry Louis. *Figures in Black: Words, Signs, and the "Radical" Self*. New York: Oxford UP, 1987.

————. Introduction. *Our Nig; or, Sketches from the Life of a Free Black, in a Two-Story White House, North. Showing that Slavery's Shadows Fall Even There*. 2d ed. New York: Random House, 1983. xi–lv.

Giddings, Paula. *When and Where I Enter: The Impact of Black Women on Race and Sex in America*. New York: William Morrow, 1984.

Holland, Josiah Gilbert. *Bitter-Sweet*. 1858. New York: Scribner's, 1892.

Marcus, Jane. *Art and Anger: Reading Like a Woman*. Columbus: Ohio State UP, 1988.

Tate, Claudia. "Allegories of Black Female Desire; or, Rereading Nineteenth-Century Narratives of Black Female Authority." *Changing Our Own Words: Essays on Criticism, Theory, and Writing by Black Women*. Ed. Cheryl A. Wall. New Brunswick, NJ: Rutgers UP, 1989. 98–126.

Welter, Barbara. *Dimity Convictions: The American Woman in the Nineteenth Century*. Columbus: Ohio UP, 1976.

Wetherell, Elizabeth [Susan Warner]. *Wide, Wide World*. New York: Putnam, 1850. Philadelphia: Lippincott, 1890.

Wilson, Harriet E. *Our Nig; or, Sketches from the Life of a Free Black, in a Two-Story White House, North. Showing that Slavery's Shadows Fall Even There*. 2d ed. New York: Random House, 1983.

Gender, Genre and Vulgar Secularism: The Case of Frances Ellen Watkins Harper and the AME Press

FRANCES SMITH FOSTER

The bibliography of early African American literature is growing and academic interest is high. Ambitious enterprises such as the Black Periodical Literature Project and the Project on the History of Black Writing have rewarded long-term investments of time and money by recovering hundreds of African American texts. The efforts of scholars such as Jean Fagan Yellin and Henry Louis Gates Jr. have confirmed the authorship of some works previously attributed to white writers. Through the careful editing by individuals such as Marilyn Richardson, Jean Humez, and William Andrews, both the texts and the contexts of several important African American women writers are now readily available for classroom use. The multiple volume the Schomburg Library of Nineteenth-Century Black Women Writers represents unprecedented cooperation between a major publisher and at least thirty of the best scholars and critics in African American literary studies. Increased availability of materials from the eighteenth and nineteenth century has come at a time when theoretical approaches and canonical assumptions have encouraged reconsideration and reinterpretation of the beginnings of the African American literary tradition.

Strictly speaking, Frances Ellen Watkins Harper is not one of the many writers restored to us by recent literary archeological projects. Like Phillis Wheatley, Frances Harper had long been included in discussions of early African American literature. Like Zora Neale Hurston and Alice Walker, she is listed in virtually every compendium of notable black women and in most modern dictionaries of American women writers. Harper's gender had not barred her inclusion in most histories of African America, including those generally focusing upon men only. She's mentioned in William Still's *Underground Rail Road* (1872), G. F. Richings's *Evidences of Progress Among Colored People* (1901), W. E. B. Du Bois's *Gift of Black Folk* (1924), Benjamin Quarles's *Black Abolitionists* (1969), and John Hope Franklin's *From Slavery to Freedom* (1967), as well as in William Wells Brown's *The Black Man, His Antecedents, His Genius, and His Achievements* (1863) and George Bragg's *Men of Maryland* (1914,

1925). Nor had her race consistently disqualified Harper from occupying an obscure niche in halls of fame generally reserved for whites only. As early as 1882 Phebe Hanaford mentioned her in *Daughters of America,* in 1891 Harper's essay, "Duty to Dependent Races" was included in the *Transactions of the National Council of Women of the United States,* and in 1922 Frances Ellen Watkins Harper was named to Women's Christian Temperance Union's Red Letter Calendar. Since the 1860s, when Lydia Maria Child included Harper's work in *The Freedmen's Book,* anthologists have usually found space for at least a few stanzas of her poetry. Frances Ellen Watkins Harper's collected poems are currently available in paperback editions from both the Feminist Press and the Oxford University Press and the myth that *Iola Leroy* is the first novel by an African American woman survives in many corners despite evidence to the contrary.

Nor may we claim that literary critics had failed to acknowledge Frances Harper as a pioneering African American writer. Benjamin Brawley, Saunders Redding, Vernon Loggins, and others had afforded Frances Harper more attention and more respect than had been their wont to do for most women writers. Though Brawley insists that she was "distinctly a minor poet," he allows that "sometimes her feeling flashed out in felicitous lines," and he includes Frances Harper in *The Negro Genius.*[1] In *To Make A Poet Black,* J. Saunders Redding deems Harper "a trail blazer, hacking, however ineffectually, at the dense forest of propaganda" but concedes that she "attempted to suit her language to her theme" and was far ahead of her contemporaries in resisting the "willful (and perhaps necessary) monopticism [that] had blinded them to other treatment and to the possibilities in other subjects."[2] Redding allows that in *Sketches of Southern Life,* especially, Harper succeeded in putting "in the mouths of Negro characters . . . a fine racy, colloquial tang" while avoiding being confined to humor and pathos that generally limited the writer of dialect. In this, Redding asserts Harper "managed to hurdle a barrier by which Dunbar was later to feel himself tripped" (42). In general, modern critics have accepted a version of Vernon Loggins's conclusion that "Mrs. Harper was in no sense the least skillful" and was "better known than the other Negro poets who were writing in the fifties," but that her popularity "is probably best explained by the fact that she was on the lecture platform circulating her books among her audiences."[3]

As a writer, Frances Ellen Watkins Harper was neither lost nor ignored for many reasons. Critics and scholars embraced Harper because her career was long and distinguished. For over sixty years, she earned her living by and devoted her life to composing poetry and prose that spoke to and about the moral, social, and political conditions of African Americans. To have ignored her literary career would have meant relinquishing one of the earliest and most enduring best-selling African American writers. Nearly a decade before the Civil War, Harper's *Poems on Miscellaneous Subjects* was published both in Boston and in Philadelphia. It was reprinted in both locations several times. At least twelve thousand copies were sold in the first four years. *Poems on Miscellaneous Subjects* continued to merit reprints annually for the next twenty years. Not only was this volume enormously successful, but Frances Harper's acknowledged canon includes at least five other volumes of poetry, many of which were enlarged and reprinted several times. To applaud her as a fiction writer is to make a stronger case for the viability of African American fiction before the Civil War for Harper's short story "The Two Offers" then joins Frederick Douglass's "Heroic Slave" as pioneering efforts in that genre. To recognize Frances Harper as a journalist whose letters and essays appeared regularly in abolitionist papers further extends the variety of genre in our antebellum tradition. And, the fact that Frances Harper's work regularly appeared in—and her activities were respectfully reported by—the white press in the United States and in England also has its appeal for many scholars. Facts such as these are useful not simply as testimony of Harper's personal achievement but as evidence of the literary experimentation and the popular acceptance of African American literature during what might otherwise seem a barren period in its published history.

Though Frances Harper has not been ignored as a writer, the critical attention afforded her work has tended to misrepresent her achievements and to misread her texts. Sometimes she has been represented as an abolitionist speaker who recited her own poetry in a very genteel fashion in order to enlist sympathy for the downtrodden slaves, but generally her longevity and popularity occasioned comments such as Blyden Jackson's that "until the advent of Paul Laurence Dunbar, Frances Ellen Watkins Harper was undoubtedly the most widely known and widely read of black American poets."[4] Such statements acknowledge both a continuity of African American poetry and the popularity of Frances Harper's poems during her own time, but they also represent her as something like a vocalized pause—a fill-in between Phillis Wheatley (usually presented as author of the earliest extant volume of poetry by a black person in the soon-to-be United States of America) and Paul Laurence Dunbar (generally proclaimed as our first "truly great" poet). In his eulogy to Frances Harper, W. E. B. Du Bois set the tone for the critics of the early twentieth century. "She was not a great singer," he wrote, "but she had some sense of song; she was not a great writer, but she wrote much worth reading. She was, above all, sincere."[5] Like Du Bois, contemporary critics continue to applaud her sincerity, and with Jackson they conclude that "superlatives are out of place in relation to Harper's art. She operated within set boundaries. Within those boundaries, however, she knew her way around and made the most of what therein was palpably hers to command" (270).

The faint praise that slights Frances Harper's artistic contributions but extols her good intentions is due in part to sexism. Until quite recently texts written by women were automatically categorized as "women's literature" and by this definition were assumed to have limited interest and importance. Even within the realm called Woman's Literature, as Mary E. Bryan in her 1860 essay "How Should Women Write?" points out, gender restrictions limited the subjects about which they could write and the attitudes they should display: "Men, after much demur and hesitation have given women liberty to write; but they cannot yet consent to allow them full freedom. . . . With metaphysics they have nothing to do; . . . nor must they grapple with those great social and moral problems with which every strong soul is now wrestling. They must not go beyond the surface of life, lest they should stir the impure sediment that lurks beneath."[6]

For African American women writers there were additional pressures to confront. Mary Helen Washington explains that they not only had to consider also the "audience whose notions of female propriety and female inferiority made it nearly impossible to imagine a complex woman character" but also "the white audience whose tastes were honed by the sentimental novel and whose conceptions of blacks were shaped by *Uncle Tom's Cabin*" and the "black audience who desperately needed positive black role models."[7] These and other conditions help explain, in part, the patronizing attitudes toward Harper's work.

But while gender bias played a real and significant role in shaping Harper's literary reputation, it is an old story these days. More interesting, I believe, is the bias of academics toward Frances Harper's chosen genre. Harper decided early in her career that she wanted to be a popular writer, to write, as she says, "songs for the people." Moreover, she chose to publish extensively in the official journals of the African Methodist Episcopal church. In the mid-nineteenth century, this was not as problematic as it is today. Then it was not Emily Dickinson or Herman Melville whose work captured the fancy of the newly literate and more leisured class. It was Lydia Maria Child, Henry Wadsworth Longfellow, Harriet Beecher Stowe, and John Greenleaf Whittier who delighted and instructed readers around family firesides. Then, religion and politics and art and science were not the rigidly separated disciplines that we would have them be today. Since the turn of the century, literary critics and scholars have been embarrassed, offended, or perhaps merely disconcerted by literature that is unabashedly sentimental, religious, or didactic.

Many of us in African American literary studies, especially, have learned to privilege the extremes: to deify the modernists and the revolutionaries and to entertain the folk or primitive over the productions that reflect the aesthetics and values of the churchgoing Christians or the black middle class and those who aspire to it. We have failed to appropriately historicize both the attitudes and the art of the mid-nineteenth century. We judge as weaknesses the propensity of our early poets for strong rhythms and predictable rhymes. We dismiss sentiment as incompatible with intelligence. We judge Harper to have relied too much upon "sentimental treatment of the old subjects to be truly innovative" while overlooking the fact that the public presentation of an African American woman who took clear unequivocal positions on issues that were politically and socially controversial was so much out of the ordinary that some people simply could not believe what they saw and heard. For example, in a letter to William Still, Harper reported: "I don't know but that you would laugh if you were to hear some of the remarks which my lectures call forth: 'She is a man,' again 'She is not colored, she is painted.'"[8]

The prejudices of twentieth-century critics and scholars have resulted not only in misrepresentations and misunderstandings of Frances Harper's canon but also in mistakes in interpreting the role and process of the African American literary tradition in general. To assume that efforts to craft a written literature, to luxuriate in fanciful language, or to weave "from threads of fact and fiction . . . a story whose mission will not be in vain if it awaken in the hearts of our countrymen a stronger sense of justice and a more Christlike humanity" are neither authentic nor admirable goals for African American writers does severe damage to our academic enterprise.[9] At the least, it posits a homogenized African American culture and attempts to proscribe the range of material and metaphysical concerns that an African American artist is free to consider. It fosters the dilemma of trying to praise the existence of writers such as William Wells Brown, Frank Webb, Frances Harper, Emma Kelly Durham, and even Charles Chesnutt while trying to ignore the melodrama, sentimentality, and gentility that form the foundation of their writing. It diminishes their achievements by depicting them as literary parrots who repeated without comprehension what others have said. Or it paints them as racial sellouts who were ashamed of the sorrow songs and translated or diminished them for the entertainment of Anglophiles. The disdain of many critics and scholars for the piety, purity, and domesticity promoted by many published African American writers of the mid-nineteenth century exacerbates a gender bias that assumes African American women writers were directing their texts to a white female readership and pandering to their expectations because these writers often employed mulatto protagonists, used dialect for their folk characters, and espoused values that are compatible with those articulated by white middle-class writers.

Feminist, historicist, and other contemporary scholars sometimes seek to ameliorate this by emphasizing these earlier writers as precursors to the later, truer literature by women and by African American men or argue that women writers be judged as generously as men writers have been. Jane Campbell's argument that "*Iola Leroy* is at least as good as *Clotel,* and Harper's romance deserves more critical attention than it has heretofore received" implies that gender equity is as strong an argument as one should make for studying *Iola Leroy*.[10] Others focus upon the political ends and means that Frances Harper intended (or that we might intend) for her work. Mary Helen Washington reminds us that Harper "put women's lives, women's activities, women's feelings into the foreground" of her texts. Hazel Carby stresses Harper's participation in the Chicago World's Fair and the formation of the National Council of Negro Women. Few, however, address the basic issue of Harper's chosen genre and her contributions within it. To this day, Harper's texts, and those like hers, are far too often taught as artifacts that exemplify Gilded Age literature, sentimental fiction, or the "romance."

The notable reluctance of many scholars to offer close readings of texts or to assess the literary aesthetics that these early writings manifest may be attributed in some cases to the imperatives of the theoretical camp in which individual critics reside, but much of it stems from embarrassment occasioned by inadequate understanding of African American cultural history. Many of us underestimate or misinterpret the texts themselves because we are not aware of the variety of sources for and the resources of their writers. For most of us, our academic training insures that we are more familiar with the aesthetics and the literary productions of Europeans than of other parts of this world. We therefore recognize similarities to Stowe, to Whittier, to Pope, to Milton, or to Shakespeare and attribute to white culture techniques, subjects, and attitudes which may be as much African, Asian, or African American.

This is understandable, but this is not an acceptable excuse for the ease with which we in literary studies have often confused the original with the imitation or improvisation with inability to replicate. Why, for example, do we tend to attribute gentility to mindless imitation of the dominant culture or to blind acceptance of Puritanism and classism when concern for decorum and ritual may just as well stem from African traditions of respect and honor? Why do we applaud the verbal agility of the trickster in folktales and extol the improvisational dexterity of the spirituals and the blues but, when it comes to the published literature, assume that a desire to be published by or read by white people necessitated abandoning such strategies and copying the conventions and convictions of others?

I do not intend these questions to be rhetorical. I believe the answers are varied and complicated. The purpose of my discussion is not to argue a revisionist theory as much as it is to describe certain findings in my own study of the publications of Frances Ellen Watkins Harper that have made these questions more compelling and critical for me. My study of the fiction, poetry, and essays about African Americans that were published by African Americans for African Americans suggests that African American writers were about the business of creating and reconstructing literary subjects, themes, and forms that best suited their own aethetics and intentions and that they assumed and did enjoy an extensive black readership.

I am persuaded that the Afro-Protestant press, especially, makes it apparent that the literary forms and content of African American writers were at once inversions, improvisations, and inventions designed to speak to, about, and for African Americans. Contrary to the situation of Ellison's *Invisible Man*, many middle-class African American writers of the nineteenth century were not merely carrying white messages in black envelopes, messages written to keep black boys, girls, women, and men running. These writers had read the texts by Eurocentric writers, white liberals, and black reactionaries, but they had also listened to their ancestors, to their kinsfolk, and to their hearts. All these sources influenced the messages they fashioned for themselves and their people as they wrote to make the crooked straight and to explain the parables that would free both their bodies and their souls.[11]

In this effort, the Afro-Protestant press proved indispensable. Much of the Afro-Protestant press was ephemeral: bulletins, programs, pamphlets, and periodicals intended for specific occasions or discrete purposes. But it also included an impressive number of separately published volumes: autobiographies, histories, philosophical treaties, political analyses, novels, and poetry. Overall, the productions of the Afro-Protestant press were as varied as the many congregations and congregants who created and who read them. In some ways, however, the African Methodist Episcopal church press is both representative and prototypical. The African Methodist church may have created the first publishing organization by African Americans. The AME Book Concern was established in 1817 to provide the literature necessary and desirable for the growth of an Afro-Protestant church a full decade before *Freedom's Journal*, which is usually cited as the first black newspaper.

As early as 1836, the AME leadership was trying to establish a quarterly journal whose mission was not to teach a catechism of received doctrines and disciplines but to provide an arena for the promulgation of the ideas, attitudes, and talents of African Americans. In 1841, the church created the *African Methodist Episcopal Church Magazine* as a means of improving the general education of its clergy. Several years before *Douglass's Monthly* (1858) or the *Anglo African* (1859), the AME press was publishing the *Repository of Religion and Literature and of Science and Art* for distribution to African American readers. Later came the *Christian Recorder*, the *A.M.E. Church Review*, and others.

The most successful AME publishing venture is the *Christian Recorder*, the longest running and, at certain periods, the largest black newspaper in this country. It was the third incarnation of Martin R. Delaney's struggling newspaper, the *Mystery*, which the AME leadership purchased and converted to the *Christian Herald* then to *Christian Recorder*. While it was the official organ of the AME church, this paper was not intended as a mere vehicle for church business or theology. Its assumption of an international readership and a multiple mission was reflected in its masthead, which for many years proclaimed: "The *Christian Recorder*. Published by the African Methodist Episcopal church in the United States, for the Dissemination of Religion, Morality, Literature and Science."

Between 1853 and 1911, when Harper was a contributor, the *Recorder* was an eight-page weekly. The number of subscribers is a matter of controversy. The microfilm collection of Bethel AME Church pegs the *Recorder*'s highest circulation at five thousand. According to an 1877 article in the *San Francisco Elevator,* the *Recorder* had eight thousand subscribers at that time. According to the *Recorder* itself, it sometimes distributed over ten thousand copies of a single issue. Certainly the *Recorder*'s goals exceeded its reality, for practically every issue exhorted ministers to secure more subscriptions, advertised premiums for subscribing, and generally bemoaned the fact that its subscribers represented such a small percentage of the membership. But, like the publishers of *Ebony* claim today, the number of subscribers does not tell the full story of a periodical's impact, for then as now the argument can be made that far more people read and are influenced by certain kinds of periodicals than actively subscribe to them.

This is certainly borne out by testimony such as that from a correspondent who wrote from St. Joseph, Missouri, in 1877 that

> the *Recorder* [is] not only our church paper, but it [is] truly the colored people's organ in the United States, and the best family paper (colored) now published. . . . Better than all, it is read and is creating a taste for reading. Fathers and mothers that cannot read, when the day's work is done, press the school children or some friend into service and the *Recorder* is read in the family circle. The sayings of the different writers are commented on, the news is discussed, and pleasant, instructive evenings are spent. It is thus giving food for thought during the day. The question is quite common now when a friend meets another to ask, "What does the *Recorder* say this week?"[12]

As my citation about the *Christian Recorder* from the *San Francisco Elevator* suggests, the Philadelphia-based *Recorder* was part of a nationwide exchange system which included many periodicals by and for whites and for blacks, periodicals that were church-sponsored as well as abolitionist, political, literary, and simply "commercial." Just as the *Christian Recorder* regularly reprinted or summarized articles from other papers—articles on Chinese immigration and Russian politics, discussions of Unitarian philosophy and Anglican liturgy, as well as short stories, poems, essays, and local news—so too did their exchange colleagues copy, summarize, or advertise material from the *Recorder.*

This discussion of Harper's AME canon focuses upon her work in the *Christian Recorder,* but I suspect it can be applied with little revision to the work of many other African American writers in most, if not all, of the nineteenth-century Afro-Protestant press. The most obvious discovery is that Harper was a far more prolific and diverse writer than we have assumed. In the course of my investigations, I have identified at least three serialized novels, two series of articles, and numerous poems and essays that appear nowhere else.[13] Second, these texts provide a context within which we can better understand Harper's concept of literature and her role as a professional writer. The ideas articulated in her essays and through her characters' dialogue provide a theoretical framework against which we might judge her own texts and her intentions. They stimulate new readings of her better known publications as they enhance our understanding of the ways in which Frances Harper crafted her writings.

The revisions and repetitions, the experiments with genre and technique, suggest that Harper was far more than an orator or elocutionist whose desire to recite her poems on the political circuit led her to make "errors of metrical construction." My findings about Harper's AME canon suggest that the *Christian Recorder* and other publications of the Afro-Protestant press are largely untapped resources from which we may discover numerous forgotten writers and texts and through which we might begin to reconstruct our concepts of early African American literature and literary aesthetics.

From materials published in the AME press, one understands that Harper was a self-conscious and conscientious artist. Like many of her contemporaries, she eschewed art for art's sake. From the pages of the *Christian Recorder*, particularly, we understand that the aesthetics of nineteenth-century African American writers were quite similar to those of the Black Arts movement of the 1960s. They believed that good art must be functional. It must serve to educate, inspire, and correct the people. It was not elitist but was constructed to reach the largest possible audience. To that end they favored poetry that approximated in print the sounds and flavor of the spoken word. This literature was intended to stir people to action and to apply its precepts to their daily lives. It used both emotion and logic to stimulate both the head and the heart.

While the comparison with contemporary Black Arts movement may appear weakened by Harper's advocacy of Christianity, it is less so when one considers that the Afro-Protestant church provided both the leadership and most of the participants for the civil rights movement. It offered space and sustenance to community groups, including the Black Panthers, SNCC, and other organizations that had the reputation of being political, revolutionary, and secular. When one recalls that the AME denomination and several others were formed as direct revolts against racial segregation and discrimination or that liberation theologists agree with Clarence Walker's concept of Afro-Protestantism as a "civil religion," then the comparison is clearly more apt.[14]

Frances Harper, for example, was part of the same Christianity that produced Nat Turner and John Brown. Harper was a church militant whose congregation included several radicals named Moses. There was the Hebrew who murdered a master to save a slave, whose arsenal of weapons included plagues of locusts and the death of all the firstborn sons of Egypt. "I like the character of Moses," Harper wrote in her 1859 essay, "Our Greatest Want": "He is the first disunionist we read of in the Jewish Scriptures. . . . He would have no union with the slave power of Egypt" (*Brighter* 103–4). There was the pistol-packing fugitive slave who literally stole thousands of dollars worth of the slave masters' property because her definition of black pride and black power superseded the law of the land. In a speech to the National Woman's Rights Convention in 1866, Harper evoked the name of Harriet Tubman, this other Moses, saying, "We have a woman in our country who has received the name of 'Moses,' not by lying about it, but by acting it out—a woman who has gone down into the Egypt of slavery and brought out hundreds of our people into liberty."[15]

In her essay "Christianity," published first in the *Christian Recorder* but included later in her book *Poems on Miscellaneous Subjects,* Harper states a theory of aesthetics that seems to have held for many. "Christianity," she asserts, is a "system claiming God for its author, and the welfare of man for its object." All literature must be subordinated to this purpose or be rejected as mere idle tales. "Learning," she writes, "may bring her ample pages and her ponderous records, . . . Philosophy and science may bring their abstruse researches and wondrous revelations—Literature her elegance, with the toils of the pen, and the labors of the pencil—but they are idle tales compared to the truths of Christianity" (*Brighter* 96–98).

Frances Harper's subordination of literature to serve a militant religion that she called Christianity did not obviate her concern for technique or talent. Rather it led her to seek out new ways in which the truths might be told and Christian soldiers might be enlisted. One innovation was her *Christian Recorder* column "Fancy Etchings."

"Fancy Etchings" appeared irregularly from February 1873 to January 1874. It was a loosely connected series of conversations between Jenny, a recent college graduate, and her Aunt Jane. In the very first column, it is clear that Harper presents literature as a means of both self-assertion and community service. Jenny's is a decidedly immodest declaration when she advises Aunt Jane to "immortalize" herself by becoming a writer. "I want you to write a book, a good book, full of hard, earnest thoughts," she says. "A book that will make people better and happier because they read it."[16] Since Aunt Jane had never attended a college, had in fact been concerned that Jenny's education might make her a snob, Jenny's suggestion implies that published literature was not the purview of the educated class alone nor were classes in creative writing or Anglo-American literature prerequisites for good books full of hard, earnest thoughts. Jenny believed that literature could provide individual fame while improving the fortunes of all and she had decided to shape her own words toward the empowerment of black women and others. Her personal goal she confessed was "to be a living loving force, not a mere intellectual force, eager about and excited only for my own welfare; but a moral and spiritual force. A woman who can and will do something for woman, especially for our own women because they will need me most."

As a recent college graduate, Jenny represented the new post-Emancipation African American woman. Aunt Jenny was a version of Harper's earlier freedwoman of the folk, Aunt Chloe. But, both the new black woman and her foremother were potential agents of change. Rather than advise her young niece to more traditional or domestic ambitions, Aunt Jenny encourages her. "Set your mark high"; she says, "Aim at perfection, and if you would succeed yourself, always be ready to acknowledge the success of others and do not place the culture of your intellect before the development of your soul. The culture of the intellect may bring you money and applause, but the right training of your soul will give you character and influence." Aunt Jane's advice to subordinate the culture of intellect to the development of soul is not to be misinterpreted as advocating a "lady's aesthetic." And, in a later column we learn that Jenny has decided to become a poet—not a quiet meditative poet of delicate odes to plants or urns—Jenny aims to become "the poet of my race." While she intends "to earn and take my place among the poets of the nineteenth century" (24 April 1873), she intends to do so as an African American woman.

In "Fancy Etchings" the voice of tradition, including the prevailing notions of appropriate gender roles, comes not from the older woman but from her brother, Uncle Gumby. In a later column, Aunt Jane asks her niece, "What does Uncle Gumby think about your being a poet?" and Jenny replies, "He says it is all moonshine, that poetry is like the measles, it generally breaks out in the young; and that in a few years I will be over, what he calls, my new fancy." Uncle Gumby's indifference we are led to understand, stems in part from naïveté. "I don't believe he hardly knows one piece of poetry from the other," Jenny says, and offers as an example his general response that "that sounds well; but I think that I have seen something like it before." But it also reveals a rigid conservatism about woman's sphere. Having shared with him one of her favorite poems, Jenny reports that he "peered at me through his spectacles and asked, 'Can you cook a beefsteak?'" (1 May 1873).

Despite his clear sexism and Philistinism, Harper does not create Uncle Gumby as an occasion for anger or ridicule. She uses him to illustrate her position in the contemporary controversy over nature and nurture. Aunt Jane laughs at Gumby's response and explains that his excessive pragmatism comes from his personal background. She explains that her older brother was born when their parents were "both poor and young . . . very anxious to get along in the world and were so engrossed in bettering their conditions, that . . . their mental state impressed itself on the mind of our brother who was born during those days of early struggle." Thus, "his intense soberness and matter of fact cast of mind, may be easily traced to his antenatal history." Aunt Jenny says she was born "under pleasanter auspices . . . [their mother], a gifted and superior woman, [had by then] found both leisure and means to gratify her intellectual and esthetic taste." Frances Harper uses Gumby as a symbol to demonstrate how physical and social sciences might be helpful in understanding not only individual but group behaviors. Through Aunt Jenny, Harper concludes, "I think the laws of transmission and hereditary descent are very little understood; and in dealing with the dangerous and the perishing classes, these laws should be largely taken into consideration" (1 May 1873).

In "Fancy Etchings" columns, Harper incorporates more ideas from science, economics, art, philosophy, and religion—generally focusing upon the ethical choices and moral values that they encompass. In one case, Aunt Jenny receives a letter from a friend who had recently attended a Mechanics Fair. This prompts a discussion between Jane and Aunt Jenny that ranges from the effect of trade fairs and labor unions upon the national economy to the role of the mulberry tree in changing Scottish culture, from the need for wealthy blacks to hire both men and women at fair wages to the mutual importance of vocational education and of liberal arts scholarship. Aunt Jenny wants to see women studying agriculture, for she predicts that in that vocation they would find "far better pay than now comes to them from washing, ironing, and plain sewing" (10 April 1873). It is important that the radical here is not the young college educated Jenny, but her intelligent and self-schooled elder aunt.

As these brief descriptions of "Fancy Etchings" show, Harper pioneered the dramatic essay as a device for reaching, teaching, and encouraging African Americans. Her column prefigured the Aunt Viney sketches of Olivia Ward Bush-Banks in 1932 and the Jesse B. Simple series that Langston Hughes wrote for the *Chicago Defender* in 1943.

Through the pages of the *Christian Recorder*, Harper advanced her theories about literature and about life. She wrote in virtually every genre and on most subjects available to nineteenth-century writers. By discussing economics and education, art and agriculture, heredity and environment, she moved beyond the boundaries of most women writers and most African American writers. In "Fancy Etchings," as in *Iola Leroy* some twenty years later, Frances Harper wove threads of fact and fiction to persuade the nation toward a "stronger sense of justice and a more Christlike humanity" and to inspire her race to "embrace every opportunity, develop every faculty, and use every power God has given . . . to rise in the scale of character and condition, and to add their quota of good citizenship to the best welfare of the nation" (*Iola Leroy* 282).

NOTES

I dedicate this article to Jean Fagan Yellin and to my colleagues in Women's Studies in Religion Program at Harvard Divinity School. Jean shared her then unpublished Harper bibliography with me and insisted that my continued research would be well rewarded. It has. The Women's Studies in Religion Program ensured that I had the time and the support to devote to this phase of the project.

1. Benjamin Brawley, *The Negro Genius: A New Appraisal of the Achievement of the American Negro in Literature and the Fine Arts* (New York: Dodd, 1937), 116.
2. Saunders Redding, *To Make a Poet Black* (1939; New York: Oxford UP, 1988), 39–40.
3. Vernon Loggins, *The Negro Author: His Development in America to 1900* (New York: Columbia UP, 1931), 247.
4. Blyden Jackson, *The History of Afro-American Literature,* vol. 1, *The Long Beginning, 1760–1895* (Baton Rouge: Louisiana State UP, 1989), 265.
5. W. E. B. Du Bois, "Writers," *Crisis* 1 (1911): 20–21.
6. Quoted in *The Heath Anthology of American Literature,* vol. 1, ed. Paul Lauter (Lexington, MA: D. C. Heath, 1990), 1,197.
7. Mary Helen Washington, ed., *Invented Lives: Narratives of Black Women, 1860–1960* (New York: Doubleday/Anchor, 1987), 75.
8. In Frances Smith Foster, ed., *A Brighter Coming Day: A Frances Ellen Watkins Harper Reader* (New York: Feminist P, 1991), 126–27. Unless otherwise noted, quotations from Harper's works are from this source and noted in the text.
9. Frances Ellen Watkins Harper, *Iola Leroy* (1892; Boston: Beacon P, 1987), 282. Subsequent references to *Iola Leroy* are from this source and referenced in the text.
10. Jane Campbell, *Mythic Black Fiction: The Transformation of History* (Knoxville: U of Tennessee P, 1986), 23.
11. From the context of my discussion, I hope it is apparent that I am using the terms *middle class* and *Afro-Protestant press* in specific ways. *Middle class* should connote the group within the African American culture that sought and supported "racial uplift" or "race pride" through education, employment, and political empowerment. Whether individual members were themselves regular churchgoers or Christians, they understood the Afro-Protestant church to be a site and source for their activities. By Afro-Protestant press, I mean both the periodicals sanctioned by or published in the name of the various church groups and the publishing organizations that the denominations established.
12. *Christian Recorder* 18 Jan. 1877.
13. I have found at least twenty poems and several variants in the *Christian Recorder* alone. Many of these previously uncollected poems are included in the collection that I edited called *A Brighter Coming Day: A Frances Ellen Watkins Harper Reader* (New York: Feminist P, 1991).
14. Clarence E. Walker, *A Rock in a Weary Land: The African Methodist Episcopal Church During the Civil War and Reconstruction* (Baton Rouge: Louisiana State UP, 1982), 2.
15. Susan B. Anthony, ed., *Proceedings of the Eleventh National Woman's Rights Convention* (New York: American News, 1866), 47.
16. *Christian Recorder* 22 Feb. 1873. Subsequent references are all from the *Christian Recorder,* and this edition, unless another is noted, is cited in the text.

WORKS CITED

Anthony, Susan B., ed. *Proceedings of the Eleventh National Women's Rights Convention.* New York: American News, 1866.

Brawley, Benjamin. *The Negro Genius: A New Appraisal of the Achievement of the American Negro in Literature and the Fine Arts.* New York: Dodd, 1937.

Campbell, Jane. *Mythic Black Fiction: The Transformation of History.* Knoxville: U of Tennessee P, 1986.

Du Bois, W. E. B. "Writers." *The Crisis* 1 (1911): 20–21.

Foster, Frances Smith, ed. *A Brighter Coming Day: A Frances Ellen Watkins Harper Reader.* New York: Feminist P, 1991.

Guillaume, Bernice F. "The Female as Harlem Sage: The 'Aunt Viney's Sketches' of Olivia Ward-Bush Banks." *Langston Hughes Review* 6.2 (Fall 1987): 1–10.

Harper, Frances E. W. *Iola Leroy; Or, Shadows Uplifted.* 1892. New York: Oxford UP, 1988.

Jackson, Blyden. *The Long Beginning, 1760–1895.* Baton Rouge: Louisiana State UP, 1989. Vol. 1 of *The History of Afro-American Literature.*

Lauter, Paul, et al., eds. *The Heath Anthology of American Literature.* Vol. 1. Lexington, MA: D. C. Heath, 1990.

Loggins, Vernon. *The Negro Author: His Development in American Literature to 1900.* New York: Columbia UP, 1931.

Redding, J. Saunders. *To Make a Poet Black.* 1939. New York: Oxford UP, 1988.

Walker, Clarence E. *A Rock in a Weary Land: The African Methodist Episcopal Church During the Civil War and Reconstruction.* Baton Rouge: Louisiana UP, 1982.

Washington, Mary Helen, ed. *Invented Lives: Narratives of Black Women, 1860–1960.* New York: Doubleday/Anchor, 1987.

Anna J. Cooper:
The International Dimensions

DAVID W. H. PELLOW

By the nineteenth century the Atlantic world had knit together a complex of historical strands connecting the three continents sharing its shores. The century was marked by slave uprisings throughout the Americas, wars of independence, civil wars, wars between republics, the abolition of slavery, and—in the closing years—the European conquest and colonization of much of Africa. African states waxed and waned, Atlantic colonies became more firmly rooted, revolutions shook Europe and the Americas, and economic systems began to yield grudgingly to pressures to end servitude and peonage in their various forms.

It was into this nineteenth-century world that Anna J. Cooper arrived. Born Annie Julia Haywood in 1859,[1] to a slave mother owned by the Haywood family of Raleigh, when that North Carolina capital was still a small and semi-rural community of about five thousand, she lived through the Civil War, abolition, Reconstruction, segregation, two world wars, the Great Depression, and into the civil rights era of the 1960s. Certainly, most simple folk far removed from the action would have little knowledge of events beyond their immediate sphere. But the young Cooper, at the core of one of the centers of learning which emerged during Reconstruction, was ideally placed to become informed and politically astute, and it is only in this context that she can be fully understood or appreciated.

In 1868 Anna enrolled in the newly opened Normal School and Collegiate Institute affiliated with the Episcopal church—which later became St. Augustine's College—and did so well that she soon became a tutor and eventually an instructor. In 1877 she married fellow instructor George Cooper, a thirty-three-year-old former tailor from Nassau, Bahamas. He died unexpectedly in 1879, just three months after he had been ordained as an Episcopal priest. Anna Cooper never remarried. She is best remembered as a feminist, an activist, and an educator—positions which she advocated eloquently in her best known work, *A Voice from the South: By a Black Woman from the South* (1892).[2]

In 1881 the young widow went to Oberlin College, where she earned her A.B. degree in 1884 in languages and an M.A. in math in 1887. She taught modern languages at Wilberforce University, in Ohio, in 1884–85, then taught mathematics, Latin, and German at St. Augustine's for two years. In 1887 she moved to Washington, D.C., to teach at the Preparatory High School for Colored Youth, which later became the M Street Colored High School (and later yet the Paul Laurence Dunbar High School). Except for a four-year hiatus from 1906–10, when she chaired the Language Department at Lincoln University in Jefferson City, Missouri, Cooper would spend the rest of her working years at this Washington school, as either principal or teacher. She taught Greek, Latin, French, and German, as well as mathematics with success and distinction.

After several summers of study—1912–13 in Paris, 1914–17 at Columbia University—during which time she also took in five orphaned grand nieces and nephews, Cooper was admitted to candidacy for the Doctorat d'Université at the Sorbonne in Paris. When she received this degree in 1925 at age sixty-six, she was only the fourth known African American woman to have earned a doctorate.[3]

As is evident in this brief introduction, the international dimensions are central to our understanding of Cooper's world view, particularly as it relates to Africa. Working at a time of black intellectual ferment, she wrote a historical dissertation on the Haitian Revolution. Cooper provides us with a unique analysis of diasporean discourse in general and Haiti as a new world narrative of containment in particular. She mapped the intersection of slavery, race, and imperialism during an era when literary critical study of Africans and the diaspora had produced the Harlem Renaissance and was about to blossom in the Négritude movement. Her critical inquiry parallels the rising tide of interest in Africa by diverse public figures such as Martin R. Delany, Alexander Crummell, Edward Wilmot Blyden, Henry Sylvester Williams, W. E. B. Du Bois, Samuel Coleridge-Taylor, Marcus Garvey, and Carter G. Woodson, to name just a few. Cooper laid the groundwork for future students of diasporean studies to think about international politics within the whole range of problems that states confront and why they often act as they do.

Most comprehensively and fundamentally, Anna J. Cooper's strength as a scholar was enhanced by her ability to understand issues on several levels, particularly those of space and time. By space I mean geography, a sense of location and place, an understanding of the world's complexities, of the interconnectedness of the centers of power and finance—particularly those on both sides of the Atlantic which engineered the exploitation of the Americas, the rise of Europe, the destruction of Native American civilizations, and the pillage of Africa. With this understanding comes the knowledge that everything is relative, and that even the racist horrors of the United States were not universal nor even inevitable, but were in fact due to certain inadequacies, omissions, or outright failures.

The other dimension, that of time, requires a sense of history; it ties in with space, and is likewise vital if one is to grasp the international connections. Cooper's sense of history is nowhere better demonstrated than in her doctoral dissertation, entitled "L'Attitude de la France à l'égard de l'esclavage pendant la Révolution," published in Paris in 1925, translated and published some sixty-three years later in the United States as *Slavery and the French Revolutionists (1788–1805).*[4] It is a study of French racial attitudes around the end of the eighteenth century, a time when France had its Revolution against an oppressive social system, and when the slaves in Saint-Domingue rose up to take their freedom, thus creating the free black country which we know today as Haiti. The eminent French historian Gabriel Debien has noted that of all the ample documentation on Saint-Domingue, archival or published, there is no known testimony from the largest constituency—the slaves themselves.[5]

However, Cooper, a scholar who had begun life as a slave, was able to bring to her study a perceptiveness and sensibility which other scholars lacked. Using both contemporary published memoirs and numerous archival documents, her finished product—which met the rigorous standards of historical scholarship set by the Sorbonne—is unique and insightful. As she studied and reflected upon the slavery system and its consequences in Saint-Domingue, Cooper compared and measured it against the society in which she herself had grown up. The knowledge that comes with this heightened awareness of time and space brings with it the realization that in other places and at other times things can be different, which, for the reformer as for the rebel, implies that they can be better. It is therefore essential to understand Cooper's world vision. Her journey in space and time indicates her perceptive assessments of the implications and interconnections of the histories and conditions of Haiti, Canada, Europe, and Africa.

Word of the successful slave revolts in the French colony of Saint-Domingue had reached America's shores even before the Haitian Republic was established there in 1804. Free blacks in the United States before the Civil War had considered Haiti—along with Liberia and Canada—as a possible destination for settlement, and indeed a number of African Americans did go there, particularly after 1824, when Haitian president Jean-Pierre Boyer invited black immigration to that Caribbean republic.[6] Haiti became an inspiration for Africans dispersed in the Americas as a symbol of hope and freedom and of triumph where slaves had risen up against injustice and by force had repossessed their own persons. Although that early migration did not result in a large movement of people, it did see the establishment of an African Methodist Episcopal church in Haiti and it set the stage for later events.[7]

Spurred by a back to Africa movement, the Emigration Convention met in Cleveland, Ohio, in 1854. Under the leadership of chair Martin R. Delany, the delegates appointed several commissioners to study possible settlement destinations.[8] One of these commissioners, the Reverend James Theodore Holly, a black abolitionist and staunch nationalist, was sent to Haiti, where, the following year, he was commissioned by that republic to recruit immigrants. According to one report, nearly two thousand people left with this impulse, beginning in 1861, but again with only modest success, as two-thirds of them were eventually repatriated.[9] In 1876 the Reverend Holly—now Bishop Holly of the Episcopalian church in Haiti—visited St. Augustine's College "to enter two of his sons and another Haitian youth in the School."[10]

The Holly presence at St. Augustine's was undoubtedly an early influence on the young Cooper. In 1876 the faculty consisted of only four people: the principal, Cooper and her husband-to-be, and a Miss Thomas, while the student body numbered little more than one hundred. Bishop Holly's visit was an important event; he officiated at both morning and evening services in the chapel and held meetings with various dignitaries.[11] And then, of course, the presence of three youths from Haiti in such a small student population could hardly have gone unnoticed. Cooper almost certainly would have shared the excitement and curiosity of her contemporaries concerning the brave people of Haiti, a country run by black people descended from slaves who had taken command of their own lives. The same Bishop Holly reappears in 1899 at the meeting of advisors who planned the London Pan-African Conference of 1900,[12] at which Cooper herself was a speaker. It is no surprise, therefore, that the London conference should have elected the presidents of Haiti and Liberia—along with Emperor Menelik of Ethiopia—honorary members of the Pan-African Association. And it should be no surprise that Cooper's interest should have led her to choose a Haitian topic for her doctoral dissertation.

Canada also influenced Cooper's intellectual development. It held a special place in the hearts and imagination of American blacks. It not only had quite a different history from the United States and Haiti, but also had abolished slavery earlier than had the United States. In spite of its segregated schools and occasional shameful acts of racially motivated violence, Canada was high on the list of desirable destinations for American blacks heading for freedom, either as runaways from slavery or as refugees from the northern states. With no widespread agricultural plantation system that required cheap and intensive labor—and consequently no extensive experience with slavery—Canada had developed only a relatively mild dose of racism, which tended to be muted by progressive legislation and a general level of tolerance.

Black settlements sprang up in "West Canada" (present-day Ontario), particularly in the region north of Lakes Erie and Ontario from Windsor to Toronto. Many blacks moved back and forth between the two countries as conditions warranted. For example, after the United States passed the second fugitive slave law in 1850, which virtually denied due process to any person anywhere of African descent, there was a surge of black emigration north, from all points between Michigan and Massachusetts. Similarly, the years after 1865 saw a movement of people coming back. Although some, like William Wells Brown, promoted Canada as an ideal place for black settlement, Martin Delany—who had lived in Chatham for a while—feared that the United States would eventually annex the region and that conditions there would deteriorate as a result.[13]

This did not happen, of course, so that during the summer of 1891, when Anna Cooper visited Toronto in a cultural exchange of black teachers from Washington, D.C., Afro-Canadian communities were flourishing. Black tenants, benefiting from favorable loan terms extended to them by black self-help organizations in Canada, were becoming successful and independent farmers, while urban blacks were moving with increasing confidence into most of the trades and professions. Cooper's letter to her mother, dated July of that year, praises the beauty of Toronto, its parks and public buildings, its streets, its houses, and its friendly people.[14] As a guest of the William Hubbard family at 51 Bathurst Street, Cooper was very close to the lakefront, the Parliament building, and the University of Ontario (now Toronto). She wrote: "A Miss Chantz who plays the piano excellently & accompanies all the leading white vocalists was there & played for us delightfully."[15]

It is likely that the visit to Canada was a pivotal experience in Cooper's life, in that it demonstrated clearly that the United States was not the only world possible. Sometimes, to understand a problem fully, one has to stand back from it and view it from a distance. I believe that Cooper's time in Canada allowed her to do just that. In her "Woman versus the Indian" she states:

> It was the good fortune of the black Woman of the South to spend some weeks, not long since, in a land over which floated the Union Jack. The Stars and Stripes were not the only familiar experiences missed. A uniform, matter-of-fact courtesy, a genial kindliness, a quick perception of opportunities for rendering any little manly assistance, a readiness to give information to strangers,—a hospitable, thawing-out atmosphere everywhere—in shops and waiting rooms, on cars and in the streets, actually seemed to her chilled little soul to transform the commonest boor in the service of the public into one of nature's noblemen, and when the old whipped-cur feeling was taken up and analyzed she could hardly tell whether it consisted mostly of self-pity for her own wounded sensibilities, or of shame for her country and mortification that her countrymen offered such an unfavorable contrast.[16]

After Haiti and Canada, Africa formed the third strand of Cooper's geopolitical orientation, and it was by far the most important. The African dimensions of her thought reflect those of an already mature tradition going back at least as far as Henry Highland Garnet (1815–82), and following such contemporaries as Martin

Delany, Alexander Crummell, and W. E. B. Du Bois, all of whom she knew personally. We find positive images in Cooper's work, such as Africa being "the fatherland of all the family,"[17] or the metaphor of black people being a sound African timber.[18] When describing the heroic achievements of Toussaint Louverture in the struggle for liberation in Haiti, she is emphatic in pointing out that he was of unmixed African descent.[19] Elsewhere she had noted that Martin Delany too was of pure African descent, so that his intelligence and accomplishments could not be attributed to any admixture of Saxon blood, as whites would often claim. Cooper's description of Delany as an "unadulterated black man" is an echo of the times.[20] For example, William Wells Brown made use of the same expression when he described Delany as "short, compactly built . . . unadulterated in race, and proud of his complexion."[21]

Black intellectuals early saw the need to reexamine history, especially that of Africa, because Eurocentric historians had for so long slanted things in order to justify Europe's impact upon the extra-European world. Ancient Egypt's ethnic identity—black or white?—was an often debated topic throughout the nineteenth century, as Scripture and the Classics were cited to sustain both sides of the argument. The erudite Volney (1757–1820), a professor of history at the prestigious École normale supérieure, had raised the question as early as 1787 with his description of the Sphinx as representing an ancient Negro king.[22] The African affinities of Egypt were likewise posited by another French scholar, the Egyptologist and linguist Champollion (1790–1832), whose works include a translation of the famous Rosetta stone.

African American intellectuals were not slow to see the importance of this position. In 1848 Henry Highland Garnet, born a slave in Maryland but the son of an African dignitary, stressed the importance of these African origins of civilization in his *Past and Present* (1848), as did William Wells Brown in *Rising Son* (1874) and Martin R. Delany in *The Origins of Races and Color* (1879). Thus Cooper is part of a long and distinguished tradition. Just as Garnet had described the early Anglo-Saxons as "degraded, living in caves, naked and practicing human sacrifice,"[23] and Brown had quoted Cicero on British slaves ("the ugliest and most stupid race I ever saw"),[24] so Cooper likewise was not dazzled by the myth of Saxon superiority, as her vivid excerpts from Tacitus and Taine attest. For example, in Cooper's quoting of Tacitus on the European barbarians, we read: "To shout, to drink, to caper about, to feel their veins heated and swollen with wine, to hear and see around them the riot of the orgy, this was the first need of the barbarians. The heavy human brute gluts himself with sensations and with noise."[25] Or, from Hippolyte Taine, the French historian: "Huge white bodies, cool-blooded, with fierce blue eyes, reddish flaxen hair; ravenous stomachs, filled with meat and cheese, heated by strong drinks. Brutal drunken pirates and robbers, they dashed to sea in their two-sailed barks, landed anywhere, killed everything; and, having sacrificed in honor of their gods the tithe of all their prisoners, leaving behind the red light of their burning, went far-ther on to begin again."[26] No, Cooper insisted in her notes to her dissertation defense, European civilization has little to brag about beyond the technical achievements, and in fact has a long way to go.[27]

A more civilized and humane culture is suggested by the African tradition, which Cooper ties neatly into the Bible and the experiences of Jesus. When Mary and Joseph fled Herod's persecution, for example, they took the infant Jesus to Africa for safety; and later, upon a certain hill at Calvary, it was an African—Simon of Cyrene—who helped the swooning Jesus to carry his bur-den.[28] The inequities which exist between black and white are based upon noth-ing more than the abusive use of force, said Cooper, and true greatness in a nation is impossible until that superior strength is used as a positive force and until the weaker fellow is respected.[29]

There was indeed a grave, abusive use of force during the last decades of the nineteenth century, when European powers undertook the military conquest and subjugation of Africa. The first Pan-African Conference, held in London in July, 1900, was in direct response to this aggression, and Cooper was among the delegates from the United States who attended. Yet, even as they met, Briton and Boer were at war in southern Africa, fighting over the lands they had earlier taken from African peoples, while elsewhere new military actions were under way, as is evidenced by the following telegram sent to the British Colo-nial Office in London, by a Colonel Willcocks from Bekwai, Gold Coast (now Ghana): "I today sent out flying column consisting of three 75-millimetre guns, two 7-pounder guns, and 800 men . . . to attack large rebel camp at Kokofu; column under the command of Lieutenant-Colonel Morland, 1st Battalion West African Frontier Force. . . . the enemy's loss 30 killed in action, and the famous rebel camp Kokofu which has resisted two attacks no longer exists. Force de-stroyed stockades, returned Bekwai 7 this evening."[30] The telegram was dated 22 July 1900.

Organized by Henry Sylvester Williams, a promising young barrister from Arouca, Trinidad, the conference was planned in 1899 by a committee which included Bishops James T. Holly (Haiti), James Johnson (Sierra Leone and La-gos), and Henry McNeal Turner (United States), the Reverends Majola Agbebi (Nigeria) and C. W. Farquar (Caribbean), and, among others, Booker T. Wash-ington, who did not attend the conference itself. Sponsored by the African As-sociation (later to become the Pan-African Association), the conference and was attended by delegates from the United States, the Caribbean, Europe, and Af-rica.[31] Chaired by African Methodist Episcopal Zion Bishop Alexander Walters from New York, this gathering of concerned activists from various professional backgrounds met in the lion's den, so to speak—the capital of the world's main colonial power.

One participant of note was Benito Sylvain, a thirty-two-year-old Haitian and co-organizer of the conference, who had studied in France, had worked as a journalist, had published his own journal, *La Fraternité*, in defense of the race, and had formed a black student association in Paris named Association de la jeunesse noire de Paris.[32] Sylvain had served in the Haitian embassy in London and had represented his country in the 1890 and 1891 Anti-Slavery Congresses in Paris and Brussels before representing the Haitian government at the court of Emperor Menelik of Ethiopia, or Abyssinia as it was then called. The connection here, between Haiti—an Afro-Caribbean state which had defeated the forces of colonialism and slavery in the early 1800s—and Abyssinia/Ethiopia—an African state which had recently (in 1896) soundly defeated an invading Italian army at Aduwa—was certainly not lost upon the participants in this conference. Another participant of note was W. E. B. Du Bois, who was very much committed to a pan-African ideal; he had designed the "American Negro Exhibit" for the Paris Exposition and traveled to Europe to install it; he served on the committee which drafted an "Address to the Nations," and would later become prominent in organizing pan-African congresses beginning in 1911.[33]

Cooper already knew Du Bois at this time, as she did a number of the other participants, including Professor Thomas J. Calloway of Hampton Institute (present-day Hampton University), who supervised the "American Negro Exhibit" at the Paris Exposition. Others Cooper knew were the Reverend H. Mason Joseph, president of the African Association and the Pan-African Conference Committee, an Antiguan then living in London who had been professor of Greek and Latin at St. Augustine's College from 1881 to 1886;[34] Anna H. Jones, a lifelong friend, linguist, and teacher from Kansas City; another friend, Fannie Barrier Williams, author and social activist from Chicago, and her sister, Ella D. Barrier, a teacher from Washington, D.C., who had been a member of Cooper's group in the 1891 Canada teacher exchange; and lastly, John L. Love, Cooper's foster son and fellow teacher from the M Street School, a member of the American Negro Academy who served as secretary of the Pan-African Conference. We know that Cooper herself spoke on the first day of the conference, although no copy of her paper "The Negro Problem in America" has been found. Mathurin, however, notes that the *Leader*'s reaction was to comment that the conditions she described were "'pathetic' in an America that calls itself Christian."[35]

Several important issues emerged from the Pan-African Conference, either in papers presented or in adopted motions, and they can be summarized as follows: First, concerns were expressed about the conditions under which Africans and people of African descent were forced to live—in the United States as well as in Africa and the Caribbean; these concerns were linked to a call for fair and responsive government. Second, some speakers, striving to rehabilitate African history, spoke of the great past of the African race with reference to Ethiopian and Egyptian influences on Greek and Roman antiquity. And third, there was serious concern for the plight of southern Africa, where, even as they spoke, the Boer War was being waged over land, language, and suppression of the Africans, who were being systematically and mercilessly dispossessed of rights and land by both sides.[36]

Finally, when all was done, the Pan-African Conference delegates issued a petition to Queen Victoria as head of the biggest colonial empire, and an "Address to the Nations of the World," directed especially at the countries which included or controlled black populations—most specifically Britain, France, Germany, Belgium, and the United States. Cooper, who evidently supported the aims and objectives of the Pan-African Association, was named to the executive committee to plan the next conference, projected for 1902.

It is difficult to assess the importance or the impact of the Pan-African Conference even at this distance, but I would suggest that it was greater than has heretofore been considered. At the very least, it was an important beginning; and at best it put the imperial powers on notice that their conduct in the world outside of Europe would not go unchallenged. Further, the Pan-African Conference forged new links between continents, as black people from Africa, Europe, North America, and the Caribbean came together in a common cause, identified common problems, and together sought common solutions. In the process a number of organizations—religious, social, and humanitarian—similarly made contact and often common cause, not the least of which were the Aborigines Protection Society,[37] the Anti-Slavery Society, the Congrès anti-esclavagiste, several temperance groups, and the British Socialist Party.

As an intelligent, informed, and intensely curious individual who had already mastered several languages, Cooper would have most likely traveled to Europe sooner or later: two shorter trips—to Canada in 1891 and the Bahamas in 1896—show she already had an interest in travel. During her 1900 trip, she toured England, Scotland, France, Germany, and Italy, and although in later years she referred to herself as having been a "mere Globe Trotter," the seriousness of her commitment to pan-Africanism is unmistakable.[38] And as a dedicated worker for the cause of uplifting African Americans, she could not fail to have been drawn to the London conference. After all, the aims and objectives of the Pan-African Association, as stated formally in London, had already been expressed by Cooper herself a decade earlier.

Cooper's attendance at the Pan-African Conference could only have enhanced her already sharp perceptions and understanding that the forces afflicting African Americans were part of the same worldwide phenomena which had likewise dispossessed her husband's people and others living in the Caribbean, and which were now gathering force to do likewise on the African continent. Her commitment may also have been costly for her career. We know that Cooper's defiance of unfair directives aimed at diluting the quality of education in the "colored" schools was probably the immediate cause of her losing her job;[39]

but having been a participant in such a "radical" event as the Pan-African Conference could not have endeared her to the conservative (and prejudiced) administrators in the Washington school system.

The Pan-African Conference scheduling (23, 24, and 25 July) was timed to coincide with several other events, including, notably, the Paris Exposition, which Cooper attended afterward. Some of the participants—Cooper among them—very likely left from London to go straight to Paris. A French newspaper of 3 August noted under "Exposition News" that a large number of travelers had been arriving at the channel port of Calais for the past three days, and that many of them were Americans.[40] Du Bois also may have been in this contingent, along with at least two other delegates, H. R. Fox Bourne of the Aborigines Protection Society and the Haitian diplomat Benito Sylvain, both of whom appear among the participants of the French Anti-Slavery Congress (Congrès anti-esclavagiste) held in Paris in conjunction with the exposition.[41] It is likely that Cooper would have attended this congress, along with two other events which are worth noting. The first was a presentation given—in French—at 3:00 P.M. on 6 August at the American Pavilion; the topic was "l'Organisation des universités américaines," and the main speaker, Adolphe Cohn, was a professor from New York's Columbia University, where Cooper would later enroll in the French graduate program.

The second must certainly have been the weekly pageant given every Wednesday evening by the colonial section of the exposition. As a major colonial power in Africa and Asia, France had ample talent from which to draw, and contemporary descriptions indicate that these events must have been spectacular. Lasting about an hour, the colonial parade would begin by the Place du Trocadéro, proceed to the Iéna Bridge, cross the River Seine to the Eiffel Tower and the Champ de Mars, and then return across the bridge and through the Jardins du Trocadéro. The participants sound like a walking cultural exhibit in this announcement: "The first group will be that from Madagascar, composed of musicians, artisans and native troops . . . about one hundred in all. The second, Tunisians, some thirty of them, [will be] followed by two sections of Africans—some twenty each Soudanais and Senegalais with their musicians. The fourth group, from Indo-China, will be composed of some one hundred subjects both artisan and military."[42] The French were obviously putting their colonial empire on display, as had the British three years earlier in June 1897, when large contingents from the far corners of the globe had converged on London to help Queen Victoria celebrate her Diamond Jubilee.

The first of these pageants in Paris was warmly received by an admiring public, according to glowing newspaper accounts. Spahis from the Algerian section, rifles slung bandolier fashion on their backs, sported white, flowing robes and rode prancing Arabian horses. They were followed by the Malagasy and then the Dahomean contingents, the first of which had in the center "Morabi, a superb Sakalava woman with tightly curled hair rolled into long tresses, being carried on a palanquin. She smiles at the public, who applaud her."

The second grouping—the Dahomean—was likewise impressive, led by "an athletic black man who carries the coat of arms of King Toffa: a leopard under a palm tree, crowned with the Black Star of Benin. Griots, marabouts and feticheurs follow. . . . A Dahomean woman, wife of a noble—who detests photographers—plays the role of the Queen, her small black head half hidden by the wings of an elaborate headdress. Her Majesty . . . is very proud in the red robe trimmed with gold, and maids of honor walk on each side of the palanquin in which she is carried."[43]

At the end of the parade the "beautiful Sakalava" and the "Queen of Dahomey" are greeted by the mayor or some other dignitary who presents them with "superb bouquets decorated with red, white and blue tricolor ribbons," which these ladies accept with grace.[44]

The irony of this scene, heavy with symbolism, would not have gone unnoticed by the pan-African delegates: two African "queens" being welcomed in Paris—capital of the second largest colonial power—while real African kings who had defended their nations were overthrown and exiled. The two Dahomey wars of 1889–90 and 1892–94, for example, which saw the defeat and exile of King Behanzin, must still have been fresh in their minds, as must have been the campaigns of the Almamy Samory Touré, who had fought French armies across much of West Africa from 1891 to 1898.

It is unlikely that Cooper or her colleagues from the London conference would have been taken in by this "show biz" display, which was intended to give an impression of amicable and mutually beneficent intercourse.[45] But that should not have prevented them from admiring the beauty and talent displayed by the African contingents, or from reflecting upon the display of power by African royalty or even noting the rather open French attitudes toward Africans, which were in obvious contrast to those of white America. All of these elements probably contributed to Cooper's decision to return to France to further her education, which she did successfully some years later.

Cooper's experiences in France require more attention than is possible here, but they may be summarized as follows. Three years after her return from Europe, Cooper met the French professor (and priest) Félix Klein. On a tour of North America, Abbé Klein visited the M Street School in Washington and was very much impressed with its dynamic and scholarly principal, Anna J. Cooper.[46] Klein proved to be a useful contact and a lifelong friend, helping her when she decided to go to France for further study. Cooper spent the summers of 1912 and 1913 studying at La Guilde internationale in Paris,[47] then matriculated to Columbia University, where she completed coursework for the Ph.D. in French during the summers 1914 to 1917. Somehow she managed to get those Columbia credits accepted by the Sorbonne, where in February 1924 her dissertation topic was approved. In March of the following year, she successfully defended her dissertation—publicly, as was the custom—and became Dr. Cooper, twenty-five years after her first visit to Europe.

Cooper's dissertation purports to deal with French attitudes toward slavery during the French Revolution, but it is just as much a study of the evolution of the plantation colony of Saint-Domingue into the Republic of Haiti, with the French Revolution as a backdrop. This work reveals the mature reflection of a lifetime scholar and shows a keen understanding of the international connections between the centers of power and the human and economic events which moved them. For example, Cooper ably shows the conflict between the various constituent interests in Haiti: the free blacks and mulattoes, the slaves, the poor and the wealthy whites. She examines the competing imperatives between profit and humanity and how allegiances shifted between black and brown, brown and white, white and black. She also examines the complexities of French society as it attempted great social and political reforms while still growing rich at the expense of captive African labor. The historic and cultural schizophrenia which resulted from this dilemma is the subject of Cooper's study. While shifting her attention back and forth across the Atlantic, she does not fail to make an occasional telling comparison with the American Revolution, including at least one irony: the French general Rochambeau who was sent to crush the revolted slaves in Saint-Domingue was the son of the general Rochambeau who earlier had been sent to help the American colonists win their freedom from England.

It is clear that Anna J. Cooper was an intellectual of international scope who came to view and understand the African American dilemma in its broadest parameters. By the time she wrote "L'Attitude de la France à l'égard de l'esclavage"—which I believe to be her major work—she had come to understand that the problems in America were not caused merely by irritating or discriminatory legislation which compelled "persons known to be colored to ride in one car, and persons supposed to be white in another," but were the product of events which spanned the globe and which had meaning in space as well as in time.[48]

NOTES

1. Dates of Cooper's birth are variously given as 1858, 1859, and 1860; I use 1859 to simplify chronology.
2. Mary Helen Washington, introduction, *A Voice from the South: By a Black Woman from the South*, by Anna J. Cooper (1892; New York: Oxford UP, 1988). Subsequent references to *Voice* are referenced in the text.
3. The three who preceded her all received their doctorates in 1921. They were Sadie Tanner Mossell Alexander (Economics, University of Pennsylvania), Eva Beatrice Dykes (English, Radcliffe College), and Georgianna R. Simpson (German, University of Chicago). I received this information from Fisk University Head Librarian

Jessie Carney Smith, who listed it in her *Black Firsts: 2,000 Years of Extraordinary Achievement* (Detroit: Gale Research, 1994).

4. Translated by Frances Richardson Keller (Lewiston, NY: Edwin Mellen, 1988).
5. Gabriel Debien, "Les Esclaves," *Histoire des Antilles et de la Guyane*, ed. Pierre Pluchon (Toulouse: Edouard Privat, 1982), 141.
6. Imanuel Geiss, *The Pan-African Movement: A History of Pan-Africanism in America, Europe and Africa*, trans. Ann Keep (New York: Holmes & Meier, 1974), 86.
7. Ibid.
8. Victor Ullman, *Martin R. Delany: The Beginnings of Black Nationalism* (Boston: Beacon, 1971), 166.
9. John W. Cromwell, "The Early Convention Movement," *American Negro Academy, Occasional Papers* No. 9 (Washington, DC: American Negro Academy, 1905), 8, cited in E. U. Essien-Udom, *Black Nationalism: A Search for an Identity in America* (Chicago: U of Chicago P, 1962), 23.
10. Cecil D. Halliburton, *A History of St. Augustine's College 1867–1937* (Raleigh, NC: St. Augustine's College, 1937), 9.
11. Ibid.
12. Owen Charles Mathurin, *Henry Sylvester Williams and the Origins of the Pan-African Movement, 1869–1911* (Westport, CT: Greenwood, 1976), 50. Geiss is probably incorrect when he identifies this Holly (J. T.) as J. F. Holly and implies that J. F. is "a descendant" of the former. Geiss 180, 141.
13. Ullman 172 and 185. It should be noted that prior to the British North American Act of 1867, Canada was a loose gathering of provinces, politically disunited and distant from the control of Westminster. The United States had already invaded Canada during the War of 1812, the year of Delany's birth, capturing and pillaging Toronto in 1813; more recently, war had been threatened in a dispute (1844–46) over the Columbia River basin, in the Oregon Territory.
14. The date is not absolutely clear on this letter as reproduced in Louise Daniel Hutchinson's excellent work entitled *Anna J. Cooper: A Voice from the South* (Washington, DC: Smithsonian Institution P, 1982), 107, as the paper has become fragile with age and the corner has crumbled. However, a photocopy made of this letter before it became too damaged does indicate more clearly the "91," which would also be in line with the "Union Jack" passage appearing in *Voice* the following year, quoted in full below. Both the original and the copy are in the Anna J. Cooper Papers, Box 23-1, Folder 5, Manuscript Division, Moorland-Spingarn Research Center, Howard University.
15. Hutchinson 107–8.
16. *Voice* 88–89.
17. "The Negro in American Literature," *Voice*, 197.
18. "What Are We Worth?" *Voice*, 238–39.
19. Anna J. Cooper, *L'Attitude de la France à l'égard de l'esclavage pendant la Révolution* (Paris: Imprimerie de la Cour d'Appel, 1925), 109. The exact quotation is as follows: "[I]l était fils d'un nègre africain de Guinée et d'une négresse, et n'avait pas une goutte de sang blanc ou mêlé dans les veines."
20. "Womanhood a Vital Element in the Regeneration and Progress of a Race," *Voice*, 30.
21. William Wells Brown, *The Rising Son; or, The Antecedents and Advancement of the Colored Race* (1874; New York: Greenwood, 1970), 461.
22. Constantin François de Chasseboeuf, comte de Volney, *Voyage en Egypte et en Syrie*, 1787.

23. *Past and Present,* 12, cited in Geiss 105.
24. William Wells Brown, *The Black Man: His Antecedents and Achievements* (Boston, 1863), 34, quoted in Geiss 107.
25. "Has America a Race Problem?" *Voice,* 157.
26. Ibid.
27. "Les idées égalitaires et le mouvement démocratique," at the Sorbonne University of Paris, 23 March 1925, translated by Cooper as "Equality of Races and the Democratic Movement" in 1945 for her classes at Frelinghuysen University, and privately printed in *The Third Step* (n.p., n.d. [Washington, DC, 1950?]).
28. "The Negro as Presented in American Literature," *Voice,* 196–97.
29. *L'Attitude* 7, and *Third Step* 35.
30. "The Ashanti Rising. Capture of Kokofu," *The Times* (London) 27 July 1900: 10.
31. A full account of the London conference may be found in Mathurin's excellent biography of Williams: *Henry Sylvester Williams and the Origins of the Pan-African Movement, 1869–1911.*
32. Mathurin 48.
33. W. E. B. Du Bois, *Writings,* ed. Nathan Huggins (New York: Library of America, 1986), 1,288.
34. I am indebted to Ted Malone, secretary and archivist of the Episcopal Diocese of North Carolina in Raleigh for help in identifying Joseph.
35. Mathurin 65. The *Leader* was a London newspaper.
36. These concerns were distilled in the following five aims and objectives of the Pan-African Association, reported in the *Colored American* 1 Feb. 1901: "1) To secure to Africans throughout the world true civil and political rights; 2) To ameliorate the condition of our brothers on the continent of Africa, America and other parts of the world; 3) To promote efforts to secure effective legislation and encourage our people in educational, industrial and commercial enterprise; 4) To foster the production of writing and statistics relating to our people everywhere; and 5) To raise funds for forwarding these purposes" (Mathurin 68).
37. "Aborigines" in the sense of peoples native or indigenous to a region, not limited to the so-named people of Australia.
38. *Third Step* 7.
39. This controversy is well documented in Hutchinson chap. 4.
40. "A travers l'exposition," *Figaro* 3 Aug. 1900: 4.
41. "L'exposition. Les congrès," *Figaro* 8 Aug. 1900: 3. One may be tempted to wonder how there could be an Anti-Slavery Congress as late as 1900. The existence of some pockets of slavery on the Swahili coast of East Africa (Zanzibar and Pemba in particular) had been noted and widely publicized during the colonial land-grab period, and was often touted as justification for a European takeover.
42. "Les fêtes coloniales du Trocadéro," *Figaro* 2 July 1900: 3. This and all other translations from the French are my own.
43. "La fête coloniale," *Figaro* 5 July 1900: 4.
44. Ibid.
45. Its impact upon the French public, that is, the people who fought the imperial wars and who paid for them through taxes, was certainly positive. The French, like the British, had taken note of an earlier Roman custom, that of parading conquered people (preferably kings and queens) through the metropole in order to whip up national pride and support for wars of conquest far from home.
46. Abbé Félix Klein, *Au pays de "La vie intense,"* 6th ed. (Paris: Plon-Nourrit, 1905), 286–90.

47. These dates, which contradict a statement in *The Third Step*, are taken from an official questionnaire filed by Cooper with the Washington school system: "Data desired relative to Group B examination, December 17, 1921" (a copy is located in the Anna J. Cooper Papers, Box 23-1, Folder 1, Manuscript Division, Moorland-Spingarn Research Center, Howard University). They are further supported by dates taken from Cooper's passport applications (1900 and 1912), courtesy of the General Reference Branch, National Archives, Washington, DC.
48. "Woman versus the Indian," *Voice*, 94.

WORKS CITED

Brown, William Wells. *The Rising Son; or, The Antecedents and Advancement of the Colored Race.* 1874. New York: Negro UP, 1970.

Cooper, Anna J. *L'Attitude de la France à l'égard de l'esclavage pendant la Révolution.* Paris: Imprimerie de la Cour d'appel, 1925.

———. Papers. Moorland-Spingarn Research Center. Howard U, Washington, DC.

———. *The Third Step.* (n.p., n.d. [Washington, DC, 1950?]).

———. *A Voice from the South: By a Black Woman from the South.* 1892. Introduction. Mary Helen Washington. *The Schomburg Library of Nineteenth-Century Black Women Writers.* Gen. ed. Henry Louis Gates Jr. New York: Oxford UP, 1988.

Debien, Gabriel. "Les Esclaves." *Histoire des Antilles et de la Guyane.* Ed. Pierre Pluchon. Toulouse: Edouard Privat, 1982.

Du Bois, W. E. B. *Writings.* Ed. Nathan Huggins. New York: Library of America, 1986.

Essien-Udom, E. U. *Black Nationalism: A Search for an Identity in America.* Chicago: U of Chicago P, 1962.

Figaro (Paris). 2 July, 5 July, 3 Aug., and 8 Aug. 1900.

Geiss, Imanuel. *The Pan-African Movement: A History of Pan-Africanism in America, Europe and Africa.* Trans. Ann Keep. New York: Holmes & Meier, 1974.

Halliburton, Cecil D. *A History of St. Augustine's College 1867–1937.* Raleigh, NC: St. Augustine's College, 1937.

Hutchinson, Louise Daniel. *Anna J. Cooper: A Voice from the South.* Washington, DC: Smithsonian Institution P, 1982.

Klein, Abbé Félix. *Au pays de "La vie intense."* 6th ed. Paris: Plon-Nourrit, 1905.

Mathurin, Owen Charles. *Henry Sylvester Williams and the Origins of the Pan-African Movement, 1869–1911.* Contributions in Afro-American and Afro Studies, No. 21. Westport, CT: Greenwood, 1976.

The Times (London). 27 July 1900.

Ullman, Victor. *Martin R. Delany: The Beginnings of Black Nationalism.* Boston: Beacon, 1971.

The "Invisible Woman" Abroad:
Jessie Fauset's New Horizon

ERICA L. GRIFFIN

One of black America's first and most influential women of letters, Jessie Redmon Fauset (1882–1961) was also the major "literary midwife" of a trio of editors that included herself, Charles S. Johnson, and Alain Locke during the Harlem Renaissance. In this capacity she discovered and published the work of writers such as George S. Schuyler, Langston Hughes, Jean Toomer, Countee Cullen, and Claude McKay in *The Crisis,* the official publication of the NAACP with W. E. B. Du Bois as its editor-in-chief. Moreover, Fauset was the most prolific novelist of the New Negro movement, producing four works whose plots emphasized the aspirations of the Northeast's emerging black middle class: *There is Confusion* (1924), *Plum Bun* (1929), *The Chinaberry Tree* (1931), and *Comedy: American Style* (1933). These novels have frequently been criticized for their excessively bourgeois characters, specifically their emphasis on "the petty excitements and disappointments of mulatto heroines in their search for happiness in love and marriage" (Singh 61).

A Phi Beta Kappa graduate of Cornell (B.A., 1905) and recipient of the M.A. in French from the University of Pennsylvania (1919), the Philadelphia-reared Fauset had developed wide-ranging interests by the time she embarked on her literary and editorial career. Her work with the *The Crisis* indicates that her personal interests reached far beyond those of her fictional divas. In addition to her accomplishments as literary editor and chief editor of *Brownies' Book: A Monthly Magazine for the Children of the Sun* (1920–21), Fauset wrote book reviews and essays on various subjects: literary movements, translations of French-Caribbean poetry, foreign politics, and the Pan-African Congress. While working on her second degree, Fauset broadened her horizons even further by traveling abroad for additional language study. She witnessed the agony of the Parisians when Germany declared war on France in 1914; memories of this devastation still haunted her upon her return to Paris in 1921 (sponsored by her Delta Sigma Theta sorority) for the Second Pan-African Congress and again during an extended tour of additional European cities as well as North Africa in 1924–25.

The six travel essays published in *The Crisis* in 1915, 1925, and 1926 are the fruits of Fauset's overseas adventures. "Tracing Shadows" (September 1915) is her firsthand account of Paris at the outbreak of World War I. "Yarrow Revisited" (January 1925) is a return to postwar "workaday" Paris as well as a reaffirmation of Fauset's racial identity. "This Way to the Flea Market" (February 1925) is a vivid picture of the life of the poor in Paris, as seen on market day. "The Enigma of the Sorbonne" (March 1925) is a historical account of the famous University. "Dark Algiers the White" (April/May 1925) is a penetrating study of the lives of oppressed women. "The Eucalyptus Tree" (January 1926) is a "reverie" of the Catacombs of Rome and Christianity. These essays exhibit Fauset's acceptance of cultural differences as well as her sensitivity to gender and racial ties, especially those to the women of Algiers. The female narrator of these pieces is accustomed to racial and sexual oppression. As a result of her identification with the suffering of others, she is able to articulate their pain.

Speaking of her novels, Fauset readily admits that "the problem story simply isn't my genre. . . . It is not my concern to solve a problem, but to tell what strikes me as a good story" (Starkey 219). The same can be said of the travel essays; she presents her readers with "a good story" overlaid with intricate themes: the senselessness of war, the subjugation of women, and the true meaning of democracy. Fauset doesn't attempt to solve the problems of the women she encounters abroad, but she identifies with them and is able to find a connection between her plight as the "invisible woman" of American society and their plight as the oppressed, marginalized "invisible" women of foreign lands.

These travel essays are worth careful study for several reasons. Firstly, Fauset adds her voice to the tradition of American travel writing in general and to the experience of other well-educated African American women such as Charlotte Forten Grimké (Port Royal, Saint Helena Island, S.C., October 1862–May 1864), Mary Church Terrell (European tour 1888–90), and Anna Julia Cooper (Paris, Guilde Internationale, 1911–14 summer study; Sorbonne, 1925, defense of dissertation) in particular. Each woman gains a greater sense of self and racial pride through travel. The humanitarian Grimké is inspired by the former slaves she educates in the Sea Islands despite her sense of cultural separation which makes her a "foreigner" in their world; the visionary Terrell finds some freedom from racial tension in Europe (despite some hostility from her fellow countrymen abroad), yet she decides to retain her Afro-American identity by returning home to work for her people rather than to accept offers of marriage from white suitors; the intellectual Cooper writes her dissertation on French attitudes toward slavery before their Revolution, thus bringing the black experience into European culture. In Europe, Fauset experiences the sense of passing without "passing"; she is treated as a first-class citizen of the United States without having to resort to the drastic measures of her race-conscious heroines. Like Terrell, she revels in an environment which is kinder to people of color than her homeland; like Grimké, she feels compassion for "foreign" people and comes to admire their strength; like Cooper, she is able to unite the plight of people of color with those of other lands in her writing.

A second point of interest in Fauset's travel essays is the emergence of a new, relaxed, and at times humorous voice, quite unlike the preachy narrators of her novels. Traveling through foreign countries, this "invisible" black woman, overshadowed in American society by her famous male counterparts and racially silenced by the "majority," expresses herself without focusing completely on the subject of American racism and her resentment of this "invisible" status next to black men in the patriarchal power structure. Writing beyond these American constraints, Fauset entertains her audience through her comparison of American and European lifestyles; moreover, she privileges the tales of other "silent" women in her discourse.

This focus on foreign women adds a new perspective on Europe in contrast to those of Fauset's male contemporaries, such as Du Bois, Locke, McKay, and Hughes. While they discussed their personal achievements abroad or told of Paris' transplanted Harlem nightlife, she tells of the everyday experience of the natives, gaining a deeper understanding of these people whose land she has "invaded." From this perspective Fauset subverts her own image as a "happy American traveler" by continually recalling her status as an "invisible" woman of color in a white and male-dominated world. Thus, Fauset forms a bond with the community of women she meets; they are equal sufferers in the gender silencing that transcends both racial and social boundaries.

Finally, Fauset incorporates her encounters with these "silenced" women into her novels. The subtle effects of her overseas experiences increase our understanding of her too-often two-dimensional female characters. The town of Chambéry serves as a backdrop for hardworking Maggie Ellersley, who seeks renewed hope during World War I in *There is Confusion.* Angela Murray uses the prize money she wins as a "white" painter from a New York art school to go to Paris in *Plum Bun.* The women and customs of Algiers are reflected in the characters of Laurentine Strange and Melissa Paul in *The Chinaberry Tree.* Paris and Toulouse become home to Olivia Cary as her life dissolves in despair in *Comedy: American Style.* Fauset goes beyond the desire to merely describe various tourist traps in her work by using the trope of the traveler, or displaced person, in her personal experience as well as in her fictional world.

In some instances, her female characters journey through life, comparing the limitations put upon them in America as women of color with the comparable "freedom" they encounter in foreign settings. For others, the journey from girlhood to womanhood includes the distinct possibility of being led down the wrong road, of sinking into the false security of marriage and becoming "displaced"; these women lose their identities in marriage and spend the remainder of their lives in silence. In addition, there are the women who travel across the color line; their "passing" leads them to their desired bourgeois standing in society—or so they hope—but again there is the danger of sinking into that false sense of security, of letting their bourgeois fantasies go too far. These fantasies eventually become realistic nightmares for women who have forgotten who they are. Like the wives of Algiers, they have willfully submitted their identities to a "higher" power: the wives to their husbands, the "passing" women to the ingrained Anglo-Saxon standard of beauty and privilege.

I will examine three of the six essays in my analysis because they give specific attention to foreign women and because they allow Fauset to illuminate life from both sides of the "veil": black, female, invisible. An encumbrance in the United States, the veil becomes a powerful asset to Fauset during her encounters overseas. Beyond the boundary of American prejudice, Fauset is allowed to experience life as a citizen of the world. The veil enables her to see more clearly through the illusion of her alleged racial and sexual inferiority and to form a bond with the foreign women, who endure their lowly status. Fauset realizes that they suffer just as keenly from the effects of war, poverty, and abuse as black women have suffered from racial hatred and segregation in America.

Empowered by her double vision in these essays, Fauset becomes both subject (American tourist) and object (invisible woman) in her own discourse. She makes her black readers aware that they are not alone in suffering from oppression, not alone in being made invisible by whites and by post-Victorian dictates of acquiescent womanhood. They are not alone in being overshadowed both personally and professionally (as Fauset certainly was by Du Bois and Locke) by their male counterparts. Fauset, the traveler, transgresses the boundaries of race and class, uniting black American women with European and North African women through their shared status as invisible members of patriarchal culture. Fauset, the author, shows us how her female characters live within—or without—their veils. For those who cross racial boundaries, success is not without its price. Renouncing one's identity as a black American woman leads to self-annihilation.

In *Travel Literature and the Evolution of the Novel,* Percy G. Adams discusses the "ingénu" figure in travel literature, a naïve character who "always grows in some important way" (276) as a result of knowledge gained from his/her journeying. Fauset adopts this narrative stance in her travel essays, particularly in "Tracing Shadows," in which the perspective of the first-time traveler is undercut by a wiser, omniscient narrator. Their naïve tourist disarms the unassuming reader with a playful double entendre on *shadow.* The shadow of her title is a metaphor for impending war and for the narrator's growing awareness of herself as "outsider" (an American) and as "other" (a woman of color). Fauset emerges as a somewhat self-contained middle-class American tourist who is enlightened as a result of a "close encounter" with the native folk during the outbreak of war.

Fauset opens "Tracing Shadows" with a picaresque tone as she carries the reader along on what begins as an idealistic European romp. The naïve traveler's initial happy-go-lucky attitude is reflected in the nicknames she gives her four fellow pleasure-seekers: "the Musician, Our Lady of Leisure, the Artist, the other Student and myself" (248). Absorbed in adventure and novelty, these Bohemians pay none too much attention to the "shadows" of impending violence around them: news of the murder of the Archduke and Archduchess of Austria, ironic celebration of the bloody Bastille Day, and an unusual "excitement prevailing in the streets" (248), of which Fauset innocently remarks: "But were not French people notably excitable?" (248). When Austria declares war on Serbia, her flippant reaction is: "It seemed ridiculous to us then—a big nation like Austria against little Servia [sic]. It was too absurd!" (248).

Money troubles are a more effective shadow for Fauset and her friends; imminent starvation and the reality of war finally make them conscious of the truer agony of the French. She sees "women weeping in the streets . . . men walking along with reddened eyes . . . whole families sending their men away in anguished silence . . . the sense of disaster, of impending fatality" (249). Fauset becomes as enveloped in misery as she had been absorbed in careless frivolity. Her increased understanding of the state of things makes her less self-centered and more compassionate toward the natives. In a dramatic moment, she refers to the painful energy around her as "a veritable twilight of the Gods" (249).

Fauset's most poignant figure in "Tracing Shadows" is the "pretty wife" of Jonathon Podd, a restaurant owner who has also gone off to fight. Mrs. Podd, "polite even in her great anguish," serves Fauset and her friends and sits in back of the restaurant with a basket: "At intervals she would choke down a sob and murmur, 'Oh mon dieu, mon dieu!'—but she kept on shelling peas" (250). Moved to admiration for the steely courage of women like Mrs. Podd, the ingénue narrator identifies with her quiet dignity: "Were peas to be shelled there were [France's] women choking back sobs, and working on with eyes too blinded by tears to see" (251). Despite her grief, Mrs. Podd subjugates her own emotions for her husband's sake. She supports his business in his absence rather than indulge in self-pity. She transcends her invisible status as wife and becomes heroic within the confines of her limited social space. She puts on a brave face for the customers, runs the restaurant, and fulfills her country's needs on the home front as many women did on both sides of the Atlantic during World War I.

Fauset retains this image of a woman who rises above her "silent" status as an silent woman to take action during wartime in *There Is Confusion* (1924). A social-climbing poor girl, Maggie Ellersey, changes her life's goal from finding an upwardly mobile husband to gaining self-reliance as a successful business-woman. This shift in her attitude stems from her YMCA efforts during the war in support of black soldiers stationed in France. She becomes a ray of sunshine for them: "[The men] were pathetically proud of her . . . glad to be allowed a sight of her bright face, to exchange a word. To be permitted to dance with her sent any one of them into a delirium of ecstatic pride" (259). Like Mrs. Podd, Maggie is "taken out of herself completely" and dives into her work. The former must forget for the time being that she may become one of many war widows: "Work must go on, life must be lived, she could not falter even though her husband had gone to an accursed war and the world for her lay in ruins" (251). The latter must also forget her personal troubles and support the black soldiers stationed in Chambéry. Fauset transfers her admiration for the French to Maggie's admiration for African American soldiers. Through them Maggie finds inspiration: "The determinedly cheerful though somewhat cynical attitude of 'the boys' . . . seemed to her the most wonderful thing she had ever witnessed" (259).

Moreover, Maggie feels a greater sense of freedom in France than at home, and she is struck by the cross, twenty-five meters high, on the Mont du Nivrolet, east of Chambéry (Fabre 116): "At sunset it stood out boldly and Maggie, looking at it daily at that hour, came to regard it as a sort of luminous symbol of faith" (*Confusion* 262). As a result of her journey to serve her black brothers overseas, Maggie has tasted equality and feels encouraged to live life to the fullest. As a result of her growth from the ingénue traveler to the wiser narrator, Fauset is able to use her character to link the African American woman's war experience with that of the French woman. Each suffers the pain of sending her men off to fight, yet each is inspired to work toward the greater goals of "Liberty, Equality, Fraternity," for her people, her country, herself.

Fauset wrote *Plum Bun* (1929) during her second visit to Paris, yet she does not make use of the setting until the end of the novel, when Angela Murray arrives in the city as an art student (Fabre 118). Determined to be free of her dependence on men, Angela Murray vows to become self-reliant after several unhappy experiences, including "passing" for white. Though Angela arrives in Paris to study painting, it is the lure of the city itself which fascinates her: "Paris at first charmed and wooed her . . . she followed the winding Seine; crossing and re-crossing the bridges" (378). However, the charm wears off and Angela, introduced to the "workaday season" of life, sees Paris in a different light: "Paris, so beautiful in the summer . . . took on another garb in the sullen greyness of late autumn . . . the hard steady grind of labour, the intent application to the business of living . . . took the place of a transient, careless freedom. Angela felt herself falling into line" (379).

This realistic view of "gay Paris" is certainly influenced by Fauset's wartime experience there. She had to relinquish her shallow pleasures and "fall into line," as is evident in her second travel essay, "Yarrow Revisited." Named after Wordsworth's nostalgic poem of the same title, the piece continues to dispel Fauset's rosy image of her first visit before the onset of war: "This is not the Paris of my student days . . . an enchanted city of gay streets, blue skies, of romantically historic monuments, a playground, a court of justice of the world" (107). The "delicious sense of laisser-aller" of the past has given way to the permanent postwar gloom of October 1924. Somberly, she notes that "the skies are drab, the days are grey and every twenty-four hours rain falls, steady, penetrating, soaking" (107). One can sense that Fauset is mindful of her 1914 visit: "Just as the weather is by no means always golden and gay, so French living is not always a thing of joy and laughter" (104). This underlying awareness of a new Paris still emerging from the war is reflected in Fauset's desire to see the realistic, gritty, day-to-day life of the French. Her experience in a cheap pension is one of damp chills and none-too-cheery inhabitants: "An old, old lady, a widow I judged from her deep black . . . another old lady, once the matron I should say of some frightfully corrective institution, erect and with a terrible, raucous voice; four or five depressed young men . . . hopelessly nondescript. The food was nondescript too" (108).

Again Fauset is especially drawn to women, marginalized and unhappy. The "old, old lady" in "deep black," possibly a war widow, could have triggered memories of the young Mrs. Podd. Is this living death her fate as well as that of other young widows?

The image of "wasted human lives" returns vividly in *Comedy: American Style* (1933). Olivia Cary, having consigned her daughter Teresa to a loveless marriage with a narrow, needling, small-town French professor, settles down in a Parisian pension curiously similar to the one Fauset describes in "Yarrow Revisited" (Sylvander 102). It is "a large house built inevitably of stone, set . . . far, far back in a courtyard. . . . Within . . . a broad winding staircase built beautifully in an open well" ("Revisited" 107). In the novel, Olivia's pension also lies in a courtyard and has a "beautiful winding staircase" (*Comedy* 322) and a chill which Olivia fights by making "a fire with a few twigs and the fewest possible briquettes. At least it looked cheerful" (322). Having been turned away from her son-in-law's equally depressing house in Toulouse, she returns to "the pension with its horrid meals . . . with its decayed and frigid gentlewomen" (326), much like herself.

Having considered herself an outcast by American society for denying her race and passing for white, Olivia, nevertheless, feels that her fondest wish has been fulfilled. She deludes herself, believing that she has escaped the stigma of blackness by becoming like these "decayed" European women.

Like her fictional divas, Fauset experiences freedom in Paris: "I find myself more American than I ever feel in America. I am conscious of national characteristics" ("Revisited" 109). Temporarily freed from her acute double-consciousness, the sophisticated Fauset indulges in the finer things of life that her white countrymen and women take for granted. She enjoys a love of leisure and comfort, of steam heat, for example, as opposed to the lukewarm European standards of heating ("Revisited" 108). Fauset struggles to reconcile American hypocrisy with the second-class status of African Americans back home. Impressed that she can have her lunch "at the first [Paris] tea room which takes my fancy" (109) without fear of segregation, Fauset comments: "[This freedom] is also something to be considered in reviewing French 'life as she is'" ("Revisited" 109). In spite of the freedom she experiences on many levels—social, racial, and cultural—Fauset notes the bitter irony of her situation (Fabre 117). Why should an American feel more at home away from home? Her characters, nevertheless, do enjoy their freedom abroad; in some cases, their foreign adventures inspire them to overcome their American oppression and return home empowered, while in other cases it makes them flee their heritage altogether.

In *Comedy: American Style,* Olivia Cary seeks life in Paris in order to flee racial barriers completely, yet because she denies her identity she is punished by being alienated from both races. In *Plum Bun,* Angela Murray receives her prize money to study abroad as an art student only because she is passing, avoiding the realities of racism by denying her heritage. Like Fauset, Angela relinquishes her ingénue persona to adopt a more mature stance; she claims her "birthright" as a woman of color by joining forces with Miss Powell and rejecting the committee's overseas scholarship and finding her own means to Paris. Once she arrives there, her true reward, aside from living without segregation, is the knowledge of her personal triumph over the stigma of passing for white. Maggie Ellersley, in contrast, finds the sensation of freedom while on foreign soil; working for "the boys" encourages her to challenge American racism by starting her own business, her chain of beauty parlors for women of color, when she returns from the war. Each character feels a certain "unusual freedom" which inspires her to transcend the limits imposed upon her by American society.

The quality of *freedom* depends on how one uses it, of course. Angela Murray uses it as a force for good, a taste of freedom that rewards her decision to stop passing; Olivia Cary uses it to become completely "white," and suffers as a consequence. She does not mature mentally or emotionally as a result of living in a segregation-free environment. Unable to see beyond her own false hopes and delusions of grandeur, Olivia continues to pass, only socializing with other "white" American women: "It is so broadening to live here. Think of the people one meets" (*Comedy* 323). Of course, the opposite is true; her life is almost as constricted in Paris as in America: she has created her own hell, living a lonely, frustrated existence as a "decayed gentlewoman" meeting only similarly frustrated women who are yet sensible enough not to believe in "the fabled freedom of Paris" (324). Maggie Ellersley celebrates the freedom she finds in France, and it helps her to pursue what before were seemingly impossible goals. In "Yarrow Revisited" Fauset stresses the importance of embracing one's heritage. Specifically, black women who do not embrace their cultural past will become even more exiled from themselves as well as from others. Having repressed their heritage, they never develop a strong identity.

Sunny North Africa is the setting of "Dark Algiers the White." Fauset's journey across the Mediterranean Sea brings into sharper focus her twin positions as subject (tourist) and object (woman of color). Like Americans and Europeans who preceded her, Fauset arrives in search of the secrets of the Dark Continent. In "Tracing Shadows" and "Yarrow Revisited," her romantic notions are quickly dispelled when she enters the "workaday" world of the Magrib. In *The Journey Narrative in American Literature,* Janis P. Stout reminds us that "the quest is, first, a journey of search, a pursuit of the unknown. . . . [The heroine] sets out with a sense of solitary exhilaration and expansion and persists in [her] commitment with an extraordinary and isolating devotion" (88).

Fauset's first impression of the Dark Continent is one of awe for this land shrouded in mystery and mysticism; the description of her approach to the city of Algiers reveals its spellbinding effect on Fauset and her fellow travelers: "Algiers . . . beyond a sea that smiled and faintly rippled: a sea warmed and gilded by the sun . . . curtained and lighted at night by stars and constellations which we had never seen; mellowed by a saffron moon climbing from below the surface of the world to the warm, rich velvet of the sky" (255).

Fauset enters the world of Algiers conscious on one hand of the barrier between herself, the American tourist, and the Algerines; on the other hand there is the link between herself, a black woman, and these people. Her quest includes the lifting of the Du Boisian veil that hides the inner nature of the Algerines, the same veil that has concealed the "souls of black folk" from the intrusion of whites in America. Because of her sincerity in and devotion to this quest, she is not a complete outsider; in embracing these shadowy people she experiences a kinship with the continent from which came her ancestors.

While riding through the city in a trolley car, Fauset is immediately drawn to the Algerine women who "suddenly [appear] from around a turning and [vanish] again in the misty night . . . clothed in white" (256). These ghostlike figures, walking the streets at dusk, enchant both narrator and reader: "a white face veil covering mouth and nose, cheeks and hair, all but two dark impenetrable eyes" (256); they seem to float above the ground. One young woman boards the trolley with her husband; Fauset, conscious of the contrast between her own status—a "free" if "invisible" African American woman—and the curious enslavement of these phantomlike creatures, examines the wife closely: "Mystery shrouded her; her two eyes stared unseeingly before her; she was like an automaton beside her lord; there was no conversation" (256). "Shrouded" denotes death and decay, as if the young wife is buried alive in her fine clothes, a delicate corpse wrapped in a beautiful winding sheet: "Her robe was wonderfully soft and white . . . the stockings encasing her dainty ankles were faintly pink . . . her shoes were russet and delicate" (256). There is a sense here of innocent fragility, an aura of imminent sacrifice in these uncanny creatures. Even old women of Algiers retain that unearthly quality which so draws Fauset: "Old and faded and wrinkled as she was her clothing and her veil lent her mystery and marvel. She was the very savor of the East" (256).

The dusky magic of Fauset's first night is destroyed by morning's cruel light, the "merciless sun." The shimmering native costumes are no longer glamorous. In fact, Fauset can see "European trousers and shoes" underneath the "flowing robes" of the men, and the women are revealed in a more realistic light: "Through the voluminous garments . . . showed the outline of misshapen bodies, broken and distorted by neglect, abuse and much bearing of children. Yet," Fauset insists, "nothing could penetrate their air of mystery" (256). She is fascinated by their mechanical acceptance of their lot: wrapped in colorful shrouds to hide their decaying flesh, living as the mere property of their "lords." Perhaps she is disturbed by the contrast between these women and herself; though she is free in comparison, they share a bond as a women of color, the link of invisibility.

In her brief encounter with the orient, Fauset comes to abandon her original "foreign" stance: privileged, distant, and prey to stereotypes. In *Orientalism*, Edward Said discusses the portrayal of oriental women by European writers. Woman, the "vessel of the Orient" (184), is an exotic, available, sexual tool, lacking the power of speech: "Women are usually the creatures of a male power-fantasy. They express unlimited sensuality, they are more or less stupid, and above all they are willing" (207). This "dumb and irreducible sexuality" makes the oriental (meaning non-Western) woman easy to control. Said quotes Flaubert, who concludes that "the oriental woman is no more than a machine" (187). In contrast, Fauset's description of the Algerine women reveals not only her awareness of such stereotypes, (note her use of the word *automaton* to describe the young wife), but an honest, compassionate feminine sympathy for these misrepresented individuals, so like the invisible women and men of the United States. Part of her awareness comes from the attitude of certain Americans toward people of color at the time, as the Harlem Renaissance was at its height. "Interest in the Negro," as Singh reminds us, "came to be focused around the cult of the primitive. It had become fashionable in the Jazz Age to defy prohibition and to find joy and abandon in exotic music and dance" (Singh 21). Interest in primitivism, a popularly misinterpreted Freudian theory, encouraged Anglo-Saxon patrons to privilege "instinct over intellect in a revolt against the Puritan spirit" (21) by celebrating what they felt was basic, namely, African and African American culture. To them the black was "simply an uninhibited and unmechanized soul" (21), closer to nature than the Anglo soul. The attitude of many white Americans influenced the European attitude toward nonwhites, and Fauset was aware of this. Women in general and women of color in particular feel the weight of their burden at the bottom of patriarchal culture throughout the world.

In the second part of "Dark Algiers the White," Fauset finds a sunken "miniature village" of "miserable shacks, swarming with women and children. . . . Somehow they strike a picturesque exotic note" (16). Again, she is influenced by the "cult of the primitive" movement, and her word choice to describe the natives is significant, if ironic. On one hand she is like the bourgeois whites who slum around Harlem for cheap (or not so cheap) thrills; unlike them, however, Fauset's interest is deeper because of her racial link to these "primitive" people. She is continually drawn to the women, and the closer she gets the better able she is to see beneath their literal and figurative veils. Though the women of the village are poor, "without face veils" like the city women, their colors are nonetheless festive and bright. She notes that "one of them . . . wears a headdress of scarlet, a green jacket with a purple collar, a cerise and yellow skirt" (16). This gay clothing is a "veil" which contradicts the reality of their lives. These women, like those of the city, are vibrantly plumaged birds of paradise, trapped in a cage of poverty, silenced by the world of men with their political and economic power, shadowed in despair. They remind Fauset once again of her comparative freedom yet draw her to their shared identity as invisible women. Fauset later finds herself an object of interest in a different area of the city to the "bronzed faces [that regard her] curiously as I stand a lonely equally exotic figure in the middle of the sunlit road" (17); ironically, the invisible woman of America is quite visible on foreign turf. She wears no veil, like the city women, and yet she is not poor like the village women; the veil she wears is beyond their vision, though not beyond their own experience.

Perhaps Fauset's most effective image is that of a household of Arab women, which she encounters in the Kasbah in the company of a French guide: "We come to a curtained door opening on a dark oblong room five feet perhaps by eight. In a moment my eyes, accustomed to the gloom, pick out three figures of women sitting on the floor near a brazier of live coals. Their backs are against the wall, their feet are bare, their hands are in their laps. They sit thus, listless, doing nothing, absolutely nothing; life slips by" (17).

Like the "automaton" young wife on the trolley and the fictional images of oriental women Said discusses in *Orientalism*, these sheltered house-dwellers live in a world of darkness. Like Mrs. Podd of "Tracing Shadows" and the "decayed gentlewomen" of the Parisian pensions, they sit and wait—for their men, for death. They suffer more, in fact, than the impoverished village women who must struggle daily, for they have nothing at all to occupy their time; they are kept "safe" at home, in their "place," so to speak, by their "lords." Such an existence is inconceivable to a career woman like Fauset; the better part of her adult life involved working first as a teacher in public schools, then as literary editor for the *The Crisis,* hosting literary socials in her home, writing, and traveling. The epitome of the well-educated, independent woman, Fauset must certainly have felt a void between herself and these women, despite the racial/sexual bond she shared with them. It would have seemed to her that all bourgeois young brides of Algiers were fated to be "shrouded" in darkness and isolation.

Fauset is definitely disturbed by what she sees of female life in sunny, "dark" Algiers. Her impressions are revealed in her third novel, *The China-berry Tree,* in the characters of Laurentine Strange and her cousin Melissa Paul, both of whom are enshrouded within a patriarchal society as they journey toward womanhood—and "invisible" wifehood. Laurentine, a dressmaker, creates lovely garments (mainly for the well-to-do white women who can afford them). The author describes her character as she has earlier examined the young Algerine wife on the trolley: "Her slender, well-moulded figure showed to every advantage in a dress of green silk and wool. . . . Her stockings of tan and her dainty yet sturdy, slender shoes . . . afforded just the necessary contrast. . . . Her black, waving hair parted smoothly in the middle and drawn to the conventional flat knot in the nape of her neck gave her a slightly foreign look" (35).

Laurentine Strange is, moreover, "distant to the point of haughtiness" (34). A beautiful, exotic, almost oriental mystery, she is inspired no doubt by the "automaton" wives Fauset saw in Algiers. Laurentine has never traveled, yet her appearance suggests the influence of distant horizons. Her haughty demeanor, in contrast to that appearance, is a characterization which challenges the "primitive" stereotype of the wildly sensual, childlike black woman; Laurentine's sensuality is tempered with a fine veil which shields her from the intrusion of the white world. On the other hand, her feminine attire is used to lure men, one of whom will become her future lord, against whom there can be no veil. She surrenders her identity to become his invisible wife. Born of black mother Sal and white, socially prominent father Colonel Halloway, she is a child of sin, ostracized by the town, and the only way to establish her good name is to marry a respectable, professional black man. Hence, Laurentine Strange lives in darkness. She depends upon the good will of a man as much as the silenced wives in the Kasbah, sitting with their hands in their laps, waiting to be told what to do. Like the young automaton bride, she is a fragile prisoner; she wears no face veil, but her heritage veils her life.

Melissa Paul is another child born of sin. As a result of her mother's affair with a married man, Melissa has no real name. She carries a false name to protect her from an intrusive world within the "deeper recesses" of the veil (Du Bois 2). Ignorant of her true parentage, she pities Laurentine, the "tragic mulatta," throughout the novel. Melissa is finally enlightened when she learns that she and her betrothed, Malory Forten, are related. "Your mother," he tells her, "was never married to any man named Paul; she—she was my father's mistress, his woman . . . and you're his child and my—my sister" (331). Malory condemns Melissa for that which is not her fault, and Melissa, like Laurentine, realizes that she must depend on her future husband's good name and judgment of her to redeem and release her from her secret ancestry. Both women, like the young Algerine wife, are automatons; their actions are monitored, and they must be particularly careful of their behavior due to their disadvantaged status as children of sin. Each woman is eventually redeemed by a lord, Laurentine by Dr. Stephen Denleigh and Melissa by Asshur Lane. Denleigh accepts Laurentine's parentage—fortunately for her—and she is now under his care. Without a forgiving husband, she lives behind her veil of shame; with such a man, however, she becomes "shrouded," for her future will always be dependent on his will.

Asshur warns the redeemed Melissa Paul to stick to the straight and narrow: "'You be good, do you hear, just as good as you can be. Don't let anything make you miss your step'" (95). His every letter to her echoes this admonition: "'Be good Melissa, remember be good until I come and after; no matter what other girls do, you be both good and careful'" (117). "Good" here has the obvious connotation of sexual as well as emotional fidelity; after all, a future wife must be above reproach. In a different scene, Asshur reveals his sense of utter content with his woman: "'You know under this tree M'lissa it's just as though we were living in a tent; on the desert' . . . Melissa murmured, 'Suppose you're the Sheik and I'm—' 'You're my favorite wife'" (89). Here Fauset links her Western and Eastern encounters with marriage. Her reference to Melissa's "living in a tent" echoes the image of idle Arab wives sitting in their dark room. But how long will this domestic security last for Melissa, even if she is the "favorite wife?" Her "Sheik" will take care of her, yet like her cousin, Melissa's future happiness depends on his judgment of her. It is ironic that he insists on her fidelity while they are courting and at the same time suggests, even jokingly, that a man could have more than one wife at his disposal—if it were legal. For both Melissa and Laurentine, marital complacency is not an option; their journey leads them down a perilous path where they must constantly watch their step. Instead of relying on their own instincts as do Maggie, Angela and even Olivia, they finally use their men as protection from the harsh world and live out their lives in shadowy rooms, becoming invisible, obedient wives within the respectable social order.

Fauset's travel essays, taken together, reveal noticeable personal development from the eager ingénue tourist to the enlightened fellow sufferer. A woman of color, she empathizes with foreign women and also becomes aware of her denied birthright as a full American citizen. The freedom Fauset feels abroad is tinged with the bitter realization that it can only last until she returns home. Through this link of oppression, she is drawn to the marginalized people of foreign lands. Some of the female travelers in her novels undergo similar realizations. Maggie Ellersley, exposed to foreign freedom in Chambéry and encouraged by the noble, if "cynical," black soldiers, feels fortified against the limits of American racism. Angela Murray finally embraces her racial identity, "falls into line," and accepts the unpleasant realities of discrimination. The "workaday season" of Paris calms and helps her to adjust to this difficult change. Other characters are not so fortunate; Fauset's third novel is a reminder that the post-Victorian black American woman has a strong, if subtle, link to the wives of Algiers. In Fauset's final novel, Olivia Cary, a tragic figure, rejects her heritage and lives her life in true darkness; her portrait is a warning to all who refuse to face the reality of life as an invisible woman, to accept the advantages of life behind the veil as well as the accompanying burdens of racism and patriarchal dominance.

As a "New Negro," Jessie Redmon Fauset realized the necessity of understanding her black American sense of "double consciousness" and of transcending its limitations. In her travels abroad she was able to observe the lives of foreign women and to write their stories, to see life beyond the world of the bourgeois black middle class in her homeland with its own peculiar enslavements. However, she is able to project her concerns as a woman of color onto the women of Paris and Algiers, recognizing universal oppression that affects her so powerfully that memories of it resurface in her novels. Both genres reveal a writer who has triumphed over her invisible status by living and writing on the less-oppressive side of her veil—as a "free" American woman rather than as the silenced African American of the twenties. For this reason a comprehensive analysis of Fauset's fiction is incomplete without tracing the trope of the woman traveler and her journeys from her early essays to her later novels.

WORKS CITED

Adams, Percy G. *Travel Literature and the Evolution of the Novel.* Lexington: UP of Kentucky, 1983.

Bone, Robert. *The Negro Novel in America.* Rev. ed. New Haven, CT: Yale UP, 1966.

Davis, Arthur P. *From the Dark Tower: Afro-American Writers 1900–1960.* Washington, DC: Howard UP, 1981. 90–94.

Donaldson, Laura E. Introduction. *Decolonizing Feminisms: Race, Gender, and Empire-Building.* Chapel Hill: U of North Carolina P, 1992. 1–12.

Donovan, Josephine. "Toward a Women's Poetics." *Feminist Issues in Literary Scholarship.* Ed. Shari Benstock. Bloomington: U of Indiana P, 1987. 98–109.

Du Bois, W. E. B. *The Souls of Black Folk.* 1903. New York: Penguin, 1989.

Fabre, Michel. *From Harlem to Paris: Black American Writers in France, 1840–1980.* Urbana: U of Illinois P, 1991.

Fauset, Jessie Redmon. *The Chinaberry Tree.* 1931. Introduction by Marcy J. Knops. Boston: Northeastern UP, 1995.

———. *Comedy: American Style.* 1933. College Park, Md.: McGrath, 1969.

——. "Dark Algiers the White." *The Crisis* 29–30 (1925–26): 255–58; 16–22.

——. *Plum Bun*. New York: Frederick A. Stokes, 1929. London: Pandora, 1985.

——. *There Is Confusion*. 1924. Boston: Northeastern UP, 1989.

——. "Tracing Shadows." *The Crisis* 10 (1915): 247–51.

——. "Yarrow Revisited." *The Crisis* 29 (1925): 107–9.

Hull, Gloria T. *Color, Sex and Poetry: Three Black Women Poets of the Harlem Renaissance*. Bloomington: U of Indiana P, 1987.

Hughes, Langston. *The Big Sea*. New York: Hill and Wang, 1981.

"Jessie Fauset." *Caroling Dusk*. Ed. Countee Cullen. New York: Harper, 1927.

"Jessie Redmon Fauset Harris." *Afro-American Women Writers: 1746–1933*. Ed. Ann Allen Shockley. New York: Meredian, 1989. 414–24.

Said, Edward W. *Orientalism*. New York: Random House, 1979.

Singh, Amritjit. *The Novels of the Harlem Renaissance*. University Park: Pennsylvania State UP, 1976.

Starkey, Marion. "Jessie Fauset." *Southern Workman* 61 (1932): 217–20.

Stout, Janis P. *The Journey Narrative in American Literature: Patterns and Departures*. Westport, CT: Greenwood, 1983.

Sylvander, Carolyn Wedin. "Jessie Redmon Fauset." *The Dictionary of Literary Biography*. Vol. 51. Detroit: Gale, 1987. 76-86.

——. *Jessie Redmon Fauset: Black American Writer*. Troy, NY: Whitson, 1981.

A Blend of Voices: Composite Narrative Strategies in Biographical Reconstruction

SANDRA Y. GOVAN

In a 1991 Harlem interview, author, scholar, and social and cultural historian John Henrik Clarke jocularly posed the paradigm of the biographer as God. "Like God," Clarke said, "biographers engage in the act of Creation." However, before they can fulfill the mandate of a godhead, particularly in the matter of black women whose lives may well be given over to public service (largely service in the capacity of behind-the-scenes nurturer and service too soon forgotten), all too often biographers must first recover and rediscover the essence of those lives. Then they may proceed to the more artistic acts of re-creation and reconstruction.

It is after the figure has first been partially restored that biographers may then begin the task of fitting together the puzzle pieces, the bits and fragments of a subject's life from a variety of sources to aesthetically re-create and reconstruct some semblance of the life/lives of their protagonist for the biography. If the writer is "good" at what he/she does, an animated person moves again. If the writer only "slickly manipulates the facts," then only a shadow, not the substance, of a figure people knew flits fitfully across the printed page.

Apart from the deity model, biographers do have other strategic aims undergirding the construction of a vital and informative text. Some, for instance, may search for the "life-myth" that has served the subject. Others attend closely to a subject's work "for clues to the life," recognizing that "public lives are not lived in isolation." Still another concern is the treatment of "amorous details"; should these be omitted for reasons of propriety or decorum, the biographer is still obligated to "probe beneath [the] public polished self." Indeed, what must be included in any honest and thoroughly grounded biographical treatment are the "doubts and vulnerabilities, the meannesses, ambitions, and private satisfactions that are hidden within a social personality" of the subject, for these "yield [the] greatest insights" (Pachter 3–15). Stretching beyond the acquisition and presentation of facts, the biographer must learn to interpret these facts, be it artistically or scientifically, in the context of all that has been learned.

In his penetrating article "Biography and Afro-American Culture," Arnold Rampersad makes several valuable observations. By far the most momentous is that for too long black biography has ignored or shunned "the role of psychology in the structure of Afro-American biographical writing" (194). Rampersad argues that while countless scholars have cited W. E. B. Du Bois's paradigm of the divided soul, the "two warring ideals in one dark body" first posited in 1903 in *The Souls of Black Folk* (215), black biography has not moved beyond this conception of black psychology. Confronted by the psychological or psychoanalytical imperative, the texts retreat, their authors withdrawing from rather than engaging in or taking "into account, the insights, discoveries, and methods of the psychologists" (198). Having surveyed the field, it is Rampersad's judgment that rather than tackling the challenge posed by psychology or admitting the utility and conceivable power of psychology as a tool, "black biography has kept a vast distance between itself and that discipline" (198).

While the stance of biographer, whether friendly, neutral, or antagonistic remains the operative guide behind the entire enterprise, this pattern is being altered to allow the participation of other voices in the project. No longer must the black biographer be *either* advocate and propagandist (often "for the race" in the case of older biographical portraits about African Americans) *or* vilifier and muckraker, castigating the subject. Like biographers of old, contemporary biographers must still rummage—through trash cans, letters, news clippings, and so on. Now, however, in addition to these traditional resources, the modern biographer can inform the work by blending these customary or typical methods more actively with voices or perspectives from other locales.

Such a composite narrative strategy encourages autobiographical testimony—from diaries, scrapbooks, letters—in an active rather than passive manner. Such a narrative blending could grant, upon verification, more privilege to oral testimony by giving peers, colleagues, friends, and associates a larger role. Their input would be neither categorically dismissed as idle gossip nor relegated to footnote status. A truly composite narrative structure seeks space not only for the voices of the literary or social and cultural historian, but, as Rampersad argues, it could also seek insights from a psychoanalytic perspective; welcome the acumen of a feminist perspective (which can have crucial applications when examining the life story of a woman); and/or encourage the artistic vision of the fictionist or filmmaker. Spike Lee's film biography of Malcolm X, for instance, attests to the rich and bold possibilities of this kind of composite structural approach.

In sum, a creative blending of the narrative format possibilities from different disciplines, from different genres, and from different modes of approaching the craft/art/science of biography can create a truly engaging "speakerly text," leading, we can hope, to a more engaging and more accurate biographical reconstruction. This, at least, is the model in mind, informing my own biographical enterprise on the life of Gwendolyn Bennett. The working title of that ongoing project is "Tapestry: The Lives of Gwendolyn Bennett." And while I quite concur with Rampersad's injunction that "remarks about biography should be made only with caution" (194), in order that readers obtain some sense of the color and complexity of that "tapestry" I will indicate a part of the trail already traversed in the struggle to recover Gwendolyn Bennett and some of the steps taken to recover her and reclaim for her a more suitable place within the canon.

Bennett's life story captured my attention during the early seventies, when as a master's candidate at Bowling Green State University, I first read several of her poems in concert with the work of other women writers from the Harlem Renaissance. Several of those we studied then, most notably Zora Neale Hurston and Nella Larsen, have since been recovered and reclaimed. Yet for Gwendolyn Bennett, deemed by Harold Cruse to be one of the "most outstanding personalities of the Harlem Renaissance," recognition has been slow in coming (23). In her day, however, Bennett's poetry was well received, even heralded. She was considered a skillful and evocative lyric poet who also made use of such recurring New Negro themes as pride *in* and celebration *of* racial heritage, the importance of cultural icons, recognizing black folk experience, and commemorating the exuberance and camaraderie of youth on the move.

Like Langston Hughes, with whom she shared a poetic sensibility, Bennett could play the race card, but she could also evoke the delicate image or sound the poignant, or angry, note. Her "To Usward," which appeared simultaneously in the May 1924 issues of *The Crisis* and *Opportunity,* was dedicated to Jessie Fauset at the integrated literary gala sponsored by Charles S. Johnson to mark the "debut" of Harlem's writers and artists. The poem celebrates the moment and illustrates the unity within diversity of the spirited younger New Negroes with whom she found a bond:

> If any have a song to sing
> That's different from the rest
> Oh let them sing before the urgency of youth's behest!

Her "Quatrains," which was published in Countee Cullen's 1927 anthology *Caroling Dusk,* paints the mood of the contemplative artist struggling with a divided artistic consciousness:

> Brushes and paints are all I have
> To speak the music in my soul
> While silently there laughs at me
> A copper jar besides a pale green bowl. (155)

Yet "Hatred" demonstrates Bennett's capacity to reveal more stark emotion. Her speaker declares in no uncertain terms:

> I shall hate you
> like a dart of stinging steel
> shot through thin air at eventide.
> Hating you shall be a game. . . .

Although her poetry was never collected into a volume, her work nonetheless received favorable attention and comment from leading critics and scholars of her day. Sterling Brown placed her work squarely within the "New Negro school" and found it "generally race conscious" (Brown 74). While he appreciated Bennett's verse in the "freer forms," James Weldon Johnson believed that she was at her best with the "delicate poignant lyric" (*Negro Poetry* 243). Alain Locke thought enough of her work to include it in *The New Negro,* and Countee Cullen asked her for contributions not only to his *Caroling Dusk* anthology but also to the little poetry magazine he guest edited, *Palms.* Clearly, in her own time Bennett was respected as the peer of and was celebrated along with Langston Hughes and Countee Cullen as a promising New Negro poet. Yet Bennett could acknowledge that poetry was not the only facet of the arts that held her interest, especially during the heady moments of the Harlem Renaissance. Reflecting upon the mood of the era years later, she fondly recalled its endless possibilities: "There was more of a freedom of one person doing several things. This was the first time I wrote prose. I also did journalistic work on *Opportunity.* And the same with anybody who felt like doing something. You didn't have to be labeled as a poet and stay right with poetry" (interview).

Despite the obvious intrinsic worth attached to a thoroughgoing study of her poetry, it was not her poetry alone, nor the fiction nor the journalism nor the illustrations, that kept bringing my attention back to Bennett despite intervening projects. Rather, it was the peculiarly elusive quality about Bennett's life, the sense of mystery connected to the information available in the 1970s about her which I found intriguing. Here was a woman who was clearly "there" and involved, and yet so little was known about her. The biographical data which appeared always recited essentially the same facts: born in Giddings, Texas, in 1902; graduated from Girls High in Brooklyn; went to Pratt Institute, graduating in 1924; and took some course work at Columbia. It was not just her work but her life which called for recovery and reclamation.

And oddly enough, in the years since Gwendolyn Bennett first caught my attention, both her career and her presence as a participant, a shaper, and a contributor to the arts community, have attracted the attention of sundry other scholars. Indeed, Bennett's status as a marginalized so-called minor figure situated within what Ronald Primeau designated as the "second echelon" of Renaissance poets, has evolved from virtual dismissals or casual mentions in texts such as Wilson Record's *Negro in the Communist Party* (1971), Nathan Huggins's *Harlem Renaissance* (1971), and Jervis Anderson's *This Was Harlem 1900–1950* (1981) to more than passing attention in more recent reexaminations of the period. Gloria Hull's *Color, Sex, and Poetry* (1987) alludes to Bennett several times and features a Bennett illustration on its cover. Other more careful, critical comments have come in the several entries composed for various biographical and critical dictionaries, including the *Dictionary of Literary Biography, The Harlem Renaissance Reexamined, Afro-American Women Writers 1746–1933* (1988), and *Notable Black American Women* (1992). Indeed, in the 1990s, Bennett's literary stock has seen some real appreciation. For the first time she has been included in a major "mainstream" college textbook, the *Heath Anthology of American Literature,* volume 2 (1990), and she finally achieved chapter status (actually, Bennett and Jessie Fauset share a chapter) with the publication of Michel Fabre's *From Harlem to Paris: Black American Writers in France, 1840–1980* (1991).

My Ph.D. dissertation, entitled "Gwendolyn Bennett: Portrait of an Artist Lost" (1980), was the first extensive treatment of Bennett. It focused on her life as an eager and willing New Negro. Following the completion of that dissertation and the recognition of its gaps, I continued my search for more about Bennett, albeit fitfully. Through the succeeding years, I had available to me limited blocks of time, derived from summer grants, spring breaks, and a research fellowship, with which to further the task of amassing facts, compiling details, tracing leads and sifting through scattered bits of data to collect and store the raw material which will eventually shape the projected "Tapestry."[1]

There have been several phases to this project, of necessity undertaken at different times and with varying degrees of skill and success. The initial step, what can be called Phase I or the "published papers phase," geared to secondary sources, was largely captured in the dissertation. This phase noted and recorded all publications by Bennett, all references to her work in literature or in art as these appeared in contemporaneous publications. All of the allusions to Bennett or to her accomplishments which repeatedly occurred in the pages of the NAACP's *Crisis* and the Urban League's *Opportunity* were tracked. I collected all of the poems, fiction, essays, and reviews by Bennett appearing in both the black and white media, including various New York newspapers and *Fire, Palms, Black Opals, Southern Workman, Ebony,* and *Topaz,* in addition to the small literary magazines or journals associated with the New Negro era. In the case of *Fire,* Bennett not only contributed a story but with Hughes, Wallace Thurman, and Bruce Nugent, among others, Bennett served on the editorial board. The highly influential Alain Locke not only included some of her poetry in the *New Negro* but subsequently placed a photograph of one of her paintings in his later work, *Negro in Art* (1940). In fact, Bennett has been included in nearly all the major anthologies edited by the leading figures of the period. Additionally, Hughes mentions Bennett favorably several times in his 1940 autobiography, *The Big Sea.*

During this phase of the research, while copying the two years of "Ebony Flute" columns which Bennett wrote for *Opportunity,* columns that served the purpose of carrying "informal literary intelligence" throughout the black arts community, thus circulating a variety or "arts" news concerning personalities or events—who had published what, who was talking to a particular publisher, who was traveling where—I chanced to look at the actual cover of a bound copy (rather than a microfilm text only version) of an *Opportunity* issue. That was the first confirmation I found that Bennett was also an artist-illustrator. Acting on the supposition that if there was one cover illustration there may be others, I subsequently discovered that during this era, Bennett had drawn five cover illustrations for both *The Crisis* and *Opportunity.* The concerted effort, then, of this initial phase was to obtain all Bennett's publications records. The next step was to locate Bennett herself. At the time Phase II of the research began I was still a student, working toward my doctorate, and Gwendolyn B. Bennett was very much alive.

Although she was not in hiding, when she retired from the hectic pace of life in New York, Gwendolyn Bennett had seemingly dropped so completely from public view that no one I contacted initially knew how to find her. She was using her married name, Mrs. Richard Crosscup, and I had been looking for "Gwendolyn Bennett." Eventually, through persistence, the right contacts, some detective work and sheer dumb luck, I found her trading in antiques, using her Kutztown, Pennsylvania, home as her base.[2] And while she was surprised by the thought of becoming the subject of a doctoral dissertation, she actually did not mind being "discovered." In fact, she seemed glad she had been "found," because the process of being recorded for posterity gave her the opportunity to share her impressions and voice her thoughts about the twenties and New Negro era, a period she clearly considered the best part of her life. Thus, in May of 1979, we held a three-day marathon interview session. During our conversations Bennett proved warm and cordial, completely willing to help a novice scholar further the doctoral process.

One of Bennett's more incisive comments about the artists of the era turned on a personal note: "It was fun to be alive and to be part of this . . . like nothing else I've ever been a part of . . . there's been nothing exactly like this . . . nothing like this particular life in which you saw the same group of people over and over again. And you were always glad to see them. You always had an exciting time with them." In a later portion of the same interview, commenting on both the supportive nature of the group and on a singular lack of envy, she argued that during the Renaissance, "the idea that you had to get an inspiration to write or paint never existed because your peers were your inspiration. Nobody was ever sorry [about] anyone's success."

Yet even as she was speaking, lending her voice to the chorus of tales told about the Renaissance, I soon recognized that what Bennett committed so graciously to the oral record would need to be verified, then supplemented or corroborated by other available secondary sources. While not gifted with second sight, I also anticipated some future backtracking, seeing the need to visit every place in which Bennett mentioned having lived during the interview, anticipating the recreation of the "sense of atmosphere" and place for the big book down the road.

It did not take a particularly keen insight to recognize Bennett as a living repository or to understand that, somehow, we had established a sympathetic relationship. I realized early on that it was advisable to conduct another extensive interview as soon as was feasible, given the vagaries of health and age. Then, too, I harbored the dream of being Gwendolyn Bennett's George Bass— of being, despite my youth and inexperience, her literary executor.[3] We had spoken of this in the months preceding our next interview, scheduled for June 1981. But sadly, tragedy struck before those plans were finalized. Richard Crosscup, Bennett's husband, suffered a heart attack in January 1979; embittered and stricken by her loss, Gwendolyn Bennett passed on 31 May 1981, a mere eighteen months later.

As might be imagined, the sudden and unexpected death of both Bennett and her husband almost derailed the projected text. The loss of her voice, the loss of the recollective tone and the rich colors that came with it, was dispiriting. Too, the absence of a second detailed interview also meant starting not quite anew but certainly charting a new plan. Thus began the second paper chase, Phase III. This time the target was Bennett's private papers, the uncollected and unpublished material, the memorabilia or "stuff" of her past, the personal mementos of every day life that had been formerly saved, quite literally, in the attic. That this sensitive material had been stored in her home was no secret because she had agreed to let me peruse it on my next visit. Fortunately, following her death the bulk of her papers were removed from her home and given unto the care of her stepdaughter, Martha Tanner, in Foster, Rhode Island. In 1982, an American Council of Learned Societies (ACLS) Summer Grant provided funding to visit Tanner, who graciously permitted me to examine, copy, and catalog all Bennett's papers before they were deposited in the archives of the Schomburg Center for Research in Black Culture, New York Public Library.

While there were some intermittent research forays during the mid-1980s (I did, for instance, go to Giddings, Bennett's birthplace), a full-time teaching load and commitments to other projects forced delays on the Bennett project until the summer of 1990. The summer began with a university research travel award to visit almost all the places where Bennett had lived and worked, and saw the paper chase begin again in earnest. A special feature of this phase was that I also met and interviewed people who had known Bennett when she lived with her first husband, Dr. Alfred Jackson, for a brief period in Eustis, Florida. This phase of the process then stretched through 1991 with the aid of a Schomburg Center Fellowship. It is not possible to describe here all of nearly twelve months' work. Suffice it to say that archival collections housed at Atlanta University and at Howard, Yale, and New York University; educational records located in various schools; the unique arts and artist oral history archive at the Hatch-Billops Collection; and of course the Schomburg's own massive files were all carefully examined. In pursuit of the details, I traveled from Florida to Washington to Pennsylvania. On my second and third trips to D.C., I worked with crucial materials in the Martin Luther King Library, the National Archives, and the Archive of American Art. In addition, upon returning to New York, the personal papers of artist Norman Lewis, held by his widow, Ouida Lewis, were graciously made available for examination. From one locale to the next, I checked newspaper accounts, clipping files, reports, letters, bills, contracts, journals, diaries, ledgers, bulletins, catalogs, yearbooks, legal proceedings, court records, interview tape transcriptions, scribbled notes on the back of envelopes—the stuff of written record, or "the facts."

While all this material is neither concentrated nor voluminous, it does offer the careful reader insights into the ethos suffusing the twenties and the shifting emphasis clearly apparent in the far more politically radicalized decades that followed. In the twenties Bennett could agonize over her writing. "I feel as though that if I don't write this year, my mouth must remain sealed forever," she wrote in a 1925 letter to Langston Hughes. This was a prophetic comment, for by the forties, the bulk of her writing was geared to generating reports for the Federal Art Project agency she directed, The Harlem Community Art Center, or toward bulletins and curriculum guides for various "left-wing" community schools. Every attempt to be thorough was made; yet, I know something was overlooked.

Beyond chasing documents, being in New York, living in Harlem, had distinct advantages, enabling me to launch Phase IV of the process: locating and interviewing colleagues, co-workers, peers, and friends of Bennett's, people who knew her after the Renaissance years, during the more politically turbulent 1930s–1940s. These interviews were vital because while repositories have been cited, by no imaginative stretch can Bennett's papers be deemed extensive; materials about her in other collections are fragmentary at best. Some respondents, Jean Blackwell Hutson and Elton Fax, were interviewed at the Schomburg; others, such as artist Ernest Crichlow or playwright Loften Mitchell, or former Harlem politico Doxey Wilkerson, spoke to me in their Brooklyn homes or in Queens or Connecticut. One informant suggested I had come "ten years too late"; that I should have tried to find people earlier when perhaps their recollections were better.

Actually, most of my informants came to light at just the right time. They still had good recall and, most important, their sense was that the of the political tenor of the country had sufficiently changed so that they no longer felt uncomfortable or threatened by disclosing and sharing their memories. People were not silenced by "sensitive" topics any longer. They were not daunted by the specter of formerly taboo subjects such as speculation about possible membership in the Communist Party nor concerned with having been politically progressive in that era and thus attuned to the Party's program for the arts and education. In this context, my informants could address questions of professionalism, of sexuality, of political activism, of jealousy and pettiness, of personality conflicts between prominent persons. They spoke about work habits or personal habits, about attitudes toward students or colleagues and about dress and personal appearance; about struggles within the community; about issues of concern to the community; about mentoring by and reactions and responses to Gwendolyn Bennett. Their various testimonies, while not scientific, added tint and shadings to the segments of her lives where before there was merely an outline. Even areas which were gray to them began to show more color for me when a pattern could be discerned from the very consistency of testimony from very different witnesses. For instance, from Bennett's own testimony I knew she tended to gain weight under stress; more than one informant commented on her love of food and the fact that she was a gourmet cook who enjoyed cooking. Couple that knowledge to information that Bennett was constantly trying to diet and a clear indication of a woman in conflict emerges.

Unquestionably, eliciting some of this information from informants was often challenging. To help them and to prepare myself for the interview process, I first constructed a letter wherein, without recourse to pedagogical theories about the genre, I attempted to define my thinking about biography as craft and then share these perceptions of the genre's function. This was a deliberate strategy embarked upon to gain trust; these people were keepers of memory and guardians of an individual's reputation—they needed to respect and trust the person to whom they confided "Gwen's" story. Interestingly, they all felt her story should be told. Only one person had reservations about issues best described as "decorum," manifested in the idea that the best biography is still hagiography and therefore anything which might diminish image should be suppressed. But those who spoke candidly and on the record to me, who responded to my letter, were very generous indeed. I include some portions of that letter here because it is an amalgam of internalized critical directives and shows my first attempts to define or shape biographical narrative.

"Any good biography," I wrote to potential contacts, "conveys to readers, in a detailed, thorough, yet lively and engaging narrative, the life of the person examined. Good biography strives to report fairly the context of the times in which the person lived, analyzing the person against the setting of his or her particular milieu. Thus, good biography is also good social and cultural history." Next, anticipating hesitations regarding intentionality I wrote: "Biography is not vicious gossip; nor is it a witch-hunt or a crusade. Its concern is neither 'bashing' old villains nor pedestal building for the 'heroic' or 'oppressed.' Its aim is not to rake open old wounds for the sake of causing pain but to bring significant parts of the past back to life so that the full story, as completely as possible, can come to life."

The largest issue indicated in the letter was cast as a quest for truth: "The intent of any true scholar's project is to enable readers to see not a cardboard figure, all one dimensional, so good and virtuous as to be saintly—but a real human being, a flesh and blood individual who encompassed, sometimes simply endured, the normal range of human emotions. That is to say, the subject laughed as well as cried—cried as well as laughed; was cheerful and pleasant—was angry and unhappy; was moody—with blue moods and red moods, and sun moods, and ice moods and the full range between. The subject fussed, loved only certain colors but hated others, was a perfectionist, craved power, was callow, showed ambition, displayed peculiar habits, said outlandish things, was a terrible organizer and worse procrastinator, loved sesame seed bagels with cream cheese or fresh fried fish and greens."

This last element was an attempt to get beyond the mask informants often donned. In guarding the reputation of the subject, I had already learned that some informants wanted either to build pedestals or present a draped figure; I was determined to shake the stand and pull the drape. The letter concluded with this plea: "I am trying to touch base and get the testimony of as many of Bennett's peers as I can. For this book to work best, to present the life story of Gwendolyn Bennett best, it needs the testimony of other voices. Take a moment, collect your thoughts, then, lend your voice so that the story of Gwen Bennett can be told in more than casual mentions."

Yet even as the database was rising, subconsciously my thoughts on crafting drifted more toward voice in biography, with blending various voices rather than the straightforward factual recitation. I am not concerned with imaginary reconstructions of dialogue or with the "art of the inferred hypotheses" as demonstrated by Joe McGinniss's *The Last Brother,* an apparently specious 1993 biography of Ted Kennedy attacked by reviewers because of its many problems. Nor am I planning to impose scarcely credible interpretations on diary or journal notations. (One recent biography turned a diary comment about the frustration of being lost in a foreign city into fear of rape and murder.) What is important to me is that the person people knew appear on the page, not flit fitfully across it as shadow rather than substance.

The best way to do that right now seems to be to use the resonance in different voices as an active part of the narrative strategy. Whether we call it "storytelling" or "individual history," when biographers fit together the puzzle pieces, the bits and fragments of a life, when we re-create and animate some semblance of that life wherein the crafting becomes so skillful that the subject functions as protagonist in her or his own story, then the biographer has found an effective narrative strategy. And I believe that treating voice will prove a highly useful tactic.

Having said that, it also seems clear that specifying the various ways we hear voice, or the ways that issues may be voiced, or that a voice may conceal issues, is a legitimate concern. Most often, both with older works and with fuller biographical portraits, the choices made by the biographer can filter and control the volume of other voices participating in the storytelling. In an interview for Gail Mandell's *Life into Art,* Arnold Rampersad privileges Hughes's autobiographical voice, the authentic voice that emerged not so much from Langston's two atypical autobiographies but from his early poems and early letters, before he became aware of posterity (60). By contrast, Rampersad concedes he has "little or no regard for the interview process" because too many people without real knowledge really want to "help" and thus are inclined to "invent" the helpful detail. Rightly, Rampersad warns of the possibility of "deep inaccuracies" (59–60).

I agree that autobiographical voice as heard in the unguarded poem or story, the lonesome or cheery voice present in "unguarded moments" heard in a diary or letter, is highly prized. And when there is a significant collection of such material, so much the better. I disagree, however, about the value assigned interviews. "Trust and verify" has been my motto; and, thus far, the additional witnesses called to testify about Gwen Bennett have been honest, if sometimes reluctant, speakers. Impressions or vaguely recalled details were often confirmed by independent verification from other sources. Where memory was thought to be unreliable, these informants conscientiously sought to cross-check their recollections with others who also knew her; thus "invention," in Rampersad's context, has yet to become an issue. Indeed there was a desire to be useful, to help with the project; my informants, however, seemed less willing to speculate or volunteer "help" when they were unsure. Almost all were forthright individuals who once led public lives themselves. This contributed to a tacit understanding of need and of task. Rather than taking refuge in created fact, during the course of free-flowing conversation is when some forgotten fragment emerged; some long buried nugget about a feature or aspect of Bennett's life when they knew her came to light, then surfaced, without fanfare, in the proverbial "unguarded" moment. It seems that not only was Bennett a gourmet cook, she was also very attentive to her clothing and she loved browsing New York shops for antiques. During the several rambling and convoluted conversations held with informants where memory eddied and swirled, my function was to listen acutely for tone, for nuance of delivery to try to detect any variance conscientiously given for my benefit. To my knowledge then, no one "invented" facts for me. Their voices spoke to a truth as each recalled it.

And again, in addition to calling upon witnesses, I am inclined to use Bennett's voice as it resonates through her scrapbooks, her Paris diary, her letters to Howard University, her reports for the Federal Art Project, and her creative work in an active rather than passive manner. This will be especially critical when the focus of my study turns to Bennett's life during the WPA years and shortly thereafter. In a way, there is some anticipation of something akin to a dialectical approach using the three voices of Bennett available to me: the youthful, wistful, encouraging and courageous voice that comes through her 1920s letters to Cullen and Hughes or her Paris diary ("There was never a more beautiful city than Paris. . . . There couldn't be!" [June 28, 1925]);[4] the bitterness, fear, capability, and adeptness reflected in written documents from the late thirties and forties; the reflectiveness present in the late oral testimony. Without question, for these reasons and others Bennett should be able to carry much of the weight of her own story. Certainly, the autobiographical impulse was one she possessed.

At one point in her life, she even outlined the life history she planned to tell; she had planned to call her uncompleted project "Rubbing Shoulders." If she followed the Hughes model, and it was likely that she would have as the two were kindred spirits in many ways, she may well have muted her voice, in the self-effacing manner she frequently adopted, painting only the image of a charming and colorful childhood of which she spoke in an interview, or seeking to evoke the bright, witty, remarkable or interesting people she came into contact with during her varied career in the arts. She might well have omitted the darker aspects of that period in her life, the fact, for instance, that her father had kidnapped her from her mother when she was only eight years old (interview).

Parenthetically, given the roseate quality of the times Bennett recalled most fondly, it is rather doubtful that she would have found in her projected volume the necessary psychic space to do any true introspection. What James Olney called the "individual's special peculiar psychic configuration" would remain masked by Bennett; what Olney judged the "moral tenor" of her being might show itself, but only in bits and snippets (20). There were many silences in Bennett's life, periods when she remained silent by choice or social circumstance and periods when silences were imposed by political constraints. Yet each of these silences is in itself telling; each one says something about the woman within. To illustrate with two brief examples: seldom did an informant report that he or she ever saw Bennett angry. Consistently, all of them often recalled a gracious, charming, warm, and generous person. But how could Bennett have avoided anger when driven from a job she loved as director of the Harlem Community Art Center and hounded, repeatedly, by the specter of the "red menace" at wherever she next worked?

In *Writing a Woman's Life,* Carolyn Heilbrun maintains that for women, anger is an emotion virtually denied. Heilbrun's thesis posits that anger is as discomforting as an "open admission of the desire for power and control over one's life," and thus something women dared not show (13). Did Bennett deny or mask her anger; or did others merely fail to see it? Certainly, Bennett was adept at masking her past; people who knew her in one context knew little about her life in another. Intriguingly, Heilbrun also maintains that "nostalgia, particularly for childhood, is likely to be a mask for unrecognized anger" (15). I'm speculating here, but it seems credible to assume that "unrecognized anger" may well be manifested in raging emotion turned inward, thus producing a silence that speaks for itself.

More than likely, Gwendolyn Bennett would concur with Arnold Rampersad's premise in the Mandell interview that in "the second half of our lives, we're not as interesting" (57). Despite her own protestations and not withstanding the dearth of published texts to analyze, the changes that occurred in the course of Bennett's life—her movement from New Negro to mentor and facilitator in the progressive arts struggle of the thirties to forgotten woman by the fifties and antiques dealer in the seventies—nonetheless conspire to make her life very "interesting" to anyone looking to tell a complete story about a woman of mystery. Although she clearly no longer had the energy to engage in the host of multiple exciting activities as she had in her youth, others who knew her also found her as interesting, although perhaps somewhat enigmatic and puzzling, at the midpoint of her life. These were the people who worked with her in the Federal Arts Project of the 1930s and early 1940s, or with her in the Negro Artist Guild, or at the community based and government targeted community schools in the late 1940s, or at Consumer Union during the 1950s and early 1960s. These are the people who had something to say about Bennett and about her life in the context of those times.

I believe there is an obligation to listen. These voices are both subjective and objective. And perhaps because Bennett is still regarded as a "minor" figure, not a public legend, there is no vested interest in inflating her memory. Hence, because of all these circumstances, I think respondents to my inquires have offered careful, deliberate, and thoughtful reflections, commenting upon the actions of a black woman artist as they observed them, in a particular social and cultural milieu, a particular time and place.

Postscript: Apart from juggling the various voices Bennett employed and those of the witnesses taking the stand to tell the story or speak the truth as they saw it, there still remains the question of authorial voice in the narrative process. According to some injunctions, despite an author's sense of commitment and concern for "narrative power," the biographer "must avoid center stage"

(Pachter 8). Yet, customarily certain stylistic trademarks stamp my prose. For instance, I prefer the active voice; I have an affection for the alliterative mode; I'm fond of the parenthetical sentence. Given these traits, my voice may intrude too pervasively into the narrative. Mine is an oral style and, typically, those perusing my prose pronounce that it "sounds" just like me. Yet as sound sense and the striking visual image are also the tools of the good creative writer, perhaps these traits can be muted, subordinated, or bent to the service of crafting dramatic moments. Recalling that the purpose of any good biographical narrative is not only the recovery, reclamation, and revelation of a life but the telling of a good story, I shall endeavor to contain my voice by shifting focus to setting, character, chronology, or evocation of mood in the recreation of circumstance rather than by calling attention to an omniscient presence.

While the procedures being contemplated are not fully operational, trying to formulate some form of composite narrative strategy or structure seems the better part of wisdom. Such a structure should create space for multiple voices, providing a place for the comment from several different resources: individuals, texts, and academic disciplines—history, sociology, psychology, art. My theory is that listening to Gwen Bennett's interior voice will be every bit as essential to the biography as is our ability as readers of Zora Hurston's narrative to hear Janie Crawford's interior voice. The trick, or rather the art, will come from a creative blending of the narrative format possibilities, using different modes, perhaps different genres, to re-create the life of Gwen Bennett inside a "speakers text." When the subject gives you the mantle and entrusts you with her story, there is an obligation to allow her to speak for herself and then to speak up and speak for her. Implicitly, when recovery and restoration is a part of the charge, some advocacy seems inherent whether the trumpet or a muffled drum roll is the instrument.

At this juncture, it looks like treating "voice" is where I have planted my flag. Regardless of whatever other "angle of consistency" seems suitable for the final text, blending the different voices raised in concert should help pull together the disparate threads of Gwendolyn Bennett's lives. Both as artist using differing media and highly regarded community figure Bennett merits more from our cultural historians. By incorporating and blending a host of voices, the intent is to make the shadowy figure of the woman embedded in the warp of the fabric more pronounced. The hues and multiple tones in the tapestry I hope one day to hang should take on a richer texture. That, at least, is the theory; bear with me; I'm working on it.

NOTES

1. My research on Gwendolyn Bennett has been supported, at various times, by an American Council of Learned Societies summer grant; several summer grants from

the University of North Carolina–Charlotte, and a New York Public Library Schomburg Scholar in Residence award funded by the National Endowment for the Humanities for 1990–91. This allowed me to live in Harlem for nine months and conduct my research in a more sustained manner.

2. Margaret Burroughs, director, DuSable African-American History Museum, Chicago, was an instrumental early contact whose help led me to Bennett.

3. Founder of Rites and Reason Theatre at Brown University, the late George Houston Bass formerly served as secretary to Langston Hughes and eventually became the executor of the Hughes estate.

4. See her 1920s letters to Cullen and Hughes or her Paris diary ("There was never a more beautiful city than Paris. . . . There couldn't be!" [28 June 1925]) Her letters are in the Beinecke Rare Book and Manuscript Library at Yale University in the James Weldon Johnson Collection. Her diary is in the New Public Library in the Schomburg Center for Research in Black Culture.

WORKS CITED

Bennett, Gwendolyn. Personal interview with Sandra Y. Govan. Mar. 1979.

Benstock, Sheri. "Authorizing the Autobiographical." *The Private Self: Theory and Practice of Women's Autobiographical Writings.* Ed. Sheri Benstock. Chapel Hill: U of North Carolina P, 1988. 10–33.

Brown, Sterling A. *The Negro in American Fiction and Negro Poetry and Drama.* 1937. New York: Arno/New York Times, 1969.

Clark, John Henrik. Interview with Sandra Y. Govan. 9 May 1991.

Cruse, Harold. *The Crisis of the Negro Intellectual.* New York: William Morrow, 1967.

Cullen, Countee, ed. *Caroling Dusk.* New York: Harper, 1927.

Govan, Sandra Yvonne. "Gwendolyn Bennett: Portrait of an Artist Lost." Diss. Emory U, 1981.

Heilbrun, Carolyn. *Writing a Woman's Life.* New York: Norton, 1988.

Huggins, Nathan. *Harlem Renaissance.* New York: Oxford UP, 1971.

Hull, Gloria T. *Color, Sex, and Poetry: Three Women Writers of the Harlem Renaissance.* Bloomington: U of Indiana P, 1987.

Olney, James. "Some Versions of Memory/Some Versions of *Bios.*" Ed. James Olney. *Autobiography: Essays Theoretical and Critical.* Princeton, NJ: Princeton UP, 1980. 236–67.

Pachter, Marc. "The Biographer Himself: An Introduction." *Telling Lives: The Biographer's Art.* Ed. Marc Pachter. Philadelphia: U of Pennsylvania P, 1981. 3–15.

Primeau, Ronald. "Frank Horne and the Second Echelon Poets." *The Harlem Renaissance Remembered.* Ed. Arna Bontemps. New York: Dodd, 1972. 247–67.

Rampersad, Arnold. "Biography and Afro-American Culture." *Afro-American Literary Studies in the 1990s.* Ed. Houston A. Baker Jr. and Patricia Redmond. Chicago: U of Chicago P, 1989. 194–230.

———. "A Conversation with Arnold Rampersad." *Life into Art.* Ed. Gail Porter Mandell. Fayetteville: U of Arkansas P, 1991. 44–67.

Record, Wilson. *The Negro and the Communist Party.* New York: Atheneum, 1971.

Before the Stigma of Race:
Authority and Witchcraft in Ann Petry's
Tituba of Salem Village

TRUDIER HARRIS

When we think of the history of African American women's texts, any number of suggestions come to mind about the subjects of their fictional worlds. We think of the slave narratives with their focus on freedom and what it meant to African American women. We think of the religious tradition, either in the spiritual narratives or what was presented in the fiction, and how that tie bound black women to their husbands, children, churches, and God. We think of conjure women, but in the tradition of those presented by Charles Chesnutt and Margaret Walker. Seldom do we extend the focus on religion and conjuration to consider how black women may have fared in the colonies in the early days of this country when women, often simply because they were women, were believed to be something other than human, even in league with the devil. One of the African American texts in need of recovering centers upon precisely that combination of factors.

American history would lead us to suspect that black women have been maligned first and foremost on the basis of their color. However, Winthrop D. Jordan's *White Over Black: American Attitudes Toward the Negro, 1550–1812* (1968) makes clear that the institutionalization of blackness with negative connotations took quite a period of development in America. Early colonists did not automatically discriminate against black people exclusively on the basis of color. The color "black" in the colonies about which Ann Petry writes in *Tituba of Salem Village* (1964; rpt. HarperCollins, 1988) was more likely to be identified with notions of evil, indeed with the devil himself, than with black human beings. I should point out, however, that the generic basis for blackness being identified with evil still holds sway in the colonies, for the devil is repeatedly referred to as "the black man" (27, 62, 202). Tituba insists that her husband John, a tall black man, pretend to be bewitched along with the young women so that the villagers will not begin to associate him with the devil.

In *Tituba*, therefore, Petry presents a slightly different view of how a black woman came to be maligned. Set in the period between 1688 and 1693 in Salem,

Massachusetts, it rewrites the history of a slave woman who was accused of witchcraft. The original Tituba, a black woman from Barbados who was purchased and brought to Massachusetts just before the height of the hysteria surrounding witch trials there, was one of the first three women accused of being in league with the devil, of having powers that no normal human being should possess. Tituba was spared hanging; her story inspired Petry to publish *Tituba of Salem Village* and the great Guadeloupan novelist, Maryse Conde, to publish *Moi, Tituba*.

With its basis in history, *Tituba* understandably presents problems of classification. Is it an historical novel, an adolescent biography, or simply a novel that evolved from a historical tidbit, perhaps like Toni Morrison's use of the brief account of Margaret Garner to develop *Beloved?* Even Ann Petry has at times seemed to waver in the classification. In autobiographical statements, as well as in critical commentary on her works, she has referred to the book as an "historical novel." She has also called it a "researched biography" and discussed it in several places as a children's book. And HarperCollins lists it with its division of Children's Books. For the purposes of this discussion, I am treating the book as a novel inspired by a set of historical circumstances.

The fact that Petry selected witchcraft for fictional development places her outside the usual parameters with which we demarcate African American writers. We ask what black women had to do with witchcraft in early America. Is that part of American history really not something that white men perpetrated against white women? Even if blacks were present during those times, were they not somehow exempt, as judged by their status of being property, from consideration as witches? The history of this novel is really the history of reaction to prevailing expectations of what black women should identify as subjects for creative development. Ann Petry, so this line of reasoning goes, strayed from the straight and narrow path of legitimate development for African American writers and paid the price by having the book ignored by the critical establishment almost immediately after it was published—although it has stayed in print for the adolescent audience.

The world that Petry creates in *Tituba* is one where imagination runs rampant, where young girls might be expected to attest to witnessing events they could not possibly have witnessed, but where grown men join them in these flights of imagination. It is a world where superstitions hold sway, where everyone can recognize a "money cat" as a harbinger of good luck, but where that same cat can be viewed as a messenger of the devil, a familiar whose presence identifies the person who feeds and pets it as a witch. It is a world where Tituba's very nature will work against her, for she has an extrasensory perception. Not only does she see visions that portend her own fate, but she has learned the skill of fortune-telling with Tarot cards. That ability to see beyond human limitations is not one that can be forgiven in this narrow-minded world. A practiced skill is thus perceived as an instantly bestowed power, a gift of the devil.

The world of Salem Village is ultimately one where the best course of human action is to blend, as invisibly as possible, into the masses of country folk. To stand out in any way is to invite disaster. The precursor bag lady, Goody Good, is therefore a likely target for accusations of witchcraft. Her individuality—not bathing, sleeping in barns, begging for food—bespeaks an independence and a separation from community that this village cannot tolerate. Pim's bright red hair sets him apart and ensures a troublemaker's existence for him. And Tituba's very natural talents are used against her. When a neighbor lady teaches her to spin thread on a flax wheel, she catches on quickly and produces thread "so fine, so strong" that her tutor "said it was like magic," "Looks like it hadn't been made by human hands" (30, 31). Her adjustment to produce occasionally broken or too thick thread is too late, for the rumors of her extraordinary hands go forth and return with a vengeance when she is tried as a witch.

Petry's world—and the logic by which it operates—is not so far removed from those of Sir James George Fraser in *The Golden Bough* and Shirley Jackson in "The Lottery." Cries to those accused, such as "'You made my cow sicken,' 'My butter wouldn't come,' 'My hens wouldn't lay'" (218), echo those in pretechnological cultures where someone would very shortly be held responsible. In worlds where people are basically farmers and at the mercy of nature, any lapses in patterns of crop production or livestock behavior might well be attributed to demonic intervention. The world can only be righted again if some convenient scapegoat is identified for physical punishment, banishment, or death. In the absence of an enlightened arena of discussion, people resort to basic animalistic urges and motivations. The fact that the book-learned Mr. Parris, former student at Harvard, is barely a cut above the lay people he claims to serve is Petry's most poignant argument for the dethroning of literacy and logic in the face of mass hysteria.

At issue in the novel is the question of authority—who has it, who wields it over whom, for what reason. Authority in the novel comes from three sources: religion (God, the Bible, the church); the forces of evil (the devil); and persons in the temporal realm who are either in league with or are opposed to the forces of evil. Ultimately, neither the power of God nor that of the devil reigns supreme. What drives the novel and determines people's fates is the power of imagination wielded by those who believe that evil is in their midst. As they cut their paths through the small New England village, nothing can stand in their wake; they use the Bible and references to the devil only as effectively as such references help them to accomplish their purpose, which usually means eradicating some undesirable person from their village, punishing those who have authority over them, or elevating their own status within their small community.

As Petry develops her novel, color becomes the secondary, not the primary motivating force for events. Certainly Tituba's position as an enslaved person in a small village society makes her vulnerable to various whims. Yet the larger force driving the community is that connected to belief in witchcraft. Witchcraft is a wonderfully democratic and leveling force, for it affects men, women, blacks, whites, Christians, and sinners. Its power resides in the fact that to be accused is to be guilty. Persons accused are guilty until proven innocent, and history has informed us that tests to determine innocence were likely as not to kill the person as to gain their freedom. In Tituba's world, therefore, the word "witch" is infinitely more fate-determining than the word "slave." Slaves can be succored and protected; witches are to be burned ("Do not suffer a witch to live"—185). Slaves can make a claim—no matter how minimal—upon their masters; witches should be cast out and killed.

Many of the traditional divisions or separations between masters and enslaved persons do not hold in the novel, for Tituba and John pray with their master's family, eat in the same room with them, share the same kind and quantity of food, and have virtually free access to the spaces within the house. As they travel on the ship from Barbados to Boston with the Reverend Parris, who has recently purchased them, Tituba and John must share "the same small cabin" with him, his sickly wife, his daughter, and his orphaned niece (9). When they arrive from Boston to their new home in Salem Village, John sits "next to the master" (67) on the settle in the kitchen as they share their first meal. There is never an indication that the master denies food to enslaved persons because they are enslaved; any scarcity in the house affects everyone equally.

The authority that came to be institutionalized in American slave relations, therefore, does not yet obtain. Tituba does, however, object to being called a "servant" when she knows in reality that she is a "slave." Servants like the bound girls and boys can escape at will and disappear among the larger population or ship to sea, as the bound boy Pim plans to do. Slaves are controlled by the bidding of their masters whether or not the masters actually separate them from the regular activities of their families' lives. The distinction between enslaved and bound persons comes to take on larger significance than mere questions of freedom of movement or physical labor.

One of the driving conflicts in the novel is the clash between indentured and orphaned white women and the authority that they imagine Tituba, an enslaved person, wields over them. The eight-year-old, adolescent Abigail Williams, the orphaned niece of Rev. Mr. Parris, is annoyed that Tituba can order her around. And not only does Tituba order Abigail around, but she boxes her ears soundly on one occasion when Abigail asserts that Tituba could be in two places if she were a witch (34). In this inversion, the orphaned child imagines that she has less status in the household than the slave. By the time Abigail is nine, she has decided, at least as far as Tituba can conclude about the matter, that she will repay this woman for the inconveniences she has suffered as a white, orphaned child. Although the accusations against Tituba do not evolve into a full-fledged conspiracy until Abigail is twelve, the girl already has the key to the one crime for which she knows Tituba will not be able to mount a defense.

For bound girls such as Mercy Lewis, who must spend their youth doing the bidding of their employers, their whiteness does not give them the privilege that enslaved Tituba has. While Tituba certainly works as hard as they do, her age, thirty-two, puts her in the relation of adult to them, and her skills—knowledge of herbs and natural cures—give her an authority that they do not have. While this knowledge will certainly become evidence against her in the accusation that she is a witch, it nonetheless clearly separates her from the younger, inexperienced, and culturally different indentured girls.

Mercy Lewis, for all her below-waistline yellow trestles of hair (the epitome of the blond icon that would come to represent the best of Anglo-American beauty), must sleep on a settle in the keeping room of the Putnam family to whom she is bound just as Tituba and John must similarly sleep in such a room and on such inconvenient beds. To her mind, the fact that she is sixteen and still a "serving wench" has severely undercut her value. Her claimed encounter with the devil positions her so that she is "a child to be treated tenderly" (162).

Petry's is a world where boredom is a powerful, but negative, stimulant to creativity. In the absence of anything comparable to movies or video games, these young women escape their confinement to house and snow by holding on to the least bit of deviation from the routine of their lives. They implore Tituba to tell their fortunes with the Tarot cards in an almost desperate kind of way. When the subterfuge to hide the cards is finally revealed and they are displayed in Mary Warren's presence, she proclaims: "It's like a show. . . . I wouldn't have missed it for anything" (124). And they are attracted to the role-playing of pretending to be bewitched without attention to the consequences of their deadly game. It adds magic to their drab lives.

The group of girls who conspire to accuse Tituba of witchcraft might also be jealous of the authority inherent in her imagination. She tells stories about the sunshine and greenery of Barbados in the midst of harsh New England winters and figuratively transports them out their immediate circumstances. Not only are the young girls being entertained during the long, cold winters, but they are also being made aware of the transformative power of words. Storytelling (the potency of words) becomes authoritative in that Tituba has the power to weave word-spells over the girls. Encouraging them to see Barbados becomes yet another piece in the web of evidence the girls concoct to show that Tituba is unusual, that her abilities are almost otherworldly.

It is perhaps not coincidental that warmth and cold are contrasts in the novel. From the point of view of those who accuse Tituba, these contrasts work symbolically to suggest that her affinity is with the legions of hell and their heat as opposed to the purity or cleanliness of the New England snow and its figurative representation of the iciness of truth. The coldness of the weather is highlighted so frequently that it also fits into the thematic detachment that goes along with persecution. The elders of the village are much too emotionally cold, much too bent on the detached superiority of their presumably objective truth, that they seem in their natural environment in the New England snow. Tituba, on the other hand, although she certainly suffers from the cold, is nonetheless one of the few people able to help others transcend the cold weather. Ironically, that very ability is one of the things that leads to her being considered a witch. The villagers also transfer their own illnesses and fears on to nature. The forest surrounding the village is sinister only because they are; their projections on to it evoke comparison to the world Nathaniel Hawthorne creates in "Young Goodman Brown," where trees and animals are thought to take the shape of the devil or of villagers in league with the devil.

The girls also conspire against Tituba because, on a couple of occasions, she refuses to use her word power for their benefit. When Tituba proclaims that she cannot "talk and keep the thread thin and straight" (111), Mercy Lewis declares: "'Then we had all this walk for nothing and there's snow coming on and the wind is blowing and it's so cold out it is like being outdoors when you are bare naked. . . . They ought to put Tituba in the press yard,' she said spitefully. 'That would make her talk'" (111). She describes the press yard almost with glee: "It's where they press the prisoners to death in the great prison in London. They roll stones on them until they die—bigger and bigger stones, heavier and heavier, until they press their insides right out. They press the ones who stand mute. They're the ones who won't answer questions. They won't say they're guilty, and they won't say they're not guilty" (111–12). Desperate for diversion, the young women remain dissatisfied even after Tituba tells them one short story.

The violence the ironically named Mercy envisions as a cure for silence is typical of the instruments of torture of her society. Indoctrinated into acceptance of such practices, the girls again do not make a humane connection between their creative lies and the deadly consequences they could effect. Strikingly, the girls have an ongoing and lusty love for violence and vengeance. When little Betsey unwittingly reveals that there are fortune-telling cards in the minister's house, Abigail "slapped her so hard that the blow left a red mark on the soft white skin" (123), but Mercy Lewis merely calls out, "Hit her again, Abigail. Hit her again," and Mary Walcott chimes in, "Good for you, Abigail" (123). They are all keenly interested when they discover that Goody Good's daughter has a doll, purportedly representing a neighbor child, into which she sticks thorns (147).

When the girls begin to have fits, the extent of their lies can be measured by the formulas of the script into which they write themselves. Oral tradition has given them the outline of a tale or tales that one can tell to claim bewitchment. The elements include reports of witches flying at night, harming the young women (especially pinching, choking, beating, and riding them), and shapeshifting themselves into animals (especially dogs and cats). To illustrate their bewitchment, the girls howl and scream, crawl or leap on all fours like dogs, hiss like cats, pretend to be out of their heads, try to burn themselves up, and fall prostrate into semi-comatose states. Someone astutely observes that "it was a strange thing that so many of these afflicted young women were orphaned nieces or bound girls or servants" (184), but no one ever draws logical extensions from that observation. It becomes known quickly, however, that the girls can be released from their afflicted states by the "touch test" (190), which Tituba and the other accused women are shortly forced to perform—as soon as they touch the young women, they become normal and sane.

The accusations of the girl/women set various levels of authority in motion. Initially, there is the authority of space. The relationship between space and authority is set up earlier when the Reverend Mr. Parris insists upon a separate room for a study, no matter how it inconveniences the members of his household. Ideas from the supernatural thus have a special place to enter. That space and what happens in it loom large in the minds of the minister's family as well as in those of Tituba and John.

Knowing full well where they will have the greatest influence, the young women go into the village, to Ingersoll's taproom, the local tavern center, to throw their fits. Their audience grows every day as people come from as far away as Boston to see them howl and crawl around on all fours. Clearly, these activities allow the young women to escape work, something for which Abigail is notorious. It also allows them access to public space, which, in their roles as presumably decorous young women, would not otherwise have been available to them. And it allows them to command male attention without explicit sexual overtones. Instead, it invites the men of the village to protect them by finding the perpetrators of the witchery. Formerly on the periphery of the community, therefore, the young women, as a result of these spells, become centered in the minds and space of their village. No other medium could have achieved this objective for them. The authority of space grants them an elevation in value.

There is also an authority of image evoked by the girls' accusations of witchcraft. It, too, has a formulaic script into which Tituba gets written. It is Mr. Parris, the preacher-writer, who, at the instigation of the girls, wields the authority of writing over Tituba. When he beats her into confessing that she is a witch, his next step is to produce a written "confession." It consists of questions and answers, ones that have obviously been used again and again with persons accused of witchcraft. The image of witch, therefore, is ultimately more important than the individual human being whose life is inscribed into those features.

The script from which Mr. Parris derives his questions contains the following elements:

> She [Tituba] had made a pact with Satan. She had signed an agreement with him, signing it in her own blood. Satan had dipped a pen in her blood and she had signed, and then Satan had given her the power to travel through space, to enter houses, to go where she pleased. She could sit here in the keeping room, and people would see her sitting at the spinning wheel, and yet at the same time she could be at Deacon Putnam's, pinching Anne and choking Mercy Lewis. She, Tituba, could be in two places at once. (195–96)

Questions such as "what familiars have you beside the cat?" and "When you journey, . . . how do you go?" (197) are merely the blotter to dry and secure the script. Tituba's fate as a guilty person is sealed as unalterably as that of an enslaved person caught in his master's smokehouse with a ham in his arms. The authority of the script has embedded in it a conclusion of guilt, and the heightened imagination that guides the writing is not about to relinquish the image it has stored, an image sanctioned by the community.

We can also think of authority as rationality and what it means, stereotypically, for men to be in control, that is, presumably thinking, when women are being submissive, that is, intuitive. Tituba has a sense of foreboding about evil things, and she has the kind of keen observation that would make less observant people believe she has some uncanny way of analyzing people. Yet in an interesting reversal of the usual stereotypical situation, the notion of rationalist *manhood* during this era seems to have disappeared. Men seem to become intuitive, subject to the *hysteria* of imagination in ways that they traditionally associate with women. Their actions raise some provocative questions about this period in American history. What did the witch hunts mean for American conceptions of manhood? How do those notions inform the creation of such an abominable character as Mr. Parris? Were the men merely transferring their own insecurities, their own madness, onto the women? Perhaps in their ever-vigilant bids to protect women and children against nature and Indians, they had lapses in which they broke down, were "feminized," and the only way they could cover that up was to blame it on witchcraft.

Women, by contrast, seem to lose authority through illness. There is a pattern in the novel of several wives of ministers in Salem Village dying of strange diseases. Before they weaken, however, they have considerable responsibility in their households and in their communities. The fact that Rev. Mr. Parris's wife cannot function in this working capacity is another symptom of the world being out of kilter, of the reins of authority being loosened or taken over by other characters. Ironically, the black woman who is accused of being a witch is much stronger physically and morally than those who own and accuse her.

On the other hand, women gain authority through their knowledge of healing, and it is in this arena that they become most susceptible to accusations of witchcraft. By easing the pain of others, as Judah White and Tituba do, women not only supplant the power of the local male doctors, but they appear to those who would accuse them of transcending the bounds of nature to which God has consigned them. By seeming to step out of their rightful place in the chain of being, particularly that of being lesser knowing than men, the very virtues that accrue to healing skills become razors with which these women cut their own throats.

And the stereotypical notions of intuition associated with them similarly become damaging. Witches, folklore tells us, always have familiars, be they birds, snakes, or cats. Animals in the novel, then, exert a different kind of authoritative evidence against the women who would be kind to them. When Tituba adopts a stray cat, those of us who know the symbolism know that she is sealing her own fate. Even more so is this true when she speaks to the cat in the presence of her overly imaginative neighbors and they conclude that the cat not only understands, but obeys her will.

Witches, then, are perceived to have authority over the natural and human worlds, and they have broken down the barriers between humanity and the supernatural in that they conspire with the devil. But who ultimately has authority over witches? Is it the Bible? White males? Civil justice? The authority seems to rest in the accusers who set in motion a series of events from which those accused have difficulty escaping. The final authority is in the word "witch" itself, for it has the power to name a reality, and that reality can be as tangible as burning up children from afar or as ephemeral as young girls believing that a cat has understood a woman or that a witch cake did indeed produce the result for which it was baked.

Tituba of Salem Village has been designated an adolescent novel, and though that is perhaps more a misnomer than not, it does explore adolescent issues. In fact, we might ask if the novel simply, finally, boils down to a case of adolescent conspiracy. It certainly seems to be a commentary (since Petry mentions it twice) on the inability of young women to be allowed to reach adulthood; although some of the "girls" who accuse Tituba are twenty, they still act like six-year-olds. What has made them so? What commentary is being made about the location of authority in the village, or processes of socialization? What comment is being made about dangerously overactive imaginations? These questions get answered in the history we bring to the novel as well as in the situations Petry depicts.

For these adolescent girls and young adult women, accusations of witchcraft become the social ladder by which they relinquish their outcast status and achieve acceptance in their communities. By accusing Tituba, Goody Good, and Good Osborne of being witches, these girl/women who have previously not had the caring and concern shown to them that legitimate offspring have, very quickly learn that almost everyone—from the owner of the busiest tavern, to the minister, to their owners, to their neighbors—becomes *concerned* about them. They become the center of attention. I cannot overestimate the value of that concern to the girls perpetuating a fraud against the community. For example, Mercy Lewis moves from sleeping on an uncomfortable wooden settle to sleeping in a down feather bed with the daughter of the man to whom she is bound. She arrives at that state when she refuses to run away with Pim, a bound boy who has concocted a scheme to shave her head and have her dress as a boy when they leave the village. Mercy changes her mind and must find an explanation for how her hair came to be cut. She tells Deacon Putnam, her master, that demons have shaved her head because she refused to sign the devil's book. He becomes concerned enough to allow her to sleep in his daughter's bed for the rest of the winter. Her reaction to that privilege is worthy of note:

> She sighed and settled deep into the warm, soft bed. She pulled the bearskin high up around her neck and finally covered her head because she could feel cold air all around her shorn nead. Tomorrow night she'd wear one of Anne Putnam's nightcaps. Just before she drifted off to sleep, she decided that this deep, soft, warm bed was better than life with the bound boy would have been. The Putnams were always saying, "Better one bird in hand than ten in the wood." (162–63)

Mrs. Parris perceptively suggests that Abigail "may want more love and attention than we have given her" (199) as the reason for the girl's so-called fits. Although Mrs. Parris recognizes Tituba's worth, and although Tituba and Judah White hunt for herbs together in the woods outside Boston, the adult women do not form a community as effectively as do the girls. Their isolation in dealing with the young women, therefore, perhaps inadvertently contributes to the license the girls feel they can take in maligning adults.

The motives of the girls are clear, but it is difficult at times to decipher why Tituba responds the way she does. There are several occasions on which Tituba senses that something is wrong, and she could alter a particular course of action; yet she follows along almost knowing that the consequences will be detrimental to her. For example, she participates in the test of the witch cake (177–82); she always lays her hands on any girl having a "fit" when she is directed to do so; and she joins in the fortune-telling games that will only serve later to establish her otherworldly clairvoyance. This clash between motivation, action, and the probable knowledge of outcome of action becomes striking enough to look at the novel from the vantage point of the authorial intrusion Petry exerts in *The Street*. Is Petry forcing Tituba to follow a path to an inevitable conclusion in the same way that she does Lutie Johnson in *The Street?* Does the novel become another case of one kind of genre, naturalism, imposed upon a world that *seems* to lend itself to that kind of interpretation, but which really operates on a different set of forces? Is an accusation of witchcraft just as determining of one's fate as living in Harlem in the 1940s? Was the attraction in recreating the historical circumstances of Tituba's experience in part motivated by Petry's belief that seventeenth-century New England and twentieth-century Harlem had more in common than not?

There is also a problem with the strange shift in point of view, for two chapters, from Tituba and Rev. Parris's household to Mercy Lewis and the Putnam household. Petry clearly had difficulty in finding a way to convey to her readers information she assumed they needed about motivation. So she violated narrative point of view in order to achieve narrative truth. These lapses give the novel a heavy-handed effect in places and push it even more toward a thematically controlled construct rather than a dramatically controlled one. Yet for all its lapses, *Tituba of Salem Village* delves into an area of literary imagination that few other black fictional works have broached; the result is one that certainly warrants this novel being reclaimed from the forgotten shelves of the African American literary library.

WORKS CITED

Hansen, Chadwick. "The Metamorphosis of Tituba, or Why American Intellectuals Can't Tell an Indian Witch from a Negro." *New England Quarterly* 47.1 (Mar. 1974): 3–12.

Jordan, Winthrop D. *White Over Black: American Attitudes Toward the Negro, 1550–1812*. Chapel Hill: U of North Carolina P, 1968.

Morsberger, Robert E. "The Further Transformation of Tituba." *New England Quarterly* 47.3 (Sept. 1974): 456–58.

Petry, Ann. "The Common Ground." *Handbook of Reflections*. Ed. Elinor Whitney Field. Boston: Horn Book, 1969. 67–72.

———. *Tituba of Salem Village*. New York: Crowell, 1964. New York: HarperCollins, 1988.

Reading Ann Petry's *The Narrows* into Black Literary Tradition

JOYCE PETTIS

First the conundrum: Why have critics almost unanimously agreed that Petry's *The Narrows* (1953) is her best work but largely ignored it and critically engaged *The Street* (1946)?[1] One answer is that *The Narrows* neither fits comfortably in a genre identified with a prominent black male writer nor wore well certain labels ascribed to it. Published just seven years after *The Street,* Petry's novel received the same disregard, misunderstanding, and partial dismissal as other fiction by black women in the 1950s.[2] That the novel defied the protest formula and decentered the questing black male undoubtedly figured in its initial neglect.

Unevenness characterized early critical response to *The Narrows.* Although Arthur P. Davis finds the work "exciting" and "fresh," he believes "it is not a strong novel." He identifies "a heavy strain on our 'suspension of disbelief,'" and "flashbacks during character crises" as weaknesses (qtd. in Bloom 5: 3088). Wright Morris in the *New York Times Book Review* condemns the novel as "a first draft of an ambitious conception that has not been labored into imaginative life" (qtd. in Bloom 5: 3085). Among recent critics, Noel Schraufnagel misreads *The Narrows* as "mark[ing] the flowering of the apologetic protest novel which had been revived," but he also considers it "the finest of Petry's three novels" (108). Sybil Weir, Margaret B. McDowell, and Vernon E. Lattin also agree that *The Narrows* is Petry's most important novel. Lattin deems it "very underrated" and calls for its being "reread and reevaluated" (72, 73). In an insightful introduction to Beacon's reprint edition, Nellie McKay considers Petry's novel "contemporary in the intricacies of its literary, philosophical, and social implications," "remarkable," and "revolutionary" (xvii).

The Narrows deserves the revaluation of Weir, McDowell, Lattin, and McKay. Reassessing fiction within its historical, cultural, and critical contexts is not necessarily a transforming act. Identifying its confluence with contemporary as well as timeless issues, however, can bring deserved attention to an undervalued text and offer it to a new audience. When such retrieval is necessary, each text brings its own challenges. For example, *The Narrows,* though different in design and concept from *The Street,* has been called a "race novel" and "apologetic protest fiction." Such labeling perhaps can be ascribed to the persistent perception of Petry as a disciple of Richard Wright, but it is a disservice to Petry's concept and her achievement in *The Narrows.*

Reassessing the novel demands approaches that are receptive to the myriad complexities and issues that Petry develops. Such readings are an "act of enlightenment," to use Mary Helen Washington's phrase, an adjusting of skewed concerns and principles, rather than a wrenching, so that Petry's work may emerge from Wright's shadow (xvii). Neither should *The Narrows* be eclipsed by Petry's achievement in either *The Street* or *Country Place* (1947), her second novel. Discovering the discrete power of an individual text is necessary before its critical well-being is merged with the author's canon. My analysis continues the dialogue already underway to reposition *The Narrows* as very significant fiction in black literary practice. It focuses on Petry's representation of three versions of womanhood in a New England segregated community. What is important is their individual philosophy for survival. The views of three contrasting women, articulated and centralized in the text through their respective courses of action, were overlooked in the haste to stamp Petry's novel according to a particularly dominant mold. Through seventy-year-old Abbie Crunch, Petry explores one response to the force of segregation and marginality. In Frances K. Jackson (called F. K.), the community undertaker, Petry explores an androgynous figure. Mamie Powther, Abbie's tenant, embodies sensuality and the thorny issue of its representation by a black woman writer. Abbie is clearly the central woman of this triad and, I would argue, the central force of the novel. The three women and the men close to them illustrate various survival philosophies in the segregated 1950s. Because Abbie's philosophy initially centers on her son Link's life and because her textual presence looms beside his, he must be an essential part of any discussion about her. Not only does he exemplify flaws in her logic but he also bridges the black and white communities in a text where that juxtaposition matters.

F. K. Jackson is the only businessperson among these women, having inherited her father's mortuary. Margaret McDowell considers her not only "the most stable and assured character in the book" but also "a tragic figure as she presides over the griefs of the black community" (136). As a funeral director, she is emotionally detached, and a precise manager. Austere black and white professional attire makes her look like the "President of the corporation" (233).

In F. K. Jackson, Petry offers a version of the female intellectual's plight during the 1950s. A gifted student, Jackson chooses not to conceal her acumen, but understands that it will deter, if not cancel, marriage. She uses her ability to operate the mortuary, thus investing her talent in her own community during a period when the dominant community would not have recognized it.

Frances's stark appearance, use of initials, lack of emotionalism, and problem-solving abilities are qualities traditionally associated with men, according to Abbie's adopted son, Link Williams. He recalls her presence in his mother's household: "She was here so often that I used to think she was my father, and you were my mother" (14). Link also takes F. K.'s male quality to another level: "Impossible to think of [F. K.] hunting a mate, handsome or otherwise. She was too brusque, too self-sufficient. Perhaps she in her own person was the dark handsome lover, and to her Abbie had been the ChinaCamiloWilliams that the male hunts for and rarely ever finds" (142). What Petry delineates here is a supportive and nurturing friendship between women, the kind that has increasingly come to be valued for its role in one's psychological health, as, for example, in the work of Toni Morrison, Paule Marshall, and Gloria Naylor. Jackson's directness and other male-perceived qualities that counter Abbie's womanly ones are developed as nothing more than that.

A middle-aged, unmarried, and successful businesswoman in the 1950s, as in the 1990s, is a target for the sexist opinion that Link offers. Contemporary readers know that models for F. K.—women who operated businesses, prospered economically, were direct and nonemotional—existed in black segregated communities. Readers are likely to embrace this portrait in fiction, recall its real-life counterparts, and dismiss Link's biased and unfounded assessment. Jackson thus allows Petry to include an important sex and gender issue, the androgynous figure: Petry also represents that figure in more extensively developed male characters Weak Knees and Bill Hod, cook and proprietor, respectively, of the Last Chance saloon in the community.

Interestingly, F. K.'s male qualities are devalued by Link Wiliams while androgynous males go unaccused. For example, the androgynous qualities of Weak Knees are conveyed through his nurturing ability and through food. His culinary skill, described through religious imagery, conveys his benevolence: "He had the dedicated look of a high priest, performing his rites, stove serves as altar, big copper hood over the stove gives it the gleam and the apartness of an altar" (83). His kitchen flooded with daylight, symbolizes his congenial nature and undercuts Abbie Crunch's opinion of his low existence. When a grief-stricken Abbie, mourning her husband, forgets Link for three months, Weak Knees feeds him in a first rite-of-adoption ceremony. The cook and Bill Hod informally adopt the young boy, and he lives with them for a few months. Nellie McKay points out that Hod's parenting, along with Abbie's, is a significant example of "multiple parenting (which further integrates Link into his community) [and] also implies an interesting critique of nontraditional versus traditional childrearing practices in most Western societies" (xii).

Petry surprises readers with Bill Hod's androgynous qualities because she first presents him from Abbie's perspective as a symbol of criminal activity in the community. Philosophically, however, Hod balances many of Abbie's non-productive ideologies when he teaches her son self-security, self-esteem, courage, and racial pride. Hod, like Weak Knees, is depicted through imagery that conveys his full humanity and complexity. For example, he moves about nude in the cool air of his bedroom, "inextricably mixed up with sunlight, and fresh, cool air" (119).

Petry's largest risk is not in creating androgynous figures. Rather, this risk may be in her delineation of Mamie Powther, a captivatingly sensuous woman. Whereas F. K. Jackson's presence is intellectual and executive, Mamie's is hedonistic. F. K.'s role compliments Abbie's while Mamie's is antagonistic. Physically placing Mamie in Abbie's home exacerbates their differences and sets up a finely wrought and enduring narrative tension. Superficial qualities identify Mamie as the outsider within the Crunch house, but her serious qualities give her security in the larger community. By juxtaposing Mamie and Abbie, Petry manages a clever criticism of black bourgeoisie ideology.

Mamie's sexuality dazzles the reader and the characters. Link likens her to the goddess Venus, but amends that to "profane goddess" (100). From Abbie's perspective, "[Mamie is] like a trumpet call sent out over the delicate nuances and shadings of stringed instruments played softly, making you jump, startled, because it didn't belong there" (25). Abbie sees her as embodying the life of the street.

One of the hazards of Mamie's sensual nature is its potential for overshadowing other dimensions of her character and for being interpreted as contributing to her powerlessness. McKay views Mamie's presence in the work as significant "in light of the negative stereotypes of this aspect of black women's lives, and the reticence of early black women writers to explore sexuality as a 'natural' part of black women's lives" (xv–xvi). For Mary Helen Washington, Mamie's presence is more problematic. She views the sexuality as objectification; Mamie is "so thoroughly framed in her husband's gaze that we know her only as he experiences her" (300). The metaphor of the framed art object with Mamie as subject always on display for the spectator offers a useful reading of Malcolm's attraction to his wife's physical qualities. In Mamie, however, using Michelle Russell's term, Petry "humaniz[es] sexuality" (131). Although Mamie's sensuosity shades most responses to her, Petry has clearly fashioned a round character, a married woman who also has a lover, but is a mother and a good cook. Mamie's personal power, her self-security, seems to derive from her easy acceptance of her sensuality. Her tastes are not dictated by other communities.[3]

Mamie's domestic contrast with Abbie is as significant as her sensual difference. Mamie's flexible attitudes toward the institutions of marriage and mothering allow her to reject marital fidelity and the strict discipline of her children. Nevertheless, she keeps her children and husband reasonably happy. She allows neither institution to oppress her. Her response to Malcolm, that she can live elsewhere if he objects to Hod's visits (she claims Hod is her cousin), confirms her liberation within the marriage. Such liberation, however, particularly in the morality of the 1950s, was as threatening as Mamie's questionable mothering practices. Her laxness, seen through Abbie's perspective of strict, traditional motherhood, might have undermined the very differences that set her apart in Petry's triad of women. That it does not is confirmation of Petry's vision for Mamie.

Washington says that Petry enables Mamie's emergence from typical female entrapment of the 1950s because nothing tragic happens to her in the end, and she sings rather than writes (302). Mamie's husband, in fact, finds her talking "more like listening to singing" (182). Indeed, Mamie's blues singing links her to the pain, disappointment, and disillusionment of The Narrows community as much as it enhances her sexuality. As Sterling Brown is reputed to have said of Ma Rainey, Mamie knows the people because she is one of them, simple and direct (65, qtd. in Duval Harrison).

Her singing, in part, may be read as her personal response to certain limitations that were part and parcel of being a black woman in the fifties. Before she met Malcolm, for example, she had tired of scrubbing steps and gone to live with a white conductor for three years. Petry addresses the issue of black women's economic dependency through both Abbie and Mamie. Part of Mamie's decision to marry Malcolm is his ability to provide for her, and understanding the significance of this quality, Malcolm enhances it as part of his courting ritual. Although Abbie has meager financial resources, she is dependent on rental income from the apartment leased to Malcolm and Mamie. The site of Mamie's blues singing—Abbie's house rather than a club—suggests its authentic origins and bridges her emotional intimacy with the black urban community. Although Mamie's songs compel Abbie's ear, Abbie dislikes blues, jazz, or boogie-woogie, all of it "a reiterated bleating about rent money and men who had gone off with other women and numbers that didn't come out" (23). Other listeners find Mamie's spontaneous and personal blues indistinguishable from spirituals.

Hazel Carby views women blues singers in fictional narrative as having been "mythologized"; such "mythologies become texts about sexuality. . . . Women blues singers frequently appear as liminal figures that play out and explore the various possibilities of a sexual existence. They are representations of women who attempt to manipulate and control their construction as sexual subjects" (749). Mamie's characterization is inconsistent with Carby's assessment. She makes no attempt to control men's perceptions of her, but, as Malcolm notes, boldly returns their gaze, measuring them as they do her.

Rather than the straitlaced, uptight, and repressive black bourgeoisie figure (recall George Schulyer's representation of middle-class black life in the "The Negro Art-Hokum"), Petry offers Mamie as a complete woman who is sexually assertive. In so doing, she reclaims and recenters sexuality from its marginalized space in the blues clubs. As important, by juxtaposing Mamie and Abbie,

Petry questions certain fixed tenets of the black bourgeoisie. Abbie represents the most repressive elements of this tradition—its rejection of women's sexuality, abhorrence and abrupt dismissal of a black economic and social underclass, preference for silence on the subject of slavery, and an aversion for black music traditions.[4]

Music, fundamental to African American cultural expression, finds no expression in Abbie. Sybil Weir makes an intriguing comparison between Abbie's facility with words and her propensity to make jingles. "[Her] gift has its roots in the rhythmic and linguistic inventiveness of black oral expression . . . yet for Abbie this oral heritage must also serve as a way to control her environment." Mamie sings, but Abbie "expresses her heritage through the structure of white nursery rhymes" (87). Petry capitalizes on this irony, having placed Abbie in close contact with her verbal heritage when she once taught children of the Gullahs before her marriage. It was the "first time [she] knew that black people could be beautiful, the fathers and mothers and the children" (251). Abby obviously has lost this valuable insight.

In the triad of women at the narrative center of *The Narrows,* Abbie Crunch dominates. Her entry and exit frame the text. Her character and its convergence with other significant characters and situations supersede the interracial romance between Link and the socialite Camilo Treadwell that early critics determined to be the narrative focus.[5] As a representative of black middle-class ideology of the 1950s, her philosophy and behavior are central to the rhythm of The Narrows community. Carby might have been recalling Abbie as she wrote about the "duty of a black heroine toward the black community [being] coterminous with her desire as a woman, a desire which was expressed as a dedication to uplift the race. This displacement from female desire to female duty enabled the negotiation of racist constructions of black female sexuality but denied sensuality and in this denial lies the class character of its cultural politics" (749).

Petry's purpose in contrasting Abbie and Mamie might well have been not only a studied disruption of these constructions but also an exposé of their divisiveness. Mamie's sensuality is given approval, even respectability, because her husband wants that quality and silently acquiesces to her infidelity to keep her. Sensuality does not make her a victim. However, Abbie's sense of duty for the race's uplifting fares less easily. Whereas Mamie's siren quality is disparaged only by Abbie, Abbie's sense of her "duty," which includes absolving the race of behavior perceived as distasteful to whites, places an intolerable burden on her young son's shoulders. She transfers the concept of racial uplift, envisioning the Race as perpetually in need of elevation and believing that each person hefts the burden, to Link. Physical appearance and class consciousness are part of the elevation process.

Racial uplift, a self-imposed task undertaken by educated middle-class blacks, was not without its drawbacks. Born of the frustration of segregation and marginality, the collective and individualistic effort was characterized by indirection concerning *exactly how* education, behavior, employment, and values would translate into changed attitudes from the majority culture. The uplift philosophy, nevertheless, was part of one's cultural inheritance until its necessity was displaced by the civil rights movement and its ethnological adjunct. Overzealous about the obligations of her inheritance, Abbie passes it on to her son. Its consequences on a young psyche are what Petry scrutinizes. For Link, the weight of the responsibility was crippling. What or who was served by it? This is one question Petry seems to ask. Young Link's fear of Abbie's disapproval of him—because Link thinks he is a disappointment to the responsibility—silences him about hurtful, racist incidents at school. His responses—lying, withdrawal, and diminished self-worth—if unattended, are utterly destructive. That the "race" is not improved by these consequences is what Petry points out through his representation. Who is well served by Abbie's uplift efforts?

In this scrutiny, Petry singles out Abbie's attitudes about race and survival for interrogation. In her middle-class correctness Abbie lives in a narrow enclosure that disallows qualities such as Mamie's sensuosity. For example, she believes racist nonsense that "colored people's houses always smell of food, ham and fried chicken and greasy greens. Sometimes I think they're all stomach and no mind," she tells young Link (124). Although a teacher before retirement, her refusal to use the word *slavery* or to conceive of a "black" historian verify her considerable knowledge deficit. Teaching Link that "the Race [has] to be cleaner, smarter, thriftier, [and] more ambitious than white people, so that white people [will] like colored people" ignores a history of racism and bigotry and places the burden on the innocent (138). Even at age seventy, Abbie seems almost as ignorant of ethnic realities as she was twenty years earlier when she was raising Link. She wonders about young men: "Something had brutalized them. But what?" (3). Through Abbie's uncritical convictions, Petry offers strong criticism of black middle-class racial ideology. Abbie's beliefs, fostered like those of any parent onto her son, unwittingly makes her a participant in his damaged spirit. Her ideology proves inadequate for her son's negotiation through a racist 1950s environment.

Petry not only situates Abbie's wrongheaded attitudes and self-defeating philosophy as poles of both the text and the community, but she also sets contrasting ideologies to resonate against them. Although Abbie's backwardness about African American history has not overly impaired her survival, it threatens her son. The contrasts to Abbie—Weak Knees and Bill Hod—offer sensitivity to a developing black ego. They tell Link that "black [is] bestlooking" (145). Through their use of exemplum and mother wit, they make him feel safe and unashamed of his black color. Their success is perhaps measurable by Link's decision to major in history and his plan to write a book about black history.

Petry complicates Abbie's position by affirming that many of her traditionally held, middle-class values still continue to enrich human life and relations. However, Abbie's preference for self-distancing from her community's social undesirables is shown to be flawed reasoning. For example, she never knows the positive influence that Hod has had on her son. She never appreciates Hod's demand that she call a physician for her husband, whose stroke characteristics she mistakes for drunkenness. Nevertheless, Abbie is responsible, loves fiercely, has integrity, and insists on order and ritual. From her son's adult perspective, she is "indestructible and wonderful," "impossible to live with, impossible to please, starchy, prideful, full of fears" (318). Her morality is impeachable. When she equates human worth with wealth and class, however, it makes her intolerant. This rigidity blinds her judgments about people, but her complexity makes her quite human and believable. She is an intriguing center in The Narrows community.

Unlike Abbie Crunch, Mamie Powther makes no claim to such cherished values. "Live and let live" is a motto that allows her to embrace living with a casualness and energy alien to Abbie (209): "There is things about white people that I will never understand. And . . . I don't intend to try. I am a hell of a lot more comfortable and it gives me a lot more honest-to-God pleasure just to write 'em all down as bastards and leave 'em strictly alone" (208–9). Mamie's substantive difference from Abbie is the difference between the laissez-faire attitude of the economic underclass and black bourgeoisie objectives. Mamie's choices are not dictated by imitation. Representative of two groups in the 1950s black community, the women's differences extend even to their physical image.

Unlike Mamie, who chooses her clothing to enhance her full-busted figure, and shows her bare legs, Abbie's image is that of the New England aristocrat, a connection affirmed by other characters and Abbie's behavior, but not her finances. Her straight back and head are like Camilo Treadwell's, according to Link, a comparison that designedly aligns Abbie with the physical bearing of the city's wealthiest white family. In her sealskin cape, restored from a handed-down coat, she still looks like a "duchess" (233). She assumes an imperial air during encounters with service people like vendors. Her home, a finely maintained, large brick house, also has an "air of aristocracy" (6).

Abbie Crunch continues a particular tradition in black fiction. She exemplifies a middle-class ideology espoused in works that include Frances Harper's *Iola Leroy* (1892), Jessie Fauset's *Plum Bun* (1929), Nella Larsen's *Passing* (1929), the aspirations of Lutie Johnson in *The Street,* and Paule Marshall's *Praisesong for the Widow* (1983). Crunch is an intriguing antecedent to such characters as Lourinda Huggs, the misdirected grandmother and domestic worker who naïvely apes the ideology and snobbery of wealthy whites in Kristin Hunter's *God Bless the Child* (1964), to Jerome Johnson in Paule Marshall's *Praisesong for the Widow,* who regresses to accepting black stereotypes, and to the ideology that infuses Macon Dead Sr.'s family in Toni Morrison's *Song of Solomon* (1977).

Abbie's acceptance of representative symbols from the dominant community proves unreliable. She trusts Malcolm Powther's appearance and bearing. As a career butler for wealthy whites, he has adopted their demeanor and tastes, including one employer's taste in women. He chooses to rent Abbie's vacant apartment because her well-kept house mirrors his partiality. Nevertheless, when Abbie finds the daughter of Powther's employees, Camilo Treadwell Sheffield, in her son's bed, she literally tosses her on the street, believing the woman is a whore. Acting furiously at the violation of her values, Abbie never realizes the problem in equating economic class with moral standards.

Petry derails and critiques several assumptions that existed about the majority culture during segregation. Principally through the Treadwell family's behavior toward, and killing of Link, she exposes the flaws in Abbie's tendency to equate wealth with civility. But primarily thorough Malcolm Powther's intimacy with them as their butler, she reveals their artificiality. Interestingly, this is achieved through using theater imagery to describe the Treadwell's dining preparation. Malcolm arranges the visual aesthetics as the director of stage lighting enhances the performance arena: "Now the food it is important, yes. But the dining room is . . . the stage" (198). Malcolm's contrived atmosphere contrasts sharply with descriptions of his own joyous responses to Mamie's food and to her preparation of it. Even in Abbie's more formal household, nothing artificial characterizes meals. The pretense of the Treadwells' dining, emblematic of other areas of their lives, is significant. Abbie has ordered her life and Link's to emulate a nonexistent ideal. Perhaps the most ironic illustration of her mistake is her conclusion that Camilo is a prostitute. Abbie's high regard for Malcolm is equally displaced, since he fingers Link for the avenging Treadwells.

Throughout the narrative, Abbie's presence and philosophy dominate. Even during the shift to Link's affair with Camilo and to Mamie and her family, Abbie's values are kept visible. Link (as the name conveys) is the literal connection between the Treadwell *ideal* and Abbie's self-modeling and philosophy. In daily contact with the Treadwell wealth and as an imitator of their mannerisms, Malcolm is a secondary bond. What Petry focuses on through Abbie's character is self-imaging after the nonexistent ideal and rejecting distinct cultural characteristics of one's community. Frances Jackson's executive comportment and intellectual prowess are pleasing to Abbie because to her they imitate the dominant culture. Similarly, her intolerance of blues and jazz, of the folk stories that her husband once narrated about his relatives, of Bill Hod's suspected qualities, and of Mamie's sensual qualities can be attributed to their difference from Abbie's idealized notion of living and conducting oneself.

F. K. Jackson, Mamie Powther, and Abbie Crunch, though different options in their community, are all survivors. F. K.'s ability to confront facts and remain emotionally detached is her deliverance. Mamie's nonpretension and singing are most probably her salvation. Abbie's self-assumed social superiority is less comforting than Mamie's elemental simplicity, but her basic values have proven essential to the harmony of the human community. Although Petry's delineation of Abbie is critical to her scrutiny of black middle-class ideology, Abbie's portrait is neither harsh nor hopeless. Having lived twenty years through self-inflicted guilt in her husband's death is strong evidence that she will survive Link's violent death as well. The last scene shows Abbie with Mamie's youngest son in hand going to offer assistance to Camilo Treadwell Sheffield, whose life might be endangered. This scene suggests Abbie as a symbol of endurance and survival in whom many lessons for the community and its youth are still vested.

Petry's decision to give the same name to both the novel and the community communicates that neighborhood and spatial concept are significant to the work.[6] Like Chicago's South Side or Manhattan's Harlem or Los Angeles' Watts, (the fictional) Monmouth, Connecticut, has its Narrows, a geographic entity where, when black people moved in, other racial groups moved out. Therefore, The Narrows is in deteriorative transition. The confinement or limitation inferred in its name, however, is merely spatial reality and not descriptive of the reality of people's experiences. Petry's well-drawn characters and philosophical matters shift and divert one's angle of concentration to create a densely textured narrative structured by concentricity and juxtaposition rather than linearity. Lives are complicated, intricate affairs, and the community is vital. Anchored in the community, the narrative engages issues that remain unresolved more than forty years after the novel's publication.

Among those issues, class as an index to one's economic status and human value proves problematic. Petry explores this concept thoroughly and successfully but, apparently for initial reviewers, so subtly that they disregarded Abbie's relation to the full narrative.[7] What are the costs of striving for social and domestic perfection, of diehard efforts to "uplift the race"? Petry asks through Abbie. How is that kind of person an asset or liability in the black community? What is the impact of race in the black community? The parallel issue is the community of the Other. During segregation, how absolute were the divisions between the two groups. What kinds of distortions existed between them? How damaging on both sides were the stereotypes? How might interracial love exist? Petry's exploration of these issues, among others, remains timely and pertinent. She examines hollow values, sham, and pretense. She depicts the assassination of black male images and the defamation of black community through the media. She scrutinizes ignorance about a race's history. She illustrates that prejudice supplants love in a disastrous interracial romance. She characterizes black males with androgynous qualities, one of whom becomes a surrogate father. She exposes the amorphous nature of labels: people seldom fit roundly or squarely in them. She concludes the story of a boy's growth to manhood, thus structuring a mini-Bildungsroman. She shows that a swinging door existed between the black and white communities and there was easy passage through it, going both ways.

In the issues raised and stories told, Petry's community is balanced by heterogeneous characters. Her narrative is lively, meticulously developed, and marked by its deftly handled, large cast of people. Complex issues are handled with evenhandedness and without didacticism. Petry's work deserves inclusion as vital fiction of the first order in the tradition of African American literature. Like *The Street*, *The Narrows* merits critical readings that will confirm its independent superiority. It is headed for a new audience whose regard for it will overwhelm its earliest critical reception. This different audience will create no conundrum for someone to solve, for they will not rush imprudently to judge any woman writer by any man's literary shadow.

NOTES

1. Until recent years, *The Street* has been analyzed as a compelling example of naturalistic fiction. Wright Morris and other initial reviewers appraised it and Petry from the recesses of Richard Wright's *Native Son*, and thus established a secondary role for the book and its author. As late as 1974, Arthur P. Davis echoed earlier assessments when he called *The Street* "hard-hitting social commentary [like that] which characterized the Richard Wright school of naturalistic protest writing" and reaffirmed its secondary status (qtd. in Bloom 5: 3084, 3087). Only recently have revisionist scholars begun disengaging *The Street* from its bruising embrace with *Native Son*. Mary Helen Washington, for example, has called attention to the subversive nature of environmental determinism because it "diminishes the effectiveness of all human energy, threatens to marginalize and repress women in particular, [and hides] an ideology that is mainly concerned with men." See Washington 298. Bell, among others, acknowledges that Petry "moves beyond the naturalistic vision of Wright and Himes in her realistic delineation of cultural myths, especially those of the American Dream" (105–6, 105–15). Yarborough is among those who read the confluence of race, gender, and class as major determinants of Lutie Johnson's oppression (33–59).
2. See Mary Helen Washington's discussion of Gwendolyn Brooks's *Maud Martha* (1953), xvi–xcii. Also, it is worthwhile to note that Ralph Ellison's *Invisible Man* (1952) eclipsed publications by black women as well as by black male writers.
3. Mamie predates several of her sensuous literary sisters. Paule Marshall's Suggie in *Brown Girl, Brownstones* (1959), Ursa in Gayl Jones's *Corregidora* (1975), and Alice Walker's Shug Avery in *The Color Purple* (1983).
4. See also E. Franklin Frazier, *Black Bourgeoisie: The Rise of the New Middle Class in the United States* (1957; New York: Collier, 1962).
5. The attraction of an interracial liaison might be understood for initial 1950s readers of *The Narrows*, but as late as 1988, the blurb highlights the romance as the narrative focus. The jacket blurb invites consideration of Gerald Graff's question: "What is the relation of this self-interpreting packaging 'to the work itself'?" He believes that these summations might at least be useful as a means of "foreground-

ing questions about how much a text is culturally processed and appropriated." (See Graff 6, 8.)

6. Melvin Dixon argues that "images of place and performance, landscape and identity in texts by several black women writers may well overturn the aesthetic primacy of the subterranean worlds depicted by Wright, Ellison, and LeRoi Jones" (83). Although Dixon does not include Petry among the women writers in his study, the connection between character, community, and identity is an essential one in *The Narrows.*

7. Although Petry's narrative engages serious issues, it is not without humor. See, in particular, the sections depicting Frances K. Jackson's household assistants—Miss Doris and her husband, Sugar—and the funeral of Deacon Hubborn Lord, pages 223–32.

WORKS CITED

Bell, Bernard W. "Ann Petry's Demythologizing of American Culture and Afro-American Character." *Conjuring: Black Women, Fiction, and Literary Tradition.* Ed. Marjorie Pryse and Hortense Spillers. Bloomington: U of Indiana P, 1985. 105–15.

Bloom, Harold, et al., eds. *Twentieth-Century American Literature.* New York: Chelsea House, 1985. Vol. 5 of *The Chelsea House Library of Literary Criticism.* 7 vols. 3083–89.

Brooks, Gwendolyn. *Maud Martha.* 1953. *Blacks.* Chicago: David, 1987.

Carby, Hazel. "It Jus Be's Dat Way Sometime." *Feminisms: An Anthology of Literary Theory and Criticism.* Ed. Robyn R. Warhol and Diane Price Herndl. New Brunswick, NJ: Rutgers UP, 1991. 746–58.

Dixon, Melvin. *Ride Out the Wilderness.* Urbana: U of Illinois P, 1987.

Duval, Daphne Harrison. "Black Women in the Blues Tradition." *The Afro-American Woman: Struggles and Images.* Ed. Sharon Harley and Rosalyn Terborg-Penn. New York: Kennikat, 1978. 58–73.

Frazier, E. Franklin. *Black Bourgeoisie: The Rise of the New Middle Class in the United States.* 1957. New York: Collier, 1962.

Graff, Gerald. "Narrative and the Unofficial Interpretive Culture." *Reading Narrative: Form, Ethics, Ideology.* Ed. James Phelan. Columbus: Ohio State UP, 1989.

Hunter, Kristin. *God Bless the Child.* 1964. Washington, DC: Howard UP, 1966.

Lattin, Vernon E. "Ann Petry and the American Dream." *Black American Literary Forum* 12.2 (Summer 1978): 69–72.

Marshall, Paule. *Praisesong for the Widow.* New York: Putnam's, 1983.

McDowell, Margaret C. "*The Narrows:* A Fuller View of Ann Petry." *Black American Literature Forum* 14.4 (Winter 1980): 135–41.

McKay, Nellie. Introduction. *The Narrows.* By Ann Petry. Boston: Beacon, 1988. vii–xx.

Morrison, Toni. *Sula.* New York: New American Library, 1973.

Naylor, Gloria. *The Women of Brewster Place.* New York: Penguin, 1983.

Petry, Ann. *Country Place.* 1947. New York: Chatham Bookseller, 1971.

———. *The Narrows.* 1953. Boston: Beacon, 1988.

———. *The Street.* 1946. Boston: Beacon, 1985.

Russell, Michele. "Slave Codes and Linear Notes." *But Some of Us Are Brave.* Ed. Gloria Hull, Patricia Bell Scott, and Barbara Smith. New York: Feminist P, 1982. 129–40.

Schraufnagel, Noel. *From Apology to Protest: The Black American Novel.* DeLand, FL: Everett Edwards, 1973.

Schuyler, George S. "The Negro Art-Hokum." *Within the Circle: Literary Criticism from the Harlem Renaissance to the Present.* Ed. Angelyn Mitchell. 1926. Durham, NC: Duke UP, 1994. 51–54.

Washington, Mary Helen, ed. *Invented Lives: Narratives of Black Women 1860–1960.* Garden City, NY: Anchor, 1987.

Weir, Sybil. "*The Narrows:* A Black New England Novel." *Studies in American Fiction* 15 (Spring 1987): 81–93.

Yarborough, Richard. "The Quest for the American Dream in Three Afro-American Novels: *If He Hollers Let Him Go, The Street,* and *Invisible Man.*" *MELUS* 8.4 (Winter 1981): 33–59.

The Unmasking of Virginia Brindis de Salas: Minority Discourse of Afro-Uruguay

CAROLL MILLS YOUNG

Virginia Brindis de Salas is the leading black woman poet of Uruguay and is considered to be the most militant among Afro-Uruguayan writers. According to Richard Jackson, her poetry comes closer to "shaking the famous black fist" (*Black Writers* 108) than that of her contemporaries, Pilar Barrios, Juan Julio Arrascaeta, and Carlos Cardoso Ferreira. Unfortunately, little about her life is known, even her date of birth has been recorded as both 1908 and 1920. Janheinz Jahn in *Schwarzer Orpheus* (1954) writes that Brindis de Salas was born in Montevideo in 1920 to José Brindis de Salas. At present, the only available date of death is 1958.

Other than Pilar Barrios (1889–1974), Virginia Brindis de Salas is only the second black Uruguayan writer of the 1940s whose work appears in book form. She published two volumes of poetry *Pregón de Marimorena* (*The Call of Mary Morena*) in 1946 and *Cien cárceles de amor* (*One Hundred Prisons of Love*) in 1949. In *Cien cárceles de amor* the editor notes that a third volume of poetry, *Cantos de lejanía* (*Songs from Faraway*), is forthcoming; nonetheless, to date the collection has not been published.

In *Pregón de Marimorena* and *Cien cárceles de amor* Brindis de Salas poetically evokes the social and cultural reality of Afro-Uruguay. Both volumes of poetry are testimonies to the oppression of her people. Although the compositions in both volumes differ widely in style, they thematically connect and reflect upon the collective experiences of Afro-Uruguay past and present. Each poem communicates a message and becomes a vehicle to excite social change. For that reason, it is the poet's mission to use a personal approach in order to involve everyone in the struggle for racial and social equality. Therefore, for Afro-Uruguayans, the poems in *Pregón de Marimorena* and *Cien cárceles de amor* represent their daily struggles to exist, the racism, the social inequities in society, the customs, the music and dance of the black Uruguayan community. This personal identification, especially with the protagonist, Marimorena, and the vivid pictures of the harsh reality that emerges from each composition are designed to awaken the spirit of every Afro-Uruguayan to change internally and to work toward external change in their society and community. For the oppressor, the poet's goal is to produce intense emotions of guilt and shame as she reports the cruel reality of Afro-Uruguay. Overall, both *Pregón de Marimorena* and *Cien cárceles de amor* represent the voice of Afro-Uruguay, a silent minority, blameless for their oppression and the socioeconomic conditions in which they live. And finally, each volume is dedicated to social change in Uruguay and exemplifies the poet's crusade for solidarity, equality, and dignity.

In sum, the literary discourse of Virginia Brindis de Salas paints the social reality of Afro-Uruguay. Unlike her white contemporaries, Delmira Agustini, Alfonsina Storni, Juana Ibarbourou, and Gabriela Mistral, Brindis de Salas did not limit herself to themes of physical love and the relationships between men and women; neither did she write of maternal love nor the problems of being a woman in Uruguayan society. We see, for the first time, what it is like to be both black and a woman in Uruguay.

Nonetheless, Brindis de Salas suffered the consequences of her forcefulness and her resistance. Her radical means to reflect the negative conditions of Afro-Uruguay often alienated her from her black colleagues who wanted to impress upon the dominant culture the intellectual genius of the black Uruguayan community. The content of her work represents a defiant discourse that illustrates the thematic emphasis of racial pride and the strength to struggle for the political, social, and economic freedom of blacks everywhere.

Pregón de Marimorena and *Cien cárceles de amor* represent both the intellectual fervor of Brindis de Salas and the cultural reality of Afro-Uruguay. In the prologue to *Pregón de Marimorena,* Julio Guadalupe, a Uruguayan poet and contemporary of Brindis de Salas, lists her among the best women poets of the River Plate area:

> Virginia Brindis de Salas, primera y única poeta negra—hasta el presente—que con esta obra sale de anonimato, es además la primera poetisa del Río de la Plata que al igual que Selva Márquez, supo aislarse—en toda la trayectoria de su libro inicial—de lo ñoño sentimental en que fueron pródigas la mayoría de las poetas americanas o que bien siguieron los pasos del romanticismo íntimo de Delmira Agustini, Eugenia Vaz Ferreyra y Alfonsina Storni. (8–9)

> (Virginia Brindis de Salas, first and only black Uruguayan woman poet, quiet and shy, unlike the majority of American women poets who lavish in popularity, has remained virtually anonymous, until the publication of this, her first book. She, like Selva Márquez, merits the same acclaim as that of Delmira Agustini, Eugenia Vaz Ferreyra, and Alfonsina Storni. [All translations from Spanish to English are my own.])

In brief, Brindis de Salas's tough-minded interpretation of Afro-Uruguay, her love for her people, her originality, her sincerity, her irony, her refusal to be a slave to traditional poetics, and her cynicism are several of the distinctive characteristics in her poetry that rank her among the best poets in the Southern Cone.

Although both volumes of poetry are important cultural documents, *Pregón de Marimorena* represents the poet's innovative attempt to reflect the social reality of Afro-Uruguay. The collection is divided into four parts: *baladas* (ballads), *pregones* (street calls or shouts), *tangos* (tangos), and *cantos* (songs). Each section of poetry is representative of a different aspect of Afro-Uruguayan culture. The themes in *Pregón de Marimorena* focus primarily on racial discrimination, supremacy of the dominant culture, black pride, Africa, and the poverty and oppression of Afro-Uruguay. Her poetic style is reflective of the folkloric traditions and oral culture of Afro-Uruguay. It is a poetry without elaborate metaphors and images, and the tone of her work ranges from anger to joy. As poet, she frees herself from the bonds of dominant discourse by taking "the shout" of the street vendor, Marimorena, her struggle, her song, and her joy, molding them into free verse.

Moreover, Brindis de Salas chooses for her stage the slums of Afro-Uruguay and poetically magnifies their deplorable condition. Her leading characters are the poor and the oppressed, and in their defense, she launches attacks at those who ignore and reject them. In contrast, she praises those, like Marimorena, who manage to overcome the tremendous conditions of misery, poverty, hunger, and prejudice. The song "Aleluya" (Hallelujah) best describes her mission as defender and "speaker" for the poor:

> ¡Aleluya!
> Son muchos
> los que van a trabajar
> Y muchos son también
> los que apenas comen
> y quisieran cantar.
> ¡Aleluya!
> Piernas
> para caminar yo tengo
> que no se detendrán
> Yo voy y vengo
> sin cesar. (58)
>
> (Hallelujah!
> there are many

who work
and many who
barely eat
who would like to sing.
Hallelujah!
Legs
I have to walk,
they won't stop,
I endlessly
go and come.)

In these lines, Virginia Brindis de Salas describes her own personal battle against the oppressor and her struggle for better living conditions for the poor of Afro-Uruguay. In turn, she defends her choice to struggle for equal rights in the ballad, "Es verdad, sí señor" (It's True, Sir, It's True):

Hay quién vive para comer
y quién come para vivir;
quién ve para creer
y quién lucha para sufrir. (20)

(There is he who loves to eat
and he who eats to live
he who sees to believe
and he who fights to suffer.)

The closing lines of the poem reveal her alliance with other black writers in the Southern Cone, the Caribbean, and the United States who have chosen to fight for and to represent the oppressed:

¿Qué yo soñé en los caminos
con Antonio y Federico
y Nicolás del Caribe
y Palés de Puerto Rico?
Es verdad, sí señor:
sí señor, es verdad. (20)

(Did I dream that I walked
with Antonio and Federico,
with Nicolás from the Caribbean,
and Palés from Puerto Rico?

It's true sir,
Yes, sir, it's true.)

Similarly, the poem "La hora de la tierra en que tú duermes" (The Hour on Earth in which You Sleep) is a call for everyone, black and white, to take off their blindfolds and join in the struggle against racial injustice:

> La hora ciega a los otros
> que viven del otro lado.
> Amigo, quítate la venda
> quítate la venda
> que a ti te ciega en este,
> quítate la venda. (21)

> (The hour blinds those
> who live on the other side.
> My friend, take off your
> blindfold.
> take it off,
> you can't see,
> take it off.)

And:

> Es hora de dejar libres
> pasiones y ocios mentales.
> Amigo bulle mi sangre
> mientras la tuya se estanca;
> quítate la venda, quítate. (21)

> (It's time to free yourself from
> your passions and mental slavery
> my friend, my blood boils
> while yours stagnates;
> take off your blindfold,
> take it off.)

In the poet's unwavering struggle to bring to light the social ills of Afro-Uruguay, the poems of *Pregón de Marimorena* became her weapon to correct them. For this reason, each poem conveys a powerful message to the ruling majority. Brindis de Salas begins her battle by depicting in her "baladas" the poverty and misery of children living in the slum areas of the black Uruguayan community. The ballad "Prez para los niños sin canto" (Prayer for the Child without a Song) illustrates their living conditions:

> Se semejan a esos patios
> de las viejas casonas
> el piso blanco y negro
> que así visten austeros
> los más amplios mosaicos.
>
> Allí están mis niños,
> ellos son los más pobres.
>
> En ese patio inmundo
> todo destartalado
> no hay hamacas, ni muñecos. . . . (25)
>
> (They look like those patios
> of the old big houses,
> black and white floors,
> thus austerely dressed
> the biggest mosaics.
> There are my children
> the poorest ones
> living in that filthy
> dilapidated patio,
> no hammocks, no dolls. . . .)

The poet continues to describe the unrelenting despair of poverty in the ballad "El cerro" (The Hillside):

> Pared y techo de adobe
> que tirita en los andrajos;
> ¿truhán que la vida robe?
> Señor en los barrios bajos. (28)
>
> (Adobe wall and roof
> that shake in this wretched mess;
> Who is the thief that
> robs these lives?
> Lord, in the slums.)

And:

> Domingo de la miseria
> abren niñas de los ojos
> y sangre dan arterias
> torne si o no al despojo.
> Tumulto de muchas cosas
> y habitación miserable
> donde la vida reposa
> en la vida deleznable. (28)

> (Sunday's misery
> the little girls open
> their eyes,
> Their arteries give blood
> but who knows if they
> are alive or not.
> Fragile lives,
> that sleep in this shabby
> room.)

In short, both ballads realistically describe the slum areas of Afro-Uruguay, where children have barely enough to eat, yet they serve as strong messages to an unjust society which victimizes innocent children by allowing them to live and to suffer in such deplorable conditions.

One of the cruel ironies of life is that those who labor so hard in physical toil are left with so little. The ballad "El pan legendario" (Legendary Bread) is reminiscent of the biblical "bread of presence," or showbread, where a group of twelve loaves of bread were kept on the table in the Holy Tent to remind the people of Israel that they were always in God's presence. Similarly, Brindis de Salas's ballad serves to remind the poor of Uruguay that they, like the people of Israel, are a chosen people and they will always be in God's presence. She praises the poor for their strength of character and indicts the lords of the land for stealing their labor. She emphasizes that without the sweat of the brow of the hardworking poor and black, there would be no bread of presence to eat:

> Provienes de la espiga
> que nace en tierra firme
> de una hermosa semilla
> que plantó el hombre humilde. (23)

(You spring forth from
the cornspike that is born
from the strong land
from a beautiful seed
that the humble black man
planted.)

Another concern of Brindis de Salas is the idea that a Christian God must be white. She rebelliously challenges this externally imposed image in her ballad "Cristo negro" (Black Christ) by portraying Christ as a black man:

Metralla contra metralla
<<que amor con amor se paga>>.
¿Un camello? Ojo por ojo;
¿A qué parábolas del cielo?

Cristo negro manoseado
por la audacia y por la fuerza,
dejarás tu mansedumbre
de cordero y tu vergüenza. (27)

(Gunshot against gunshot
"Love is repaid with love"
A wagon full of bullets?
An eye for an eye.
To what parables from
heaven do these belong?

Black Christ,
Abused by audacity and power
You will bequeath your
meekness and your shame.)

This shocking image of a black Christ shows the poet's rejection of the religious hegemony of the majority culture. For Brindis de Salas, the black Christ typifies the bloodshed and suffering of Afro-Uruguay.

Symbolically, the shocking image of a black Christ in a dominant white society is representative of the bloodshed and suffering of Uruguay's black citizens:

Sangre y llaga mucho enseñan.
Mejor amo es la Justicia

que las lágrimas del valle
del esclavo venerable. (27)

(Bloodshed and bruises,
teach a lot
a better teacher is Justice,
than a valley full of tears,
cried by the venerable slave.)

Above all, she concludes, justice is better than the abusive treatment of black men and women.

In the poet's continued attempt to change the social ills of Uruguay and to draw more attention to the day-to-day struggles of the poor, she captures the cry or call of the black street vendor, the *pregón*, and brings this poetic form to the reader's attention. The pregón is an example of one of the oldest oral art forms in Uruguay that originated during slavery. During the colonial period, black men and women were used to do domestic tasks that were most often burdensome and unpleasant. After these tasks were completed, the slaves were required to go through the streets and sell their wares for their masters. It was very common to see black women who were especially skilled in making candy, *empanadas* (meat pies), or cakes selling their goods in the street. From sunup to sundown the public announcements or the calls of the black street vendors filled the air with their rhythmic and melodious sounds (*Pregones* 31). According to Rubén Carámbula, those black town criers who sold their wares through the streets of colonial Montevideo were characterized and recognized by their typical songs, often a kind of short melody, with an initial syllable in the middle or the end of the pregón sustained (*Negro y tambor* 199).

In the second division of *Pregón de Marimorena* there are three pregones in which the reader accompanies Marimorena, the central figure of each pregón, on her daily journey to sell the local newspaper. In this section, Brindis de Salas connects the past to the present by emphasizing the pregón as an art form, and the pregón becomes symbolic of the figurative enslavement of the poor in black Uruguay. Marimorena, although free, is still enslaved by society. In each pregón the reader relives the daily experiences of Marimorena as she struggles to exist. The first pregón is suggestive of the pain and sacrifice of Marimorena's day-to-day survival:

Tu voz,
que nunca arrulló
a tus hijos
ni a tus nietos
y es voz de paria

arrulla mimosamente
toda la prensa diaria. (34)

(Your voice
that never lulled
your children
nor your grandchildren
to sleep.
It's the voice of a
lowly woman
that lulls sweetly the
call of the daily paper.)

Marimorena earns only a few pennies daily from peddling papers from sunrise to sundown. Yet her long hours of labor are unappreciated by those whose papers she sells:

Cuánto te deben
Marimorena
esos que escriben
y que tú pagas
con tus vintenes,
con tus pregones,
por la mañana
y por la tarde
miles de veces. (35)

(How much do they owe you,
Marimorena,
for the papers they write,
the ones you pay for
with your hard work,
and your shouts,
in the mornings,
in the afternoons,
a thousand times.)

Unaware of the political propaganda, the egotism of the newspaper owners and the ideologies they advocate, Marimorena, illiterate and unconcerned, struggles to sell their papers to feed her family. For this purpose, Marimorena endures the burdens of her job.

In the second pregón, Brindis de Salas sheds light on the working conditions that Marimorena must tolerate:

> No hay sol que te arredre nunca,
> ni lluvia que te aglutine.
> y si se empapa tu nuca
> o chapotean tus botines,
> vas adelante y pregonando
> como heraldo en los mitines
> y es un concierto tu anuncio
> de todos los diarios juntos. (37)

> (There's no sun that
> frightens you,
> nor rain that weakens
> you.
> If your clothes are soaked,
> you keep peddling papers,
> like an herald angel.
> Your shouts of the daily
> newspapers form a
> harmonious chorus.)

As Brindis de Salas closes the pregón, she attacks those who become wealthy from the painful labor of Marimorena, who barely earns enough to buy bread:

> Oigan políticos,
> periodistas,
> que aquí hacen gordas sus vistas;
> pues miren como ha vivido
> Marimorena
> señores tan egoístas,
> que nada nunca les ha pedido. (38)

> (Listen! Politicians,
> Journalists,
> those who pretend not
> to see her,
> look at how she lives,
> Marimorena,
> You selfish men,

she has never asked
you for anything.)

The final pregón calls attention to all the men and women, like Marimorena, who earn a living selling papers on the streets of Uruguay:

Cuantos hombres
que cargan y descargan
Sudados
y sucios de tinta
entre perniciosos vahos. (39)

(So many men who load and
unload papers,
Sweaty and ink-soiled,
among the harmful fumes.)

In sum, the final pregón serves as a tribute to all those who are the foundation of the Uruguayan economy and whose cries of suffering and pain are daily reminders of their struggle to survive. And finally, Brindis de Salas ends her last pregón with praise of Marimorena:

Y Mari Marimorena
que Mari mezcla de sol,
    ¡y luna llena!
Y Mari Marimorena;
que Mari de triste voz
    ay que pena!
Y Mari Marimorena
qué Mari que no logró
aún su cena! (42)

(Marimorena,
Mari, a blend of sun
    and full moon!
Marimorena,
Mari, your sad voice
    Ah! What a shame!
Mari, Marimorena
    You haven't even
earned enough for your
supper yet!)

Like many of the black Uruguayan writers, Virginia Brindis de Salas looked back to her African roots for a sense of identity and personal liberation from the dominant society. This sense of freedom and identity is illustrated in her use of the *tango* as a poetic form. It is a rhythmic composition that is symbolic of the dance, the tango, originally created and choreographed by African slaves. According to Nestor Ortíz Oderigo, the word *tango* is a genuine Africanism that is a corruption of the name Shango, god of thunder and of storms in the mythology of the Yorubas from Nigeria in West Africa (Lewis 21).

Usually, ritualistic dances and songs would accompany the evocation of such gods. When transferred to the New World setting, these dances and songs would take the same name as the secret society. Thus, the present-day tango and the present-day *candombe* are derivatives of ritualistic dances of slaves who were transported to Brazil and the River Plate area (Carámbula 177). To illustrate this Afro-Uruguayan tradition, Brindis de Salas includes three tangos in *Pregón de Marimorena*. She captures the fast moving rhythmic pace of the dancers, singers, and their musical instruments in the tango below:

> (Danza
> que bailaron los esclavos,
> parche y ritmo
> en su elemental rueda de gallo.
> Yimbamba—yimbamba
> Yimbamba—yambambé;
> son tus caderas
> y tus pies.) (46)

> (The Dance,
> that the slaves danced,
> drum and drumbeat,
> the dance of the
> peacock.
> Yimbamba—yimbamba
> Yimbamba—yambambé;
> Your hips sway,
> and your feet move.)

The drum language, "yimbamba—yambambé," mixed with the Spanish words adds to the intensity of the dance. Likewise, the onomatopoeic reproduction of the song and the sounds of the piano, a medium size drum of African origin that produces a baritone sound, evoke the ceremonial calling of the gods and the ritualistic dancing and celebration of the participants:

Aheeé,
canta el chico
Ahooó
canta el "piano"
. . . .
Yumba que yumba
yumba que yumba,
¡Chás—chas! (46)

(Aheeé
the young man sings
Ahooó
the piano plays
. . . .
Yumba, yumba
Yumba, yumba
Chas—chas!)

Brindis de Salas's poetic reproduction of the tango is another example of minority discourse that evolved from the slave experience of black Uruguayans.

In the last division of *Pregón de Marimorena,* Brindis de Salas includes four songs written for Afro-Uruguay. Each song links the past to the present and captures the spirituality and essence of black Uruguay. The first song, "Canto para un muchacho negro americano del sur" (Song for a South American Black Boy), encourages black elders to pass on to black youth the torch of their ancestry, pride, and wisdom:

Muchacho con orgullo de bantú
que cantas:
Ya ho . . . ,
ge . . . , ge . . . ,
ge . . . , ge . . . ,
tangó!
Abuelito,
gramillero
siempre lo recuerdas tú
dile a este muchacho americano
qué era el Bantú. (50)

(Boy with the pride of the
Bantú

who sings
Ya ho . . . ,
ge . . . , ge . . . ,
ge . . . , ge . . . ,
tangó
Grandfather,
Griot,
You, who remembers it,
Tell, to this South
American black boy,
who were the Bantú.)

The poet strengthens her argument about the importance of being guardians of Afro-Uruguayan culture by contrasting the youth and innocence of the young boy in the first verse to the wisdom of the grandfather in the next, who is the keeper of Afro-Uruguayan traditions and customs. Most important, Brindis de Salas enhances the grandfather's role as one of the most respected men of the black Uruguayan community, the *gramillero*. Traditionally a "medicine man" and the leading figure of the tango and the candombe, the gramillero is one of the most popular and well-known figures of Afro-Uruguayan culture (Carámbula 61). As a result, the gramillero represents for the poet a storehouse of knowledge, the narrator of Afro-Uruguayan history, especially the legacy of those Bantu-speaking slaves who were brought to Montevideo. It is his task, therefore, to inform black Uruguayan youth of their African heritage and to instruct them in the traditions and customs of Afro-Uruguay. The remaining songs of the collection represent the poet's attempt to instruct and to inform Afro-Uruguay of its African heritage.

In contrast to *Pregón de Marimorena* stands *Cien cárceles de amor*, published in Montevideo in 1949. In the prologue, Isaura Bajac de Borjes describes *Cien cárceles de amor* as laments of Afro-Uruguay. The poems are often of pain and suffering, at times emotionally intense, contrasted with the oppression of blacks in the diaspora and the freedom and beauty of Africa. Brindis de Salas's mission is to attack the oppressor with a sarcastic and bitter voice. Her use of free verse exemplifies her rebellious voice in her refusal to be a slave to traditional patterns of poetry. In a letter to Brindis de Salas, Humberto Zarrilli describes the collection as "el más completo de poesía negra que se publica en el Uruguay" (*Cien cárceles de amor* 7). Zarrilli, a contemporary of Brindis de Salas, considered *Cien cárceles de amor* the most representative of Afro-Uruguayan literature.

The Chilean poet Gabriela Mistral acclaimed *Cien cárceles de amor* as an artistic success and described Virginia Brindis de Salas as the first black literary figure to connect Afro-Uruguay across continental lines. In a letter to her, Mistral assured Brindis de Salas that *Cien cárceles de amor* would open the world to Afro-Uruguay. Mistral writes:

> . . . cante querida Virginia que Ud. es la única y la figura entre su raza del Uruguay; en Los Angeles se conoce su poesía, en el Oeste. . . . Por amigos diplomáticos sé de Ud., de sus tareas, y quiera Dios que este libro sea la llave que abra el cofre de dicha a la única negra valiente y decidida que yo conozco en el Uruguay. (*Cien cárceles de amor* 9–10)

> (Sing beloved Virginia, you are the only one of your race that represents Uruguay. Your poetry is known in Los Angeles and in the West. I have learned of your recent work through diplomatic friends, and, may God grant that this book be the key that opens coffers of luck to the only brave black Uruguayan woman that I know.)

In the concluding remarks of the letter, Gabriela Mistral encouraged Brindis de Salas to travel to Los Angeles and to spread her talent and the message of Afro-Uruguay throughout the world. Because of a lack of sufficient biographical data, it is not clear whether Brindis de Salas visited Los Angeles in the late 1940s. As a witness for history, Mistral tells us that Brindis de Salas was well received as an artist and her poetry was recognized for its aesthetic merit and her portrayal of the black experience in Uruguay.

Cien cárceles de amor is a collection of some twenty-three poems with five poems dedicated to poets such as Marta De Mezquita, Elvira Comas Vieytes, Montiel Ballesteros, and José C. Santos. Brindis de Salas's use of sarcasm in her selection of title, *One Hundred Prisons of Love,* is indicative of the tone and themes throughout the collection. She uses a straightforward approach to attack and criticize the cruel abuses that Afro-Uruguay suffered and still suffers. The poems are at times bitter and angry and emphasize themes of spiritual and physical pain, forgiveness, despair, hope, and freedom. While her compositions vary thematically, Brindis de Salas's interest is the universality of the human experience of oppression, identity, and self-affirmation.

Although not all of the poems in *Cien cárceles de amor* deal specifically with the black experience in Uruguay, my analysis will focus on those texts which do. Brindis de Salas opens *Cien cárceles de amor* with a brief essay dedicated to the black race and her uncles, Claudio Brindis de Salas, an Argentine violinist, and Gabino Ezeiza, an Argentine *payador* (troubadour). She laments their death and regards them as immortal. It is her mission to capture the soul and spirit of these great men of color and to immortalize their spirit through her poetry. Her uncles symbolize the black experience—one in which men and women labored and suffered in silence but are no longer remembered. The poet dedicates *Cien cárceles de amor* to them and to the countless other black men and women who still struggle to survive and to hope for a better world in which to live.

The compositions "Abuelito Mon" (My Beloved Grandfather), "La criada de color" (The Black Servant Girl), "Navidad Palermitana" (A Palermo Christmas), "Cantos" (Songs), "Negros" (Black Men and Women), and "Lamento negro" (A Black Man's Lament) move away from the ballads, songs, and folk customs of Afro-Uruguay seen in *Pregón de Marimorena* and present a more personal and straightforward interpretation of the black experience in Uruguay.

"Abuelito mon" is a poem written in memory of the poet's ancestors who worked the sugarcane fields of Uruguay. In the poem, rum becomes symbolic of the pain and toil of black men and women whose sweat and tears produced the drink for the white man's pleasure. This drink, writes the poet, evokes a painful memory of an unjust society, a drink which she will not allow to touch her lips:

> Me cabe el cañaveral
> en cuatro dedos de ron.
> Poco paga el yanqui ya
> por este millón de cañas
> que el negro sembró y cortó.
> Mas no me trago este trago,
> porque es trago de sudor.
>
> (I can fit the canefield
> in a swig of rum.
> The Yankee can't pay
> enough for the millions of
> cane reeds that the black man
> has sown and cut.
> I can't swallow this swig,
> because it's a swig of sweat.)

The poet criticizes the power of a capitalist society, "el yanqui" (Yankee) who pays blacks little and earns millions of dollars. For Brindis de Salas, el yanqui is viewed as the twentieth-century slave owner of Afro-Uruguayans. Therefore, it is the poet's quest to rid Uruguay of its oppressor, and in her battle against the oppressor, her poetry becomes her weapon:

> Cantando tal vez no pueda
> pasar algodón de seda . . .
> Mas como quiero cantar
> bien claro, me voy a echar

todo el Caribe en un trago.
Y este viaje yo no pago
si ya el viajero es el mar.
Y mataré con mi boca
lo que con balas no mato. (21)

(Perhaps singing I can't
turn cotton into silk,
But I want to sing clearly,
I'm going to pour out the
Caribbean in a swig.
And this time, I will
not pay, since the traveler
is the sea.
I will kill with my verses
what bullets cannot.)

The poem ends on a bitter and angry note. In the lines below, Brindis de Salas contrasts the sleeping, contented yanqui with the look of sadness and despair of the black man. Again, she reinforces her refusal to drink that which robbed her ancestors from their freedom. The poem strongly suggests to Afro-Uruguayans not to drink *el ron*, which empowers the yanqui with wealth and control:

Pero como el negro suelta
agua—triste como yo.
Mientras el yanqui en el bar
duerme su siesta de ron.
Este trago no me trago
por ser trago de sudor. (22)

(The black man's sweat runs like
water, sorrowful like me.
While the Yankee in the bar
sleeps off his rum.
I can't swallow this swig,
because it's a swig of sweat.)

In the richly lyrical "La criada de color," Brindis de Salas describes the psychological and physical pain a black woman endures as a domestic servant. One hears overtones of "We Wear the Mask" by Paul Laurence Dunbar (1872–1906) in this poem drenched in anger. The opening lines of the poem evoke the beauty of Africa, which symbolizes the lost freedom of the young woman and of all Afro-

Uruguayans. Brindis de Salas depicts the young woman as a humble servant who wears an artificial smile of happiness. This smile represents the mask many Afro-Uruguayans have worn in order to avoid the outrages and offenses of a harsh society:

> La risa agudizada sobre sus dientes blancos,
> Guarda en lo más profundo castigos de otra raza;
> Como pasión ferviente de querer libertarse,
> Del ímpetu despótico con que se le rebaja. (25)

> (A striking smile upon her white teeth
> guards the deepest punishments of another race;
> like the burning desire of wanting to be free,
> from the tyrannical violence that demeans her.)

The concluding lines of the poem are reflective of the stigmas of racial inferiority and the emotional torture Afro-Uruguayans endured in an unjust society:

> Por eso es que en su risa como grito estridente
> Hay recuerdos remotos del Pasado al Presente.
>   Y ahí se "desencaja"
>   Fuera de todo ambiente:
> Y evoca los vestigios de ahogadas rebeldías,
> Que curvan reverencias como de servidumbres,
> Agrietando su rostro que hasta padece y se aja.
>   Mientras se resquebraja
>   Con débil pesadumbre,
> Es la amarga tortura de tener miedo al ¡amo!!! (26)

> (For that reason her smile like a clamorous shout
> evokes memories from the Past to the Present.
>   It is a smile of anger
>   That echoes her surroundings
> A smile that brings forth drowned rebellions and
> reverent bows of servitude,
> Her face aches with grief until she suffers
>   and withers away
>   with insurmountable agony
> It is the painful fear of the Master!)

Brindis de Salas ends the poem on a critical note as she attacks the dominant culture for the agony it has caused the black servant girl and Afro-Uruguay.

In spite of the angry voice of Brindis de Salas in the poems "Abuelito mon" and "La criada de color," she addresses the issue of her own identity in "Cantos":

> Yo negra soy
> Porque tengo la piel negra
> ¡Esclava no! . . .
> Yo nací de vientre libre,
> Badagris Badagris, dictador
> de la puñalada y el veneno.
> Espíritu vuelto de los cañaverales
> del Tafiá, Padre del rencor
> y de la ira,
> negro: implora al
> Legbá, Dembolá, Uedó, Avidá.
> Yo negra soy,
> porque tengo la piel negra.
> ¡Esclava no! (32)
>
> (I'm a black woman,
> because I have black skin.
> I am not a slave!
> I was born free
> Badagris Badagris, ruler
> of grief and wrath.
> Spirit from the canefields
> Tafía, the god of malice
> and of ire,
> Black man, plea to Legbá,
> Dembolá, Uedó, Avidá.
> I am a black woman,
> because I have black skin.
> I am not a slave.)

The poet feels that her skin color should not continue to bind her to the social structures of slavery. Therefore, in an act of rebellion, she calls upon the Afro-Uruguayan gods of anger, Legbá, Dembolá, Uedó, and Avidá, for strength. The evocation of their names brings forth the power and strength to rid the country of its racial and social inequities. As a proud black woman, Brindis de Salas affirms her racial heritage by refusing to call upon Christian gods and insists that one's beliefs and skin color should not determine one's place in society.

On a lighter note is the poem "Navidad Palermitana" (A Palermo Christmas). Here, the poet offers a beautiful description of the "barrio Palermo," an

Afro-Montevidean community, on Christmas night. The poem vividly depicts shining stars, a round white moon, colorful decorations, and men and women dancing the candombe:

> Cielo con muchas estrellas
> Y luna blanca y redonda.
> Que linda que fue en Palermo
> La noche de Navidad.
> Enfarolada de cañas
> Y de vinachos guerreros.
> La negrada entusiasmada
> Hacia repicar los cueros.
> Candombe de Navidad,
> Candombe de sol caliente. (24)

> (Starlit sky,
> White round moon,
> how beautiful Palermo was
> on Christmas night.
> Lampposts adorned with
> canereeds
> Wine-drunken men,
> The enthusiastic crowd
> made the drum beat,
> Christmas candombe,
> Hot sun candombe.)

For the poet, the Christmas celebration evokes memories of her ancestors and the customs they brought from Africa. In the next lines, Brindis de Salas draws attention to the ancestral drum, a symbol of strength and survival. The drum, like her people, has survived the oppressive conditions of slavery:

> Reminiscencia africana
> Que reviven los morenos
> En nuestra fiesta cristiana.
> Recinto de los esclavos
> Del viejo Montevideo,
> En donde por vez primera
> Repico mi tamboril. (24)

> (Memories of Africa
> that my people relive

on this day of Christian
celebration.
In the slave quarters
of Old Montevideo,
where for the first time
I played my tamboril.)

For the poet, the Christmas celebration is the past, the present, and the future
of Afro-Uruguay:

Porque hoy los negros son libres
En esta tierra Oriental. (24)

(Because today black men
are free in the land of
the Banda Oriental.)

Although Brindis de Salas is critical of society and her anger and bitterness are
straightforward, she is also optimistic. In the poem "Lamento negro" (Black Lament) she describes the pain and misery Afro-Uruguayans have endured while
never having lost their hope for freedom and a better future. She begins the
poem with the following rhetorical question:

¿Sabe, compañero,
Qué cosa me hicieron?,
Todo me estropearon;
Es una crueldad.
Pronto llega el día
Que todo concluye
Y entonces el negro
Tendrá libertad.
Andembo y andembo.
No cobrar la infamia
Que Pancho sufrió.
Qué importa que el alma
Se encuentre oprimida
Si un rayo de luz
Nos puede dar vida!!! (37)

(Brother, do you know
what they did to me?
They destroyed my life;

It's a shame.
Soon the day will come
when it will all end
and the black man
will be free.
Andembo and andembo.
Don't hate this cruelty
that Pancho suffered.
It doesn't matter that the
soul may be oppressed
if a ray of light
can give us hope!)

"Lamento negro" is a sensitively written poem in which Afro-Uruguay is blame-less for the oppression and for the racism it suffers. It is a poem of survival, of hope and of strength, in which the poet encourages faith in the struggle from oppression.

While the poetry of Brindis de Salas has received much critical acclaim, her life remains shrouded in mystery. How could a writer who received consid-erable respect as the voice of Afro-Uruguay be ignored for so many years after her death? There are several possible answers to this riddle.

Between the years 1948 (just before the publication of *Cien cárceles de amor*) and 1960, Uruguay began to experience a severe economic crisis. There were increased political and social tensions, economic stagnation, inflation, and currency devaluation (Weinstein 33–36). It would be safe to conjecture that given the economic climate of Uruguay, Brindis de Salas and her supporters were unable to secure the proper funds needed for the publication of her third volume of poetry, *Cantos de lejanía*. In addition, her militant attitude as a black woman writer and the lack of solidarity among black intellectuals since the death of Pilar Barrios (1889–1974) may have led to the exclusion of her work among her peers. Although Gabriela Mistral read the works of Brindis de Salas while in Los Angeles, there is only one other document that indicates that her work was accessible to the outside world. In 1954, her poem "Tango Número Tres" appeared in German translation in the anthology *Schwarzer Orpheus* ed-ited by Jahnheinz Jahn.

Most recently, her poems have appeared in the international anthology of black women writers, *Daughters of Africa* (1992), by Margaret Busby and *Voices of Négritude* (1988) by Julio Finn. Over the last ten years, critics such as Rich-ard L. Jackson, Marvin A. Lewis, Ann Venture Young, and Lemuel A. Johnson have taken steps in their studies of Brindis de Salas to bring her work to the outside world and to draw attention to her as an artist.

The literary discourse of Virginia Brindis de Salas adds to the interpretation of the black experience in Uruguay and, for that matter, in the diaspora. Her work represents the many works by black writers that have been neglected or overlooked in Latin America, especially in South America. I concur with Lemuel Johnson that "it is doubly regrettable that both volumes of [her] poetry are now out of print" (*Afro-Hispanic Review* 28). Perhaps in years to come, more works by Brindis de Salas will be recovered and the mystery of her life will unfold. The project of reclamation will necessitate more studies on Afro-Uruguay and other black writers of the Southern Cone. It is hoped that it will stimulate future scholars to engage in a dialogue between issues of race, sex, and nationality as we rethink our comparative pan-American identities.

WORKS CITED

Brindis de Salas, Virginia. *Cien cárceles de amor*. Montevideo, 1949.

———. *Pregón de marimorena*. Montevideo: Sociedad Cultural Editora Indoamericana, 1946.

Busby, Margaret, ed. *Daughters of Africa*. New York: Pantheon, 1992.

Carámbula, Rubén. *Negro y tambor: poemas, pregones, danzas leyendas sobre motivos del folklore afro-rioplatense*. Buenos Aires: Editorial Folklorica Americana, 1952.

———. *Pregones del Montevideo colonial: Candombe, comparsa de los negros lúbolos*. Montevideo: Editores Mosca, 1987.

Finn, Julio. *Voices of Négritude*. London: Quartet, 1988.

Jackson, Richard L. *Black Writers in Latin America*. Albuquerque: U of New Mexico P, 1979.

Jahn, Janheinz. *Schwarzer Orpheus*. Munchen: Hanser Verlag Munchen, 1954.

Johnson, Lemuel. "'Amo y espero': The Love Lyric of Virginia Brindis de Salas and the African American Experience in the New World." *Afro-Hispanic Review*. 3.3 (1984): 19–29.

Lewis, Marvin A. *Afro-Hispanic Poetry, 1940–1980: From Slavery to "Negritud" in South American Verse*. Columbia: U of Missouri P, 1983.

Mullen, Edward. "Afro-Hispanic and Afro-American Literary Historiography: Comments on Generational Shifts." *CLA Journal* 38.4 (June 1995): 371–89.

Pereda Valdés, Ildelfonso. *El Negro en el Uruguay: pasado y presente*. Montevideo: Revista del Institutes Historico y Geografico, 1965.

Weinstein, Martin. *Uruguay: Democracy at the Crossroads*. Boulder, Colo.: Westview, 1988.

Young, Ann Venture. *The Image of Black Women in 20th Century South American Poetry*. Washington, DC: Three Continents P, 1987.

Young, Caroll. "The New Voices of Afro-Uruguay." *Afro-Hispanic Review* 14.1 (Spring 1995): 58–64.

Selected Bibliography

Aaron, Daniel. "The 'Inky Curse': Miscegenation in the White American Literary Imagination." *Social Science Information* 22.2 (1983): 169–90.

Adams, Percy G. *Travel Literature and the Evolution of the Novel.* Lexington: UP of Kentucky, 1983.

Anthony, Susan B., ed. *Proceedings of the Eleventh National Women's Rights Convention.* New York: American News, 1866.

Awkward, Michael. *Inspiriting Influences: Tradition, Revision, and Afro-American Women's Novels.* New York: Columbia UP, 1989.

Baker, Houston A., Jr. *The Journey Back: Issues in Black Literature and Criticism.* Chicago: U of Chicago P, 1980.

Balutansky, Kathleen M. "Naming Caribbean Women Writers." *Callaloo* 13.3 (Summer 1990): 539–50.

Baym, Nina. *Woman's Fiction: A Guide to Novels by and about Women in America, 1820–1870.* Ithaca, NY: Cornell UP, 1978.

———. *Novels, Readers, and Reviewers: Responses to Fiction in Antebellum America.* Ithaca, NY: Cornell UP, 1984.

Bell, Bernard W. "Ann Petry's Demythologizing of American Culture and Afro-American Character." *Conjuring: Black Women, Fiction, and Literary Tradition.* Ed. Marjorie Pryse and Hortense Spillers. Bloomington: U of Indiana P, 1985. 105–15

Bennett, Gwendolyn. Personal interview with Sandra Y. Govan. Mar. 1979.

Benstock, Sheri. "Authorizing the Autobiographical." *The Private Self: Theory and Practice of Women's Autobiographical Writings.* Ed. Sheri Benstock. Chapel Hill: U of North Carolina P, 1988. 10–33.

Berrian, Brenda. *Bibliography of Women Writers from the Caribbean (1831–1986).* Washington, DC: Three Continents P, 1989.

Bewell, Alan. "An Issue of Monstrous Desire: Frankenstein and Obstetrics." *Yale Journal of Criticism* 2 (Winter 1988): 105–28.

Bhabha, Homi K. "Introduction: Narrating the Nation." *Nation and Narration*, London: Routledge, 1990: 1-7.

Bloom, Harold, et. al., eds. *Twentieth-Century American Literature.* New York: Chelsea House, 1987. Vol. 5 of *The Chelsea House Library of Literary Criticism.* 7 vols. 3083–89.

Bone, Robert. *The Negro Novel in America.* Rev. ed. New Haven: Yale UP, 1966.

Brawley, Benjamin. *The Negro Genius: A New Appraisal of the Achievement of the American Negro in Literature and the Fine Arts.* New York: Dodd, 1937.

Brindis de Salas, Virginia. *Cien cárceles de amor*. Montevideo, 1949.

———. *Pregón de Marimorena*. Montevideo: Sociedad Cultural Editora Indoamericana, 1946.

———. *Pregones del Montevideo colonial: Candombe, comparsa de los negros lúbolos*. Montevideo: Editores Mosca, 1987.

Brodie, Fawn M. *Thomas Jefferson: An Intimate History*. New York: Bantam, 1974.

Brooks, Gwendolyn. *Maud Martha*. 1953. *Blacks*. Chicago: David, 1987.

Brown, Sterling A. *The Negro in American Fiction and Negro Poetry and Drama*. 1937. New York: Arno/New York Times, 1969.

Brown, William Wells. *The Rising Son; or, The Antecedents and Advancement of the Colored Race*. 1874. New York: Negro Universities P, 1970.

Busby, Margaret, ed. *Daughters of Africa: An International Anthology of Words and Writings by Women of African Descent: From the Ancient Egyptian to the Present*. New York: Pantheon, 1992.

Campbell, Jane. *Mythic Black Fiction: The Transformation of History*. Knoxville: U of Tennessee P, 1986.

Carámbula, Rubén. *Negro y tambor: poemas, pregones, danzas leyendas sobre motivos del folklore afro-rioplatense*. Buenos Aires: Editorial Folklorica Americana, 1952.

———. *Pregones del Montevideo colonial: Candombe, comparsa de los negros lúbolos*. Montevideo: Editores Mosca, 1987.

Carby, Hazel V. "It Jus Be's Dat Way Sometime." *Feminisms: An Anthology of Literary Theory and Criticism*. Ed. Robyn R. Warhol and Diane Price Herndl. New Brunswick, NJ: Rutgers UP, 1991. 746–58.

———. *Reconstructing Womanhood: The Emergence of the Afro-American Woman Novelist*. New York: Oxford UP, 1987.

Chase-Riboud, Barbara. *Sally Hemings*. New York: Avon, 1979.

Christian, Barbara. "Afro-American Women Poets: A Historical Introduction (1982)." *Black Feminist Criticism: Perspectives on Black Women Writers*. New York: Pergamon, 1985: 119–25.

———. *Black Women Novelists: The Development of a Tradition, 1892–1976*. Westport, CT: Greenwood, 1980.

———. "Somebody Forgot to Tell Somebody Something." *Wild Women in the Whirlwind*. Ed. Joanne M. Braxton et al. New Brunswick, NJ: Rutgers UP, 1990. 326–41.

Clark, John Henrik. Interview with Sandra Y. Govan. 9 May 1991.

Cooper, Anna J. *L'Attitude de la France à l'égard de l'esclavage pendant la Révolution*. Paris: Imprimerie de la Cour d'appel, 1925.

———. Papers. Moorland-Spingarn Research Center. Howard University. Washington, DC.

———. *The Third Step*. Washington, DC: Privately printed, n.d.

———. *A Voice from the South: By a Black Woman from the South*. 1892. Introduction. Mary Helen Washington. *The Schomburg Library of Nineteenth-Century Black Women Writers*. Gen. ed. Henry Louis Gates Jr. New York: Oxford UP, 1988.

Cowper, William. *The Poems of William Cowper*. Ed. J. C. Baily. London: Methuen, 1905.

Cruse, Harold. *The Crisis of the Negro Intellectual*. New York: William Morrow, 1967.

Dabney, Virginius. *The Jefferson Scandals: A Rebuttal*. New York: Dodd, 1981.

Dake, Finis Jennings. *Dake's Annotated Reference Bible*. Lawrenceville, GA: Dake Bible Sales, 1963.

Davies, Carole Boyce, and Elaine Fido, eds. *Out of the Kumbla: Caribbean and Literature*. New York: Africa World P, 1990.

Davies, Carole Boyce, Elaine Fido, and Anne Adams Graves, eds. *Ngamibika: Studies of Women in African Literature*. New York: Africa World P, 1986.

Davies, Carole Boyce, and 'Molara Ogundipe-Leslie, eds. *International Dimensions of Black Women's Writing*. New York: New York UP, 1995. Vol. 1 of *Moving Beyond Boundaries*.

———. Davies, Carole Boyce, and 'Molara Ogundipe-Leslie, eds. *Black Women's Diasporas*. New York: New York UP, 1995. Vol. 2 of *Moving Beyond Boundaries*.

Davies, Carole Boyce and Elaine Fido, eds. *Out of the Kumbla: Caribbean Women and Literature*. New York: Africa World P, 1990.

Davis, Arthur P. *From the Dark Tower: Afro-American Writers 1900–1960*. Washington, DC: Howard UP, 1981. 90–94.

Davis, Charles T., and Henry Louis Gates Jr., eds. Introduction. *The Slave's Narrative*. Oxford: Oxford UP, 1985. xi–xxiv.

Davis, David Brion. *The Problem of Slavery in the Age of Revolution: 1770–1823*. Ithaca, NY: Cornell UP, 1975.

Davis, Thadious M. *Nella Larsen, Novelist of the Harlem Renaissance: A Woman's Life Unveiled*. Baton Rouge: Louisiana State UP, 1994.

Debien, Gabriel. "Les Esclaves." *Historie des Antilles et de la Guyane*. Ed. Pierre Pluchon. Toulouse: Edouard Privat, 1982.

Dixon, Melvin. *Ride Out the Wilderness*. Urbana: U of Illinois P, 1987.

Dodson, Joanne. "The Hidden Hand: Subversion of Cultural Ideology in Three Mid-Nineteenth-Century American Women's Novels." *American Quarterly* 38.2 (Summer 1986): 233–42.

Donaldson, Laura E. Introduction. *Decolonizing Feminisms: Race, Gender, and Empire-Building*. Chapel Hill: U of North Carolina P. 1992. 1–12.

Donovan, Josephine. "Toward a Women's Poetics." *Feminist Issues in Literary Scholarship*. Ed. Shari Benstock. Bloomington: U of Indiana P, 1987. 98–109. [100].

Douglass, Frederick. *The Life and Times of Frederick Douglass*. 1881. Rev. ed. 1892. Rpt. New York: Collier, 1962.

Doyle, John Robert, Jr. *Thomas Pringle*. New York: Twayne, 1972.

Du Bois, W. E. B. *The Souls of Black Folk*. 1903. New York: Penguin, 1989.

———. "Writers." *The Crisis* 1 (1911): 20–21.

———. *Writings*. Ed. Nathan Huggins. New York: Library of America, 1986.

duCille, Ann. *The Coupling Convention: Sex, Text, and Tradition in Black Women's Fiction*. New York: Oxford UP, 1993.

Dunbar-Nelson, Alice. *Give Us Each Day: The Diary of Alice Dunbar-Nelson*. Ed. Gloria T. Hull. New York: W. W. Norton, 1984.

Essien-Udom, E. U. *Black Nationalism: A Search for an Identity in America*. Chicago: U of Chicago P, 1962.

Fabre, Michel. *From Harlem to Paris: Black American Writers in France, 1840–1980*. Urbana: U of Illinois P, 1991.

Farrison, W. Edward. "Clotel, Thomas Jefferson, and Sally Hemings." *CLA Journal* 17.2 (Dec. 1973): 147–74.

Fauset, Jessie Redmon. *The Chinaberry Tree*. 1931. Introduction by Marcy J. Knops. Boston: Northeastern, 1995.

———. *Comedy: American Style*. 1933. College Park, Md.: McGrath, 1969.

———. "Dark Algiers the White." *The Crisis* 29–30 (1925–26): 255–58; 16–22.

———. *Plum Bun*. 1929. London: Pandora, 1985.

———. *There Is Confusion*. 1924. Boston: Northeastern UP, 1989.

————. "Tracing Shadows." *The Crisis* 10 (1915): 247–51.

————. "Yarrow Revisited." *The Crisis* 29 (1925): 107–9.

Feal, Rosemary Geisdorfer. "The Afro-Latin American Woman Writer: Drumming with a Difference." *Afro-Hispanic Review* 14.2 (Fall 1995): 10–12.

Ferguson, Moira. Introduction. Prince, Mary. *The History of Mary Prince, A West Indian Slave, Related by Herself.* By Mary Prince. 1831. Ann Arbor: U of Michigan Press, 1993. 3-41.

————. *Subject to Others: British Women Writers and Colonial Slavery, 1670–1834.* New York: Routledge, 1993.

Figaro (Paris). 2 July, 5 July, 3 Aug., and 8 Aug. 1900.

Finn, Julio. *Voices of Négritude.* London: Quartet, 1988.

Firmat, Gustavo Pérez, ed. *Life on the Hyphen: The Cuban-American Way?* Austin: U of Texas P, 1994.

————. *Do the Americas Have a Common Literature?* Durham, NC: Duke UP, 1990.

Foster, Frances Smith. "Adding Color and Contour to Early American Self-Portraitures: Autobiographical Writings of Afro-American Women." *Conjuring: Black Women, Fiction, and Literary Tradition.* Ed. Marjorie Pryse and Hortense J. Spillers. Bloomington: U of Indiana P, 1985. 25–38.

Foster, Frances Smith. *Witnessing Slavery.* 1979. Madison: U of Wisconsin P, 1994.

————, ed. *A Brighter Coming Day: A Frances Ellen Watkins Harper Reader.* New York: Feminist P, 1991.

Fowler, Carolyn. *The College Language Association: A Social History.* Ann Arbor: University Microfilms, 1988.

Frazier, E. Franklin. *Black Bourgeoisie: The Rise of the New Middle Class in the United States.* 1957. New York: Collier, 1962.

Garrison, Dee. "Immoral Fiction in the Late Victorian Library." *American Quarterly* 28.1 (Spring 1976): 71–89.

Gates, Henry Louis. *Figures in Black: Words, Signs, and the "Racial" Self.* New York: Oxford UP, 1987.

————. Introduction. *Our Nig; or, Sketches from the Life of a Free Black, In a Two-Story White House, North. Showing that Slavery's Shadows Fall Even There.* 2d ed. New York: Random House, 1983. xi–lv.

————, ed. *Reading Black, Reading Feminist: A Critical Anthology.* New York: Meridian, 1990.

Geiss, Immanuel. *The Pan-African Movement: A History of Pan-Africanism in America, Europe and Africa.* Trans. Ann Keep. New York: Holmes & Meier, 1974.

Giddings, Paula. *In Search of Sisterhood: Delta Sigma Theta and the Challenge of the Black Sorority Movement.* New York: William Morrow, 1988.

————. *When and Where I Enter: The Impact of Black Women on Race and Sex in America.* New York: William Morrow, 1984.

Govan, Sandra Yvonne. "Gwendolyn Bennett: Portrait of an Artist Lost." Diss. Emory University, 1981.

Graff, Gerald. "Narrative and the Unofficial Interpretive Culture." *Reading Narrative: Form, Ethics, Ideology.* Ed. James Phelan. Columbus: Ohio State UP, 1989.

Guillaume, Bernice F. "The Female as Harlem Sage: The 'Aunt Viney's Sketches' of Olivia Ward-Bush Banks." *Langston Hughes Review* 6.2 (Fall 1987): 1–10.

Gwin, Minrose C. "Green-Eyed Monsters of the Slavocracy: Jealous Mistresses in Two Slave Narratives." *Conjuring: Black Women, Fiction, and Literary Tradition.* Ed. Marjorie Pryse and Hortense J. Spillers. Bloomington: U of Indiana P, 1985. 39–52.

Halliburton, Cecil D. *A History of St. Augustine's College 1867–1937.* Raleigh, NC: St. Augustine's College, 1937.

Hansen, Chadwick. "The Metamorphosis of Tituba, or Why American Intellectuals Can't Tell an Indian Witch from a Negro." *New England Quarterly* 47.1 (Mar. 1974): 3–12.

Harper, Frances Ellen Watkins. *Iola Leroy; Or, Shadows Uplifted.* 1892. Boston: Beacon, 1987.

Harrison, Daphne Duval. "Black Women in the Blues Tradition." *The Afro-American Woman: Struggles and Images.* Ed. Sharon Harley and Rosalyn Terborg-Penn. New York: Kennikat, 1978. 58–73.

Hawkes, Terence. *Shakespeare's Talking Animals: Language and Drama in Society.* London: Edward Arnold, 1973.

Heilbrun, Carolyn. *Writing a Woman's Life.* New York: Norton, 1988.

Heller, Dana. *The Feminization of Quest-Romance: Radical Departures.* Austin: U of Texas P, 1990.

Hemenway, Robert E. *Zora Neale Hurston: A Literary Biography.* Urbana: U of Illinois P, 1977.

Holland, Josiah Gilbert. *Bitter-Sweet.* 1858. New York: Scribner's, 1892.

Holloway, Karla F. C. *Moorings and Metaphors: Figures of Culture and Gender in Black Women's Literature.* New Brunswick, NJ: Rutgers UP, 1992.

Hubbard, Dolan. "Why CLA Still Prospers." *Black Issues in Higher Education* (25 Aug. 1994): 57.

Huggins, Nathan. *Harlem Renaissance.* New York: Oxford UP, 1971.

Hughes, Langston. *The Big Sea.* 1940. New York: Hill and Wang, 1981.

Hull, Gloria T. *Color, Sex, and Poetry: Three Women Writers of the Harlem Renaissance.* Bloomington: U of Indiana P, 1987.

Hunter, Kristin. *God Bless the Child.* 1964. Washington, DC: Howard UP, 1966.

Hutchinson, Louise Daniel. *Anna J. Cooper: A Voice from the South.* Washington, DC: Smithsonian Institution P, 1982.

Jackson, Blyden. *The History of Afro-American Literature.* Vol. I. Baton Rouge: Louisiana State UP, 1989.

Jackson, Richard L. *Black Writers in Latin America.* Albuquerque: U of New Mexico P, 1979.

Jacobs, Harriet A. *Incidents in the Live of a Slave Girl: Written by Herself.* Ed. Jean Fagan Yellin. Cambridge: Harvard UP, 1987.

Jahn, Janheinz. *Schwarzer Orpheus.* Munchen: Hanser Verlag Munchen, 1954.

James, Stanlie M. and Abenia P. A. Busia. *Theorizing Black Feminisms: The Visionary Pragmatism of Black Women.* New York: Routledge, 1994.

Jameson, Fredric. Foreword. Roberto Fernandez Retamar. *Caliban and Other Essays.* Trans. Edward Baker. Minneapolis: U of Minnesota P, 1989.

JanMohamed, Abdul R., and David Lloyd. "Introduction: Minority Discourse—What Is to Be Done?" Ed. JanMohamed and Lloyd. *Cultural Critique: Special Issue: The Nature and Context of Minority Discourse II* 7 (Fall 1987): 5–17

Jefferson, Thomas. *Notes on the State of Virginia.* 1787. Chapel Hill: U of North Carolina P, 1955.

"Jessie Fauset." *Caroling Dusk: An Anthology of Verse by Negro Poets.* Ed. Countee Cullen. New York: Harper and Brothers, 1927.

"Jessie Redmon Fauset Harris." *Afro-American Women Writers: 1746–1933.* Ed. Ann Allen Shockley. New York: Meredian, 1989. 414–24.

Johnson, Barbara. "My Mother/My Self." *A World of Difference.* Baltimore: Johns Hopkins UP, 1987. 144–54.

Johnson, Lemuel. "'Amo y espero': The Love Lyric of Virginia Brindis de Salas and the African American Experience in the New World." *Afro-Hispanic Review* 3.3 (1984): 19–29.

Jordan, Winthrop D. *White over Black: American Attitudes toward the Negro, 1550–1812.* Chapel Hill: U of North Carolina P, 1968. 430–36.

Kermode, Frank. "John." *The Literary Guide to the Bible.* Ed. Robert Alter and Frank Kermode. Cambridge: Harvard UP, 1987. 440–66.

Kissel, Howard, "Sally Hemings: Little Fictional Embroidery." *Chicago Tribune* 3 July 1979, sec. 2: 4.

Klein, Abbé Félix. *Au pays de "La vie intense."* 6th ed. Paris: Plon-Nourrit, 1905.

Larson, Charles R., ed. *An Intimation of Things Distant: The Collected Fiction of Nella Larsen.* New York: Anchor, 1992.

Lattin, Vernon E. "Ann Petry and the American Dream." *Black American Literary Forum* 12.2 (Summer 1978): 69–72.

Lauter, Paul, et al., eds. *The Heath Anthology of American Literature.* Vol. I. Lexington, MA: D. C. Heath, 1990.

Lewis, Marvin A. *Afro-Argentine Discourse: Another Dimension of the Black Diaspora.* Columbia: U of Missouri P, 1996.

———. *Afro-Hispanic Poetry, 1940–1980: From Slavery to "Negritud" in South American Verse.* Columbia: U of Missouri P, 1983.

Loggins, Vernon. *The Negro Author: His Development in American Literature to 1900.* New York: Columbia UP, 1931.

Lorde, Audre. "Poetry Is Not a Luxury." *Sister Outsider: Essays and Speeches.* Trumansburg, NY: Crossing P, 1984. 36–39.

Marcus, Jane. *Art and Anger: Reading Like a Woman.* Columbus: Ohio State UP, 1988.

Marshall, Paule. *Praisesong for the Widow.* New York: Putnam's, 1983.

Mathurin, Owen Charles. *Henry Sylvester Williams and the Origins of the Pan-African Movement, 1869–1911.* Contributions in Afro-American and Afro Studies, Number 21. Westport, CT: Greenwood, 1976.

McDowell, Margaret C. *"The Narrows:* A Fuller View of Ann Petry." *Black American Literature Forum* 14.4 (Winter 1980): 135–41.

McHenry, Susan. "'Sally Hemings': A Key to Our National Identity." *Ms* (Oct. 1980): 35–40.

McKay, Nellie. Introduction. *The Narrows.* By Ann Petry. Boston: Beacon, 1988. vii–xx.

Moers, Ellen. "Female Gothic." *Literary Women.* Garden City, NY: Doubleday, 1976. 92.

Morrison, Toni. *Jazz.* New York: Knopf, 1992.

———. *Sula.* New York: New American Library, 1973.

———. "Unspeakable Things Unspoken: The Afro-American Presence in American Literature." *Michigan Quarterly Review* 28 (Winter 1989): 1–34.

Morsberger, Robert E. "The Further Transformation of Tituba." *New England Quarterly* 47.3 (Sept. 1974): 456–58.

Mullen, Edward. "Afro-Hispanic and Afro-American Literary Historiography: Comments on Generational Shifts." *College Language Association Journal* 38.4 (June 1995): 371–89.

Naylor, Gloria. *The Women of Brewster Place.* New York: Penguin, 1983.

Olney, James. "Some Versions of Memory/Some Versions of *Bios.*" *Autobiography: Essays Theoretical and Critical.* James Olney. Princeton, NJ: Princeton UP, 1980. 236–67.

O'Daniel, Therman B. Introduction. *A Twenty-Five-Year Cumulative Author-Title Index to the CLA Journal (1957–1982).* Baltimore: J. H. Furst, 1985): xi–xxx.

O'Neale, Sondra. "A Slave's Subtle War: Phillis Wheatley's Use of Biblical Myth and Symbol." *EAL* 21.2 (Fall 1986): 144–65.

Pachter, Marc. "The Biographer Himself: An Introduction." *Telling Lives: The Biographer's Art.* Ed. Marc Pachter. Philadelphia: U of Pennsylvania P, 1981. 3–15.

Paquet, Sandra Pouchet. "The Heartbeat of a West Indian Slave: *The History of Mary Prince.*" *African American Review* 26 (Spring 1992): 131–46.

Pereda Valdés, Ildelfonso. *El Negro en el Uruguay: pasado y presente.* Montevideo, 1965.

Petry, Ann. "The Common Ground." *Handbook of Reflections.* Ed. Elinor Whitney Field. Boston: Horn Book, 1969. 67–72.

Petry, Ann. *Country Place.* 1947. New York: Chatham Bookseller, 1971.

——. *The Narrows.* 1953. Boston: Beacon, 1988.

——. *The Street.* 1946. Boston: Beacon, 1985.

——. *Tituba of Salem Village.* 1964. New York: HarperCollins, 1988.

Poovey, Mary. "My Hideous Progeny: Mary Shelley and the Feminization of Romanticism." *PMLA* 95 (May 1980): 332–47.

Primeau, Ronald. "Frank Horne and the Second Echelon Poets." *The Harlem Renaissance Remembered.* Ed. Arna Bontemps. New York: Dodd, 1972. 247–67.

Prince, Mary. *The History of Mary Prince, A West Indian Slave, Related by Herself.* 1831. London: Pandora, 1987.

Rampersad, Arnold. "Biography and Afro-American Culture." *Afro-American Literary Studies in the 1990s.* Ed. Houston A. Baker Jr. and Patricia Redmond. Chicago: U of Chicago P, 1989. 194–230.

——. "A Conversation with Arnold Rampersad." *Life into Art.* Ed. Gail Porter Mandell. Fayetteville: U of Arkansas P, 1991. 44–67.

Randolph, Laura B. "Thomas Jefferson's Black and White Descendants Debate His Lineage and Legacy." *Ebony* 48.7 (July 1993): 25–29.

Reckley, Ralph. "The Love-Hate Syndrome of Master-Slave Relationships in Sally Hemings." *20th Century Black American Women in Print.* Ed. Lola E. Jones. Baltimore: Morgan State UP, 1991. 33–43.

Record, Wilson. *The Negro and the Communist Party.* New York: Atheneum, 1971.

Redding, J. Saunders. *To Make a Poet Black.* 1939. New York: Oxford UP, 1988.

Ruoff, A. La Vonne Brown, and Jerry W. Ward Jr., eds. Introduction. *Redefining American Literary History.* Ed. Brown and Ward. New York: MLA, 1990. 1–5 .

Rushworth, John. *Historical Collections of Private Passages of State, Weighty Matters in Laws, Remarkable Proceedings.* 8 vols. London: D. Browne, 1721–22.

Russell, Michele. "Slave Codes and Linear Notes." *But Some of Us Are Brave.* Ed. Gloria Hull, Patricia Bell Scott, Barbara Smith. New York: Feminist P, 1982. 129–40.

Said, Edward W. *Orientalism.* New York: Random House, 1979.

Schraufnagel, Noel. *From Apology to Protest: The Black American Novel.* DeLand: Everett Edwards, 1973.

Schuyler, George S. "The Negro Art-Hokum." 1926 *Within the Circle: Literary Criticism from the Harlem Renaissance to the Present.* Ed. Angelyn Mitchell. Durham, NC: Duke UP, 1994. 51–54.

Sekora, John and Darwin T. Turner, eds. *The Art of Slave Narrative: Original Essays in Criticism and Theory.* Macomb: Western Illinois UP, 1982.

Shelley, Mary Wollstonecraft. *Frankenstein, or, The Modern Prometheus.* 1818. New York: New American Library, 1965.

Shockley, Ann Allen, ed. *Afro-American Women Writers: 1746–1933.* New York: Meredian, 1989.

Singh, Amritjit. *The Novels of the Harlem Renaissance.* University Park: Pennsylvania State UP, 1976.

Smart, Ian Isidore. *Nicolás Guillén: Popular Poet of the Caribbean.* Columbia: U of Missouri P, 1990.

Smith, Robert P. Jr. "Rereading *Banjo*: Claude McKay and the French Connection." *CLA Journal* 30.1 (Sept. 1986): 46–58.

Smith, Valerie. *Self-Discovery and Authority in Afro-American Narrative.* Cambridge: Harvard UP, 1987.

Sollars, Werner. "'Never Was Born': The Mulatto, An American Tragedy?" *Massachusetts Review* 27 (1986): 293–316.

Spillers, Hortense J., ed. *Comparative American Identities: Race, Sex, and Nationality in the Modern Text.* New York: Routledge, 1991.

Starkey, Marion. "Jessie Fauset." *Southern Workman* 61 (1932): 217–20.

Stout, Janis P. *The Journey Narrative in American Literature: Patterns and Departures.* Westport, CT: Greenwood, 1983.

Sylvander, Carolyn Wedin. "Jessie Redmon Fauset." *The Dictionary of Literary Biography.* Vol. 51. Detroit: Gale, 1987: 76–86.

————. *Jessie Redmon Fauset: Black American Writer.* Troy, NY: Whitson, 1981.

Tate, Claudia. "Allegories of Black Female Desire; or, Rereading Nineteenth-Century Narratives of Black Female Authority." *Changing Our Own Words: Essays on Criticism, Theory, and Writing by Black Women.* Ed. Cheryl A. Wall. New Brunswick, NJ: Rutgers UP, 1989. 98–126.

————. *Domestic Allegories of Political Desire: The Black Heroines' Text at the Turn of the Century.* New York: Oxford UP, 1992.

Times (London). 27 July 1900.

Traylor, Eleanor W. Response. *Afro-American Literary Study in the 1990s.* Ed. Houston A. Baker Jr. and Patricia Redmond. Chicago: U of Chicago P, 1989. 128–34.

Ullman, Victor. *Martin R. Delany: The Beginnings of Black Nationalism.* Boston: Beacon, 1971.

Veeder, William. *Mary Shelley and Frankenstein: The Fate of Androgyny.* Chicago: U of Chicago P, 1974.

Walker, Alice. *In Search of Our Mothers' Gardens.* New York: Harcourt, 1983.

Walker, Clarence E. *A Rock in a Weary Land: The African Methodist Episcopal Church During the Civil War and Reconstruction.* Baton Rouge: Louisiana UP, 1982.

Wall, Cheryl A., ed. *Changing Our Own Words: Essays on Criticism, Theory, and Writing by Black Women.* New Brunswick, NJ: Rutgers UP, 1989.

Washington, Mary Helen, ed. *Invented Lives: Narratives of Black Women 1860–1960.* Garden City, NY: Anchor, 1987.

Weinstein, Martin. *Uruguay: Democracy at the Crossroads.* Boulder, Colo.: Westview, 1988.

Weir, Sybil. "*The Narrows*: A Black New England Novel." *Studies in American Fiction* 15 (Spring 1987): 81–93.

Welter, Barbara. "The Cult of True Womanhood, 1820–1860." *Dimity Convictions: The American Woman in the Nineteenth Century.* Athens: Ohio UP, 1976. 21–41.

Wetherell, Elizabeth [Susan Warner]. *Wide, Wide World.* 1850. Philadelphia: Lippincott, 1890.

Wheatley, Phillis. *The Poems of Phillis Wheatley.* Ed. Julian D. Mason. 1966. Rev. and enl. Chapel Hill: U of North Carolina P, 1989.

Wheatley, Phillis. *The Poems of Phillis Wheatley.* Ed. John Shields. *The Schomburg Library of Nineteenth-Century Black Women Writers.* Gen. ed. Henry Louis Gates Jr. New York: Oxford UP, 1988.

White, Deborah Gray. *Ar'n't I a Woman: Female Slaves in the Plantation South.* New York: Norton, 1985.

Williams, Kenny J. Introduction. *Essays.* By Ann Plato. New York: Oxford UP, 1988. xxvii–liii.

Williams, Sherley Anne. *Dessa Rose.* New York: Berkley, 1986.

Willis, Miriam DeCosta. "Afra-Hispanic Writers and Feminist Discourse." *NWSA Journal* 5.2 (1993): 204–18.

———. *The Memphis Diary of Ida Wells Barnett.* 1994. Boston: Beacon P, 1995.

Willis, Miriam DeCosta, ed. *Blacks in Hispanic Literature: Critical Essays.* Port Washington, NY: Kennikat, 1977.

Wilson, Harriet E. *Our Nig; or, Sketches from the Life of a Free Black, In a Two-Story White House, North. Showing that Slavery's Shadows Fall Even There.* 1859. New York: Random House, 1983.

Wilson, Judith. "Barbara Chase-Riboud: Sculpting Our History." *Essence* 10.8 (Dec. 1979): 12–13.

Yarborough, Richard. "The Quest for the American Dream in Three Afro-American Novels: *If He Hollers Let Him Go, The Street,* and *Invisible Man.*" *MELUS* 8.4 (Winter 1981): 33–59.

Young, Ann Venture. *The Image of Black Women in 20th Century South American Poetry: A Bilingual Anthology.* Washington, DC: Three Continents P, 1987.

Young, Caroll. "The New Voices of Afro-Uruguay." *Afro-Hispanic Review* 14.1 (Spring 1985): 58–64.

Contributors

Emma Waters Dawson is Professor of English and Chair, Department of Languages and Literature at Florida Agricultural and Mechanical University, Tallahassee, Florida, where she teaches courses in literary criticism and African American literature. An avid scholar of literature by and about African American women, she has published on the works of Jean Toomer, Zora Neale Hurston, Alice Walker, Gwendolyn Brooks, and Sherley Anne Williams. She is currently at work on a coauthored text, *Toni Morrison: A Bio-Bibliography,* to be published by The Greenwood Press.

Frances Smith Foster, Professor of English and Women's Studies at Emory University, is author of *Witnessing Slavery: The Development of the Ante-bellum Slave Narrative* and *Written By Herself: Literary Production by African American Women 1746–1892.* She has edited two volumes of Frances Harper's works: *A Brighter Coming Day: A Frances Ellen Watkins Harper Reader* and *Minnie's Sacrifice; Sowing and Reaping; Trial and Triumph: Three Rediscovered Novels by Frances E. W. Harper.* The latter work was awarded the College Language Association Book Award for 1994.

Sandra Y. Govan is Associate Professor of English at the University of North Carolina, Charlotte. She has received several research awards, including a 1982 American Council of Learned Societies grant to pursue biographical work on Gwendolyn Bennett. Govan contributed two essays to the *Dictionary of Literary Biography* and has had several articles in *Black American Literature Forum,* and she has served as guest editor of the *Langston Hughes Review.* Her varied literary and popular culture interests range from black women writers to Ishmael Reed, from black writers within the canon to those outside in science fiction. She is Book Review Editor for *Obsidian II* and Coordinator of the Ronald E. McNair Postbaccalaureate Achievement Program.

Erica L. Griffin, a Ph.D. candidate in English at the University of Georgia, has a biographical entry on Johnson Publishing Company President Linda Johnson Rice forthcoming in *Notable Black American Women.* Her interests include Black women novelists from the Civil War to World War II, the Victorian Novel, and Creative Writing.

Trudier Harris is Augustus Baldwin Longstreet Professor of American Literature in the English Department at Emory University. She has published articles and book reviews in such journals as *Callaloo, Black American Literature Forum, Studies in American Fiction, Southern Humanities Review,* and *Southern Cultures.* Among her authored books are *Fiction and Folklore: The Novels of Toni Morrison* (1991) and, most recently, *The Power of the Porch: The Storyteller's Craft in Zora Neale Hurston, Gloria Naylor, and Randall Kenan* (1996). She also coedited three volumes of the *Dictionary of Literary Biography* series on African American writers and edited three additional volumes. She recently edited *New Critical Essays on Go Tell It on the Mountain* for Cambridge University Press. Currently she is coediting *The Oxford Companion to African American Literature* and *The Norton Anthology of Southern Literature.* She is also composing a series of essays for publication as a volume.

Dolan Hubbard, Associate Professor of English and African American Studies at the University of Georgia, is the author of *The Sermon and the African American Literary Imagination* (1994). He is a contributor to *The Oxford Companion to Women's Writing in the United States* and *The Oxford Companion to African American Literature.* He is editor of the *Langston Hughes Review* and immediate past president of the College Language Association (1994–96).

Debra Walker King is Assistant Professor of English at the University of Florida, Gainesville. She has published articles in *Names: The Journal of the American Name Society* and *Philosophy and Rhetoric.* She is a contributor to *The Oxford Companion to African American Literature.* Her present work includes a book-length study of names as used in African American literature.

David W. H. Pellow is Professor of French at North Carolina Central University, Durham. He taught French, World History, and Caribbean Literature at Fisk University in Nashville, Tennessee, before moving to NCCU. His primary specialty is nineteenth-century French and Caribbean literature; secondary areas include twentieth-century francophone literature and history. He has published in *Studi Francesi* and *Études Baudelairiennes* and is a contributor to *Notable Black American Women* (1992).

Joyce Pettis, Associate Professor of English at North Carolina State University, has published in *College English, African American Review, MELUS, Sage,* and *North Carolina Literary Review,* among other journals. She has chapters in *Southern Women Writers: The New Generation, Rejuvenating the Humanities,* and *Perspectives of Black Popular Culture.* She is the author of *Toward Wholeness in Paule Marshall's Fiction.* The latter work was awarded the College Language Association Book Award for 1995.

Helena Woodard, Assistant Professor of English at the University of Texas, Austin, earned the doctorate at the University of North Carolina at Chapel Hill. She specializes in eighteenth-century British literature, African British literature, and African American literature. She is a contributor to *The Oxford Companion to Women's Writing in the United States.* She is currently completing a manuscript on eighteenth-century African British writers.

Caroll Mills Young is Associate Professor of Spanish at Indiana University of Pennsylvania. Her primary teaching and research interests are Afro-Latin literature and culture, black women writers, comparative literature, and issues on multicultural education. She has been awarded several grants to study the black experience in both Argentina and Uruguay. Young has published articles in journals such as the *Afro-Hispanic Review* and the *College Language Association Journal.* Her recent publication is "New Voices of Afro-Uruguay" in *Afro-Hispanic Review* (Spring 1995).

Index

abolition, 22, 60, 63, 68
academic critics, xviii
Adams, Abigail, 3
Adams, Percy G., 78–79
Africa, and black intellectuals, xv, 61, 64–66, 69, 141; in antiquity, 65, 67; and the Bible, 66; and the Caribbean, 68
African American literary tradition, xiv–xv, 2, 50
African Methodist Episcopal Church, 49, 52, 62; and Afro-Protestant Press, 51, 52, 53; *Christian Recorder,* 52–54, 55; *see also* Harper, Frances E. W.
Afro-Canadian, 64
Agbebi, Majola, 66
Agustini, Delmira, 130
American Negro Academy, 67
American romance, 1
Anderson, Jervis, 94
Andrews, Willliam, 46
Arrascenta, Juan Julio, 129
autobiography, 31, 32, 101

Bajac de Borjes, Isaura, 143
Baldwin, James, xix
Ballesteros, Montiel, 144
Barnett, Ida Wells, xiv
Barrier, Ella D., 67
Barrios, Pilar, 129, 151
Bass, George, 96
Baym, Nina, 37, 39
Bennett, Gwendolyn, xiii, xviii, xix, 92–103; anthologized, 94–95; and Communist Party, 98; and the Federal Art Project, 97, 101; and the Harlem Community Art Center, 97, 101–2; marriage, 95–96, 97; *Opportunity,* 92, 93, 94–95; and *The Crisis,* 92, 94–95

Benstock, Shari, xv
Berrian, Brenda, xiv
Bildungsroman, 126
biography, 32, 91, 98–103
Black Arts movement, 54
black autobiography, 20
black feminist discourse, xi, xii–xv, xx, 2, 6, 8, 18, 35, 44, 48–49, 78, 82, 88, 105, 117, 119–23, 151
Black Panthers, 54
Blues, 51, 120, 124
Blyden, Edward Wilmot, 61
Boer War, 68
Bourne, H. R. Fox, 69
Boyd, Melba Joyce, xiv
Boyer, Jean-Pierre, 62
Bragg, George, 46
Brawley, Benjamin, 47
Brindis de Salas, Claudio, 144
Brindis de Salas, José, 129
Brindis de Salas, Virginia, xiii, xv, xix, xx, 129–52; and African Diaspora, 132, 141, 143, 152; and African roots, 131, 137, 141–42, 147–49; and Afro-Uruguayan writers, 129, 130, 141; and a black Christ, 136–37; and *Cantos de lejanía,* 129, 151; and *Cien cárceles de amor,* 129–30, 143–51; and her poetics, 131, 137, 141; and *Pregón de Marimorena,* 129–43, 145; and the Southern Cone, 131, 132, 152

Britain, antislavery movement, 17, 20, 22, 24
Brodie, Fawn, 1, 5
Brown, John, 54
Brown, Sterling A., 93
Brown, William Wells, 46, 50, 64, 65
Bryan, Mary E., 49
Bryon, 15
Burke, Edmund, 3
Busby, Margaret, 151
Bush-Banks, Olivia Ward, 57

call-and-response, xv
Calloway, Thomas J., 67
Campbell, Jane, 50
Carámbula, Rubén, 137, 141
Carby, Hazel, xiv, 22, 50, 120, 121
Carlyle, Thomas, 3
Champollian, Jean François, 65
Chase-Riboud, Barbara, xvi, 1–12; and black folklore, 2
Chesnutt, Charles, 50, 105
Chestnut, Mary Boykin, 3
Child, Lydia Maria, 23, 47, 49
Christian, Barbara, xiv, 6, 9
Civil Rights Movement, xiii
Civil War, 60
Clarke, John Henrik, 90
Cohn, Adolphe, 69
Coleridge-Taylor, Samuel, 61
College Language Association, xi
Conde, Maryse, 106
Cooper, Anna J., xiii, xviii, 60–71, 76–77; *A Voice from the South*, 60; and the Bible, 66; and black intellectual tradition, 65–66; and the Grand Tour, 68; on Haitian Revolution, 61–63, 65, 71; at Lincoln University, 61; and M. Street Colored High School, 61, 70; and Pan-African Conference, 63, 66–70; and St. Augustine's College, 60–61, 63, 67; "The Negro Problem in America," 67; visits Toronto, 64; "Women vs. the Indian," 64
Cooper, George, 60
Cowper, William, 19
Crichlow, Ernest, 97
Crosscup, Richard, 95–96.
Crummell, Alexander, 61, 65
Cruse, Harold, 92
Cugoano, Ottobah, 20
Cullen, Countee, 75, 92, 93, 101

Cult of True Womanhood, 1, 17, 18, 22, 31, 34–36, 44

Darwin, Charles, xvi
Davis, Arthur P., 116
Davis, Carol Boyce, xiv
Davis, Thadious, xiv
Dawson, Emma Waters, xvi
De Mezquita, Marta, 144
Debien, Gabriel, 62
DeCosta-Willis, Miriam, xiv
Delany, Martin R., 52, 61, 62, 64, 65
Delta Sigma Theta sorority, 75
diasporean studies, 61
Dickinson, Emily, 49
Dodson, Joanne, 36
domestic fiction, xiii
Douglas, Margaret, 3
Douglass, Frederick, xvi, 3; and *Douglass's Monthly*, 52; "The Heroic Slave," 48
Du Bois, W. E. B., xviii, 3, 20, 46, 61, 65, 67; eulogy to Harper, 48; *Gift of Black Folk*, 46; and Pan-African Conference, 67–70; 75, 77, 78, 83; *The Crisis*, 75; and *The Souls of Black Folk*, 78, 83, 91, 96
Dunbar, Paul Laurence, 48, 146
Dunbar-Nelson, Alice, xiv
Durham, Emma Kelly, 50

Ebony, 53, 94
Ellison, Ralph, xix, 51
Emperor Menelik of Ethiopia, 63, 66
Engels, Friedrich, 3
English nationalism, 18, 19
Equiano, Olaudah, 20, 27
Ezeiza, Gabino, 144

Fabre, Michel, 80, 94
Fanon, Frantz, 20
Farquar, C. W., 66
Fauset, Jessie, xiii, xviii, 75–88, 92, 93; *Comedy: American Style*, 75, 77, 81–83; "Dark Algiers the White," 83–86; *Plum Bun*, 75, 77, 80–82, 123; *The Brownies Book*, 75; *The Chinaberry Tree*, 75, 77, 86–87; *The Crisis*, 75–76, 86; *There is Confusion*, 75, 77, 79–80; "Tracing Shadows," 78–79, 83, 85; "Yarrow Revisited," 81, 83
Fax, Elton, 97
Feal, Rosemary Geisdorfer, xv

Ferguson, Moira, 15, 20, 22, 23
Ferreira, Carlos Cardoso, 129
Ferreyra, Eugenia Vaz, 130
Fido, Elaine, xiv
Finn, Julio, 151
Foster, Frances Smith, xiv, xvii, xviii, 42
Franklin, John Hope, 46
Fraser, James George, 107
Freedom's Journal, 52
French Revolution, 27, 62, 71

Garnet, Henry Highland, 64, 65
Garrison, Dee, 36
Garvey, Marcus, xviii, 61
Gates, Henry Louis, xiv, xviii, 20, 44, 46
Giddings, Paula, 34
Gilded Age, 50
Godwin, William, 15, 16, 27
Gothic fiction, 15
Govan, Sandra Y., xviii
Graham, Maryemma, xiv
Greenblatt, Stephen, 16
Griffin, Erica L., xviii
Grimké, Charlotte Forten, 76,77
Gronniosaw, James Ukawsaw, 20
Guadalupe, Julio, xx, 130
Gwin, Minrose, 7

Haiti (Saint-Domingue), 62, 63; and AME
     Church xvii, 62; and black immigration,
     62–63; *see also* Cooper, Anna J.
Hamitic Hypothesis, 20
Hanaford, Phebe, 46
Harlem Renaissance (the New Negro Era), xiii,
     61, 75, 84, 92, 93, 94–96
Harper, Frances E. W., xiv, xvii, xviii, 46–57;
     and Afro-Protestant Press, 51–54; "Duty to
     Dependent Races," 47; and "Fancy Etch-
     ings," 55–58; and *Iola Leroy,* 47, 50, 57,
     123; and National Council of Negro
     Women, 50; and National Women's Rights
     Convention, 55; "Our Greatest Want," 55;
     and *Poems on Miscellaneous Subjects,* 47,
     48, 55; and *Sketches of Southern Life,* 47;
     and "The Two Offers," 48; and Women's
     Christian Temperance Union, 47
Harris, Trudier, xiv, xix
Hawkes, Terence, 16, 17
Heilburn, Carolyn, 102
Hemenway, Robert E., xiv

Hemings, Sally, xvi, 1–12
Holloway, Karla F. C., xiv
Holly, James T., 63, 66
hooks, bell, xiv
Hubbard, William, 64
Huggins, Nathan, 94
Hughes, Langston, 57, 75, 77, 92, 93, 94, 95,
     97, 101
Hull, Gloria, xiv, 94
Humez, Jean, 46
Hunter, Kristin, 123
Hurston, Zora Neale, xiii, xiv, 46, 92, 97, 103
Hutson, Jean Blackwell, 97

Ibarbourou, Juana, 130

Jackson, Blyden, 48
Jackson, Richard, 129, 151
Jackson, Shirley, 107
Jacobs, Harriet, xiv, 23
Jahn, Janheinz, 129, 151
James, Daniel, 18
Jameson, Fredric, xvi
Jazz Age, 84
Jefferson, Martha Wayles, 7
Jefferson, Thomas, xvi, 1–11
Johnson, Barbara, 16
Johnson, Charles S., 75, 92
Johnson, James, 66
Johnson, James Weldon, 93, 151, 152
Jones, Anna H., 67
Jordan, Winthrop D., 105
Joseph, Gloria, xiv
Joseph, H. Mason, 67
Joyce, Joyce, xiv

Kennedy, Ted, 99
King, Deborah Walker, xvii
Kissel, Howard, 11
Klein, Félix, 70

Larsen, Nella, xiii, xiv, 92, 123
Larson, Charles R., xiv
Lattin, Vernon E., 116
Lauter, Paul, xi
Lee, Spike, 91
Lewis, Marvin A., 141, 151
Lewis, Norman, 97
Lewis, Ouida, 97
Locke, Alain, xviii, 75, 77, 78, 93, 94–95

Loggins, Vernon, 47
Longfellow, Henry Wadsworth, 49
Lorde, Audre, xi, 20
Louverture, Toussaint, 65
Love, John L., 67

Madison, Dolly, 1
Madison, James, 1
Mandell, Gail, 100, 101
Marcus, Jane, 36
Márquez, Selva, 130
Marshall, Paule, 118, 123
Marx, Karl, xvi
Mathurin, Owen Charles, 67
McDowell, Deborah, xiv
McDowell, Margaret B., 116
McGinnis, Joe, 99
McKay, Claude, 75, 77
McKay, Nellie, 116
Melville, Herman, 49
Memmi, Albert, 20
Mill, John Stuart, xvi
Milton, John, 51
miscegenation, 2–9
Mistral, Gabriela, 130, 143–44, 151
Mitchell, Loften, 97
Moravian Church, 18, 23
Morris, Wright, 116
Morrison, Toni, xvii, 6, 106, 118, 124
Mosaic Law, 42
mulatto, 3, 4, 33, 71

Nardal, Paulette, 20
National Council of Negro Women, 51
Naylor, Gloria, 118
Neoclassical tradition, xii, 17, 19
neofeminist discourse, 17
New Historicism, 16
New World black literature, xi, xv
Nugent, Bruce, 94

Oderigo, Nestor Ortíz, 141
Olney, James, 101

Pachter, Marc, 90, 102–3
Pan-African Conference, London, 63, 69–70, 75, 77–78, 83
pan-African discourse, xviii
Paquet, Sandra Pouchet, 15, 19
passing, theme of, 76

Pellow, David W.,H., xviii
Petry, Anne, xv, xix, 105–14, 116–26; and on black women's sexuality, 119; and Country Place, 117; the female intellectual, 117; and Richard Wright, 117; and The Narrows, 116–26; and The Street, 116, 117, 123, 126; and Tituba, 105–14
Pettis, Joyce, xix
Poovey, Mary, 16, 17, 20, 24
Pope, Alexander, 51
postmodern, xvii
Primeau, Ronald, 93
Prince, Mary, xv, xvii, 15–28
Pringle, Thomas, 16, 18, 22, 25, 28
Puritanism, 51

Quarles, Benjamin, 46
Queen Elizabeth, 26, 68, 69

Rampersad, Arnold, xix, 91–92, 100, 101
Randolph, Martha Jefferson, 7, 8
Reckley, Ralph, 10
Reclamation and reconstruction, projects of, xiii, xix, 11, 46, 47
Record, Wilson, 94
Redding, Saunders, 47
Richardson, Marilyn, 46
Riching, G. F., 46
Romance, 15, 19, 50
romantic literary tradition, 17
Rushworth, John, 19
Russell, Michelle, 119

Said, Edward, 84, 85
Santos, José C., 144
Schraufnagel, Noel, 116
Schuyler, George S., 75, 120
science fiction, 15
sentimental literary tradition, 19, 20
sentimental novel, 31, 32, 33, 36, 39, 43, 50, 51
Serrat, Alberto Brito, xix, xx
Shakespeare, 16, 17, 26, 51
Shelley, Mary, xvi, xvii, 15, 16, 17, 20, 22–28
Shelley, Percy B., 15, 16, 27
Singh, Amritjit, 84
slave narratives, xiii, xviii, 15, 19, 20, 31, 32, 33, 42
Smith, Barbara, xiv
Smith, Valerie, xiv

Sorrow Songs. *See* Spirituals
Southworth, E. D. E. N., 37
Spear, Chloe, 32
Spillers, Hortense J., xiv
Spirituals, 50, 51
Still, William, 46, 50
Storni, Alfonsina, 130
Stout, Janis P., 83
Stowe, Harriet Beecher, 3, 40, 49, 51
Strickland, Susanna, 16, 18, 23, 25
Student Nonviolent Coordinating Convention
    (SNCC), 54
Sylvain, Benito, 66–67, 69

Taine, Hippolyte, 65
Tanner, Martha, 96
Tate, Claudia, 36
Terrell, Mary Church, 76
Thurman, Wallace, 94
Toomer, Jean, 75
Touré, Almay Samory, 70
Truth, Sojourner, 32
Turner, Henry McNeal, 66
Turner, Nat, 9, 10, 11, 54

Veeder, William, 15
Victorian age, 31, 36, 39, 78, 88
Vieytes, Elvira Comas, 144
Volney, 65

Walker, Alice, xiv, 46
Walker, Clarence, 54
Walker, Margaret, 105
Wall, Cheryl A., xiv
Walters, Alexander, 66
Warner, Susan, 36, 38, 39, 40, 41

Washington, Booker T., 66
Washington, George, 1
Washington, Martha, 1
Washington, Mary Helen, xiv, 8, 49, 50, 117,
    119–20
Wayles, John, 7
Webb, Frank, 50
Weinstein, Martin, 151
Weir, Sybil, 116
Welter, Barbara, 34
Wheatley, Phillis, xi, xii, xiii, xiv, 27, 46, 48
Whittier, John Greenleaf, 49, 51
Wilkerson, Doxey, 97
Williams, Betsy, 18
Williams, Fannie Barrier, 67
Williams, Henry Sylvester, 61, 66
Williams, Sherley Anne, xiv, 10
Wilson, Harriet, xiii, xiv, xvii, 31–44
Wilson, Judith, 2
Wollstonecraft, Mary, 15
Wood, John, 18, 21, 22, 23
Woodard, Helena, xvii
Woodson, Carter G., 61
Wordsworth, William, 81
World War II, 7
World's Fair, Chicago, 50–51
Wright, Richard, xv, xix, 117

X, Malcolm, 91

Yellin, Jean Fagin, xiv, 46
Young, Ann Venture, xiv, 151
Young, Caroll Mills, xix

Zarrilli, Humberto, 143

Recovered Writers/Recovered Texts was designed and typeset on a MacIntosh computer system using PageMaker software. The text is set in Bodoni, chapter titles are set in Bodoni and Franklin Gothic Heavy. This book was designed by Todd Duren, composed by Wolf Song Design, and was printed and bound by Thomson-Shore, Inc. The recycled paper used in this book is designed for an effective life of at least three hundred years.